Serbian Fairy Tales:

Hero Tales and Legends of the Serbians

By

Woislav M. Petrovitch

and

Chedo Miyatovich

Contents

Preface 10
Introduction 18
Chapter I: Historical Retrospect 25
    The Coming of the Serb 25
    Early Struggles 26
    Internecine Strife 27
    Doushan the Powerful 29
    The Royal Prince Marko 30
    The Treachery of Brankovitch 31
    The Final Success of the Turks 32
    The Miseries of Turkish Rule 33
    Serbia again Subjugated 34
    King Peter I 36
Chapter II: Superstitious Beliefs & National Customs ... 38
    General Characteristics 38
    Paganism and Religion 39
    The God Peroon 40
    The God Volos 40
    The Sun God 40
    The Veele 41
    Predestination and Immortality 45
    Good and Evil Spirits 45
    Witches 47
    Vampires 48

Nature Worship	49
Enchanters	50
Sacrificial Rites	51
Funeral Customs	52
Classic and Mediæval Influence	54
The Spread of Christianity	55
Superstition	57
Marriage	61
Marriage Negotiations	63
The Wedding Procession	64
The Arrival	66
The Return from Church	68
Slava (or Krsno Ime)	69
The Slava Eve Reception	71
Slava Toasts	73
The Ceremony at Church	74
The Slava Feast	75
Christmas Eve	76
Christmas Day	80
The Dodola Rite	82
Whitsuntide	83
Palm Sunday	83
St. George's Day	84
Chapter III: Serbian National Epic Poetry	**86**
The Importance of the Ballads	86

The Goussle 88

Chapter IV: Kralyevitch Marko; or, the Royal Prince Marko 91

    The Marko Legends 91

    The Bad Faith of Voukashin 93

    The Horse Sharatz 94

    PRINCE MARKO TELLS WHOSE THE EMPIRE SHALL BE 96

    Marko is Summoned 99

    Marko tells the Truth 101

    PRINCE MARKO AND A MOORISH CHIEFTAIN 104

    The Entrance of the Moor 106

    The Sultana's Dream 106

    The Princess appeals to Marko 108

    Marko prepares to succour the Princess 109

    Marko greets the Princess 110

    The Moor in Istamboul 112

    Sharatz and Bedevia 112

    Marko and the Moor 113

    PRINCE MARKO ABOLISHES THE WEDDING TAX 115

    Marko visits the Moor 117

    Marko pays for All 119

    PRINCE MARKO AND BOGDAN THE BULLY 120

    The Bully fears to meet Marko 124

    PRINCE MARKO AND GENERAL VOUTCHA 124

    The Arrival of Marko 126

- Marko captures General Voutcha 128
- **PRINCE MARKO'S WEDDING PROCESSION** 130
  - The Wedding Procession 133
  - The Unfaithful Koom 133
  - The Escape of the Maiden 135
- **PRINCE MARKO AND THE MOORISH PRINCESS** .. 138
  - The Moorish Princess 139
- **PRINCE MARKO AND THE VEELA** 142
  - The Pursuit of the Veela 143
- **PRINCE MARKO AND THE TURKISH HUNTSMEN** 146
  - The Vengeance of Marko 148
- **PRINCE MARKO AND MOUSSA KESSEDJIYA14** 149
  - Marko is Sent for 151
  - Marko orders a Sword 153
  - Marko meets Moussa 155
- **THE DEATH OF PRINCE MARKO** 158
  - Marko learns his Fate 159
  - The Finding of Marko 161
- **Chapter V: Banovitch Strahinya** 166
  - Historical Data 166
  - The Falcon Banovitch 167
  - Banovitch seeks the Turk 169
  - The Faithless Wife 171
  - The Combat 172
  - The return of the Falcon 175

Chapter VI: The Tsarina Militza and the Zmay1 of Yastrebatz 177

    Militza tells the Tsar 177

    Vook as Champion 179

Chapter VII: The Marriage of Maximus Tzrnoyevitch . 182

    The Ballad 182

    The Story 182

    The Message from the Doge 185

    The Wedding Procession sets out 189

    The Wedding Gifts 192

    The Princess learns of the Deception 194

    Milosh's Offer 195

    The Violence of Maximus 197

    Maximus becomes a Turk 198

Chapter VIII: The Marriage of Tsar Doushan the Mighty 200

    Doushan sends Theodor to Ledyen 200

    The Princess Roksanda 201

    The Procession Starts 203

    Milosh Joins the Procession 207

    The Leap of Koulash 209

    The Fight for Koulash 210

    The First Test 212

    The Second Test 215

    The Third Test 216

    The Fourth Test 217

The Departure of the Serbians 220

The Contest with Balatchko 222

Chapter IX: Tsar Lazarus and the Tsarina Militza.........224

The Tsarina's Forebodings 224

News of Battle 226

The Trusty Miloutin 227

Historical Note 228

Chapter X: The Captivity and Marriage of Stephan Yakshitch1 231

The Veela's Warning 231

Stephan and the Sultan 232

Stephan at Tyoopria 233

Stephan at Novi Bazar 234

Stephan and the Vizier's Daughter 236

The Ending of the Ballad 238

Historical Note 238

Chapter XI: The Marriage of King Voukashin 241

The Message to Vidossava 241

Vidossava's Treachery 242

The Winged Horse 243

Momtchilo's Dream 244

The Ambuscade 244

Brother and Sister 246

The Death of Momtchilo 247

The Punishment of Vidossava 248

Historical Note 249
Chapter XII: The Saints Divide the Treasures1 251
　The Bard begins! 251
　The Wrath of God 252
Chapter XIII: Three Serbian Ballads 254
　I. The Building of Skadar (Scutari)1 254
　II. The Stepsisters 262
　III. The Abduction of the Beautiful Iconia 267
Chapter XIV: Folk Lore 270
　I. The Ram with the Golden Fleece 270
　II. A Pavilion neither in the Sky nor on the Earth1 279
　III. Pepelyouga 285
　IV. Animals' Language 292
　V. The Stepmother and her Stepdaughter 299
　VI. Justice and Injustice 304
　VII. He Who Asks Little Receives Much 308
　VIII. Bash Tchelik or Real Steel 314
　IX. The Golden Apple-tree and the Nine Peahens 336
　X. The Bird Maiden 351
　XI. Lying for a Wager 355
　XII. The Maiden Wiser than the Tsar 361
　XIII. Good Deeds Never Perish 367
　XIV. He Whom God Helps No One Can Harm 377
　XV. Animals as Friends and as Enemies7 384
　XVI. The Three Suitors 397

XVII. The Dream of the King's Son 403
XVIII. The Biter Bit 410
XIX. The Trade that No One Knows 424
XX. The Golden-haired Twins 437
Chapter XV: Some Serbian Popular Anecdotes 447
St. Peter and the Sand 447
Why the Serbian People are Poor 447
The Gipsies and the Nobleman 448
Why the Priest was drowned 449
The Era from the other World2 449
A Trade before Everything 452
The Condition 453

Preface

Serbians attach the utmost value and importance to the sympathies of such a highly cultured, great, and therefore legitimately influential people as is the British nation. Since the beginning of the twentieth century there have been two critical occasions[1]—the annexation of Bosnia and Herzegovina by Austria and the war against the Turks—when we have had opportunities to note how British sympathies, even when apparently only platonic, can be of great practical importance for our nation. It is quite natural that we should desire to retain and if possible deepen and increase those sympathies. We are proud of our army, but we flatter ourselves that our nation may win sympathy and respect by other than military features of its national character. We wish that our British friends should know our nation such as it is. We wish them to be acquainted with our national psychology. And nothing could give a better insight into the very soul of the Serbian nation than this book.

The Serbians belong ethnologically to the great family of the Slavonic nations. They are first cousins to the Russians, Poles, Czechs, Slovaks, and Bulgars, and they are brothers to the Croats and Slovenes. Since the Church has ceased to be the discordant and disuniting element in the life of the nations, the Orthodox Serbians and the Roman Catholic Croats are practically one and the same people. But of all Slavonic nations the Serbians can legitimately claim to be the most poetical one. Their language is the richest and the most musical among all the Slavonic languages. The late Professor Morfill, a man who was something of a Panslavist, repeatedly said to me: "I wish you Serbians, as well as all other Slavonic nations, to join Russia in a political union, but I do not wish you to surrender your beautiful and well-developed language to be exchanged for the Russian!" On one occasion he went even so far as to suggest that the future United States of the Slavs should adopt as their literary and official language the Serbian, as by far the finest and most musical of all the Slavonic tongues.

When our ancestors occupied the western part of the Balkan Peninsula, they found there numerous Latin colonies and Greek towns and settlements. In the course of twelve centuries we have through intermarriage absorbed much Greek and Latin blood. That influence, and the influence of the commercial and political intercourse with Italy, has softened our language and our manners and intensified our original Slavonic love of what is beautiful, poetical, and noble. We are a special Slavonic type, modified by Latin and Greek influences. The Bulgars are a Slavonic nation of a quite different type, created by the circulation of Tartar blood in Slavonian veins. This simple fact throws much light on the conflicts between the Serbians and Bulgarians during the Middle Ages, and even in our own days.

Now what are the Serbian national songs? They are not songs made by cultured or highly educated poets—songs which, becoming popular, are sung by common people. They are songs made by the common people themselves. Up to the middle of the nineteenth century the Serbian peasantry lived mostly in agricultural and family associations called *Zadrooga*. As M. Petrovitch has stated, the sons of a peasant did not leave their father's house when they got married, but built a wooden cottage on the land surrounding the father's house. Very often a large settlement arose around the original home, with often more than a hundred persons, men and women, working together, considering the land and houses as their common property, enjoying the fruits of their work as the common property too. All the members of the Zadrooga considered the oldest member of such family association as their chief, and it was the usual custom to gather round him every evening in the original house. After questions of farming or other business had been disposed of, the family gathering would be enlivened by the chieftain or some other male member reciting an epic song, or several such songs, describing historic events or events which had lately happened. At the public gatherings around the churches and monasteries groups of men and women would similarly gather about the reciters of songs on old kings and heroes or on some great and important event.

In Hungarian Serbia (Syrmia, Banat, Bachka) poor blind men often make it a lucrative profession to sing old or new songs, mostly on old heroes and historical events or on contemporary events. But in other parts of Serbia (Shumadiya, Bosnia, Herzegovina, Montenegro, Dalmatia) very often well-to-do peasants recite the hero songs to crowds of listeners of both sexes. It is a curious fact noticed already by Vouk S. Karadgitch that the reciters of the heroic songs are hardly ever young men, but generally men of middle age, and still more frequently old men. It is as if old men considered it their duty to acquaint the young generation with the principal events of the nation's history and their principal heroes. You may find still many an illiterate person in Serbia, but you will not find one who would not be able to tell you something about Stephan Nemanya, the first king of mediæval Serbia, about his son St. Sava, Tsar Doushan, his young son Ourosh, King Voukashin, the Royal Prince Kralyevitch Marko, Tsar Lazar, and the heroes who fell in the famous battle at Kossovo (1389). It can be said that the Serbian peasants wrote their own national history by composing and reciting it from one generation to another in the rhythmical ten-syllabic blank verse. The *gooslari* and the monks kept the national political consciousness and the national Church fully alive through the five centuries in which they were only Turkish *Rayah*, a mass of common people doomed to be nothing better than slaves to their master, the Turk. We would to-day not have known anything about the persistent guerilla war, which the best and boldest men of the nation were relentlessly carrying on against the nation's oppressor since the beginning of the sixteenth century until the first rising of Shumadia under Karageorge in 1804, if we had not the so-called *Haïdoochke Pesme* (the Songs on Haïdooks). Long before the history of *The Resurrection of the Serbian National State* had been written by Stoyan Novakovich, the learned President of the Serbian Academy, the bard Vishnyich described that resurrection in songs of great beauty and power. And the victories of the Serbian army over the Turks and Bulgars in the war of 1912–13 are already sung by the improvized bards in the inns and at the great gatherings of the people at the village fairs and around the churches on great church festivals. Of course, a Serbian who has heard on hundreds of occasions national songs recited learns to recite them himself, although he may not be able to accompany his recitation on the *goussle*. Nor does he find it difficult, by using many stereotyped lines of old and well-known songs, to tell the story of a recent event. When in 1873, as Minister of Finance, I was defeated in the Budget debate at the Skoupshtina, my defeat was recited to the people in blank verse the same evening, and the next day.

Besides the songs which relate, more or less accurately, actual events, many a national song relates a legend or a tradition. They have been created, no doubt, under the influence of the priests and monks, and are appropriate recitations to the crowds who come to the church festivals. I am glad to see that M. Petrovitch has included in his collection the song which is probably the oldest among all Serbian songs. It is called "The Saints partition [or divide] the Treasures," and it gives expression to an evidently very old tradition, which remembers a sort of catastrophe which befell India, and which probably was the cause of the ancient ancestors of the Slavs leaving India. It is most remarkable to find an echo of an Indian catastrophe in the national songs of the Serbians.

That the Serbians had national songs in which they described the exploits of their national heroes was noted in the fourteenth century. Nicephoras Gregoras, sent by the Byzantine Emperor on a diplomatic mission to Serbia, relates having heard the Serbians sing their national songs on their heroes. The records of several diplomatic missions, going from Vienna or Buda to Constantinople during the sixteenth century, relate that the members heard people sing heroic songs. In that century we have the first attempt to reproduce in print some of those national songs, as, for instance, by the Ragusan poet Hectorovich. In the eighteenth century fuller efforts were made by the Franciscan monk Kachich-Mioshich and by Abbé Fortis. But it is to the self-taught founder of modern Serbian literature, Vouk Stephanovitch Karadgitch, that the greatest honour is due, as has been shown by M. Petrovitch in his Introduction and elsewhere.

M. Petrovitch must have experienced what the French call *embarras de richesses*. It was not so easy to select the songs for an English translation. But he has given us some of the finest Serbian epic songs as samples of what the Serbian national poetry is capable of creating. I regret only that he has not included a few samples of what the Serbian village women and girls are able to produce in the way of lyrical poetry. Perhaps on some other occasion he will make an *amende honorable* to our countrywomen.

I wish to add yet a few words to what M. Petrovitch has said about our greatest national hero, the Royal Prince (Kralyevitch) Marko. As he has pointed out, Marko is a historical personality. But what history has to say about him is not much, and certainly not of the nature to explain how he became the favourite hero of the Serbian people. He was a loyal and faithful vassal of the Sultan, a fact hardly likely to win him the respect and admiration of the Serbians. Yet the Serbians throughout the last five centuries have respected, admired, loved their Royal Prince Marko, and were and are now and will ever be proud of him. This psychological puzzle has stirred up the best Serbian and some other historical students and authors to investigate the matter. It is evident to all that most of the songs on Marko must have been composed under the mighty influence of his personality upon his contemporary countrymen. Dr. Yagich, Dr. Maretich, Professor Stoykovich and St. Novakovich all believe that his athletic strength and personal appearance were responsible for much of the impression he made. All agree that his conduct in everyday life and on all occasions was that of a true knight, a *cavaliere servente*, a *chevalier sans peur et sans reproche*. Even his attachment and unfailing readiness to serve the Sultan was counted in his favour, as proof of his absolute loyalty of character. Probably that very loyalty was appreciated by the Sultan and enabled Marko not rarely to appeal to the Sultan in favour of his people, especially when some prisoners or slaves were to be liberated and saved. He was certainly the protector of poor and suffering men and women, and went to their rescue at all and every personal risk and cost. He must have given real proofs of his devotion to the cause of justice; that is what endeared him to his generation as well as to the generations which followed. He must have been known during his life for his fear of God and his respect and tender love for his mother. The Serbians painted him from the model which his own personality and his actual deeds offered to the nation. One of the most beautiful features of his knightly character as described by the national bards is his love of and pity for suffering animals. I regret that my friend Petrovitch did not give a sample of the songs which glorify that feature of our national hero, as, for instance, the song "Marko and the Falcon" (Vouk. ii. 53), or "Marko and the Eagle" (Vouk. ii. 54), in each of which it is described how when once Marko fell ill on a field, an intense thirst tormenting him and the scorching sun-rays burning his face, those birds out of gratitude for the kindness Marko showed them once, brought to him water in their beaks and spread their wings to shade his face against the sun.

By far the best study on the Serbian national hero has been written by the Russian professor M. Halanski, who explains the puzzle by the natural sympathy of the people for a 'tragic hero.' The historical Marko was certainly a 'tragic hero.' Nothing proves that better than his last words before the battle of Rovina began (1399), and which M. Petrovitch quotes in the text.

I ought to add that there is also a theory that the Serbian nation, so to say, projected itself in the Royal Prince Marko, depicting its own tragic fate, its own virtues and weaknesses, in the popular yet tragic personality of Marko. No doubt Marko must have been in some way the representative type of a noble Serbian, otherwise he could not have found the way to the soul and heart of his people. Yet that theory is hardly modest, for my taste.

It may interest our British friends to know that a relation of the dynasty of which Marko was the last representative, a certain Prince John Mussachi, in a historical memoir stated that Marko's father, King Voukashin, was the descendant of a certain nobleman named Britanius or Britanicus![2] We should be proud if it could be proved that the ancestors of our national hero were in some way connected with the Britons.

    CHEDO   MIYATOVICH
Member of the Royal Serbian Academy of Sciences
BELGRADE
June 28, 1914

---

[1]This was written one month before an even more critical situation confronted the Serbian nation.

[2]Mussachi's memoir in Karl Hopf's *Chroniques Græco-Romaines*.

Introduction

More than once in the following pages I have lamented my inability to translate into English verse the spirited ballads of our national bards; never until now have I realized the error involved in the dictum of my teachers of literature—true as it may be from one point of view—that beautiful thoughts are to be more freely expressed in prose than in a poetic form, which is necessarily hampered by rules of prosody and metre. Undoubtedly, good prose is worth more than mediocre verse, but how if the author be a master poet?

Serbian epic poetry undoubtedly deserves the attention of the English literary world, and I venture to express the hope that some day another English poet will be attracted as was Sir John Bowring by the charm of our ballads, and like him will endeavour to communicate to readers of English the alluring rhythmic qualities of the originals.

In the first half of the nineteenth century various German poets transversified some of our national ballads, and I cannot but boast that among the number was even Goethe himself. Alas! he was compelled to use Italian versions, for he was ignorant of the Serbian language, unlike his worthy countryman Jacob Grimm, who, after having learnt our musical tongue that he might acquaint himself with the treasures written in it, wrote: "The Serbian national poetry deserves indeed a general attention.... On account of these ballads I think the Serbian will now be universally studied."

A Tcheque[1] writer, Lyoodevit Schtur, speaking of the Slav poetry, wrote: "The Indo-European peoples express each in their own manner what they contain in themselves and what elevates their souls. The Indian manifests this in his huge temples; the Persian in his holy books; the Egyptian in pyramids, obelisks and immeasurable, mysterious labyrinths; the Hellene in his magnificent statues; the Roman in his enchanting pictures; the German in his beautiful music—the Slavs have poured out their soul and their intimate thoughts in ballads and tales."

I think that it is not too much to claim that of all the Slavs, Serbians have most profusely poured out their souls in their poetry, which is thoroughly and essentially national. So much could not safely be said about their tales and legends, which, to my mind, seem less characteristic. Indeed, by their striking analogy with the folk lore of other nations they help to demonstrate the prehistoric oneness of the entire Aryan race. For example, it would be ridiculous for any nation to lay exclusive claim, as 'national property,' to such legends as "Cinderella"[2] and certain others, which are found more or less alike in many languages, as is well known to those who have any considerable acquaintance with European folk lore.

From time immemorial the Serbian has possessed an exceptional natural gift for composing heroic ballads. That gift was brought from his ancient abode in the North; and the beautiful scenery of his new surroundings, and contact with the civilized Byzantine, influenced it very considerably and provided food for its development, so that it came to resemble the Homeric epic rather than any product of the genius of the

Northern Slav. The treasure of his mental productions was continually augmented by new impressions, and the national poetry thus grew opulent in its form and more beautiful in its composition. The glorious forests of the Balkans, instinct with legend and romance, to which truly no other forests in Europe can compare; the ever-smiling sky of Southern Macedonia; the gigantic Black Rocks of Montenegro and Herzegovina, are well calculated to inspire even a less talented people than the Serbian inhabitants of those romantic regions for the last thirteen centuries.

The untiring Serbian muse pursued her mission alike upon the battlefield or in the forest, in pleasant pastures amid the flocks, or beneath the frowning walls of princely castles and sacred monasteries. The entire nation participated in her gracious gifts; and whenever a poet chanted of the exploits of some favourite national hero, or of the pious deeds of monk or saint, or, indeed, of any subject which appeals closely to the people, there were never lacking other bards who could make such poetic creations their own and pass them on with the modifications which must always accompany oral transmission, and which serve to bring them ever more intimately near to the heart of the nation. This characteristic of oral transmission explains the existence of varying versions of some of the most popular songs.

Through many centuries, and more especially during the blighting domination of the Turk, Serbian national literature was limited to a merely oral form, save that the untiring monks, inviolable within the sacred walls of their monasteries, spent their leisure, not in inscribing the popular ballads and lyric songs of their nation, but in recording the biographies of other monks or of this or that princely patron.

Those Serbians who could not endure the oppressive rule of the Ottoman, and who in the seventeenth century emigrated with their Patriarch Arsen Tcharnoyevitch to the level fields of Southern Hungary—there to adopt in the course of the two subsequent centuries the pseudo-classicism of the West—considered it *infra dignitatem* to write about such vulgar subjects as popular poetry and tradition. The gifted descendants of those lamentable slaves of the cunning Austrian and Pan-Russian influences wasted their talents in vain and empty imitation of pseudo-classic productions from Italy and France, and, by conjugating zealously the Serbian and Old-Slavonic verbs in the Russian fashion they created a monstrous literary jargon which they termed *Slavyano-Serbski* (*i.e.* Slavo-Serbian). And if any Serbian author should have presumed to write in the melodious and genuine Serbian as universally spoken throughout his fatherland, he would have been anathematized by those misguided Slavo-Serbian 'classicists' who fondly believed that by writing in a language hardly comprehensible even to themselves, because of its utter inconsequence and arbitrary changes, they would surely become distinguished in the history of their nation's literature.

The 'classicists' received their deserts in the first half of the nineteenth century, when they were overwhelmed by the irresistible torrent of the popular movement headed by the self-taught Serbian peasant, VOUK STEPHANOVITCH-KARADGITCH, whose name will remain for ever great in the history of Serbian literature.

Karadgitch has been called justly "the father of Serbian modern literature." His numberless opponents, who began by heaping upon him every opprobrious epithet which their pens or tongues could command, ended, after more than fifty years of fruitless resistance, by opening wide their arms to him.

Karadgitch framed a grammar of the popular Serbian language, banishing all unnecessary graphic signs and adapting his thirty-lettered alphabet to the thirty sounds (five vowels and twenty-five consonants) of his mother tongue—thus giving it an ideal phonetic orthography, and establishing the golden rule, "*Spell as you speak and speak as you spell.*"[3] He also travelled from one village to another throughout Serbia, zealously collecting and inscribing the epic and lyric poems, legends, and traditions as he heard them from the lips of bards and story-tellers, professional and amateur.

In his endeavours he was powerfully seconded by the Serbian ruling princes, and he had the good fortune to acquire the intimate friendship of those distinguished philologers and scientists of the last century, Bartholemy Kopitar, Schaffarik, and Grimm. Helped by Kopitar, Karadgitch succeeded in compiling an academic dictionary of the Serbian language interpreted by Latin and German equivalents. This remains to this day the only reliable Serbian dictionary approaching to the Western standard of such books. His first collection of Serbian popular poems was published in Vienna in 1814. It contained 200 lyric songs, which he called *zenske pyesme* (*i.e.* 'women-songs'), and 23 heroic ballads, and the book created a stir in literary circles in Austria, Serbia, Germany, Russia, and other countries. Seven years later Karadgitch published at Leipzig a second edition in three books. This contained 406 lyric songs and 117 heroic poems. From this edition Sir John Bowring made his metrical translation of certain of the lyric and epic poems, which he published in 1827 under the title *Servian Popular Poetry*. He dedicated the book to Karadgitch, who was his intimate friend and teacher of Serbian.

I have reproduced three of Bowring's ballads in this book that English readers may have a better idea than they can obtain from a mere prose rendering of the original verse. As to the poetic merits of these metrical translations I will not presume to offer an opinion, but I may be permitted to say that I have not seen a more faithful translation of our national ballads and lyric songs in English or in any other language. Considering the difficulties to the Anglo-Saxon student of any Slavonic language (more especially Serbian) it is surprising that there should be so few defects in Bowring's work. Sir John must have possessed an uncommon gift for acquiring languages, as he has also translated from each of the other Slavonic tongues with—so I am informed—similar accuracy and precision.

The third edition of Karadgitch's work appeared in Vienna at intervals between the years 1841 and 1866. It had now grown to five volumes and contained 1112 lyric songs and 313 heroic ballads. It is from this edition that I have selected the hero-tales in this book; and if I should succeed in interesting a new generation of English readers in the literature of my country it will be my further ambition to attempt the immeasurably harder task of introducing them in a subsequent volume to our popular lyric poetry.

It remains only to tender my most grateful acknowledgment to my esteemed friend M. Chedo Miyatovich for his invaluable advice and encouragement, and for his generous willingness to contribute the preface which adorns my book.
    W. M. P.

---

[1] *Tcheque* is a better synonym for the solecism *Bohemian*.

[2] In Serbian *Pepelyouga*, where *pepel*, or—with vocalized *l*—*pepeo*, means 'cinder' or 'ashes'; *ouga* being the idiomatic suffix corresponding to the Italian *one* or English *ella*, etc.

[3] See *Servian Conversation Grammar*, by Woislav M. Petrovitch, ed. Julius Groos, Heidelberg, 1914 (London: David Nutt, 212 Shaftesbury Avenue, W.C.), Introduction, pp. 1–8.

Chapter I: Historical Retrospect

The Coming of the Serb

Prior to their incursion into the Balkan Peninsula during the seventh century, the Serbians[1] lived as a patriarchal people in the country now known as Galicia. Ptolemy, the ancient Greek geographer, describes them as living on the banks of the River Don, to the north-east of the sea of Azov. They settled mostly in those Balkan territories which they inhabit at the present day, namely, the present kingdom of Serbia, Old Serbia, Macedonia, Bosnia and Herzegovina, Montenegro, Dalmatia, Batchka, Banat, Croatia, Sirmia and Istria. The ancient inhabitants of those regions, Latins, Illyrians, Thracians, Greeks and Albanians, were easily driven by the newcomers toward the Adriatic coast. Their Emperor, Heraclius (A.D. 610–641), unable to oppose an effective resistance, ceded to the Serbians all the provinces which they had occupied, and peace was thus purchased. The pagan and uncultured Serbian tribes now came into constant intercourse with the civilized Byzantines, and soon were converted to Christianity; for it is an almost invariable fact that when one people conquers or subjects another people, the more civilized of the two, whether the vanquished or the victorious, must necessarily impose its civilization and customs on the more barbarous. But the Serbians only embraced Christianity to any large extent with the beginning of the ninth century, when the two brothers Cyrillos and Methodius—the so-called Slavonic apostles—translated and preached the teaching of Christ in the ancient Slav language, then in common use among all southern Slavs of that time.

Early Struggles

As the Serbians, during the seventh and eighth centuries, were divided into tribes, they became an easy prey to the attacks of the Byzantines, the Bulgars and the Francs, although they never were subjugated by any of those neighbours. The Serbians, however, were forced to realize that only by concentration of their power could they offer resistance as a nation, and a serious effort was made to found a State on the banks of the River Morava, with Horea Margi (now called Tyoupriya) as its capital, in the early part of the ninth century. Owing to Bulgarian hostility, however, this proved abortive.

A fresh attempt to form an independent State was made by the Djoupan (Count) Vlastimir, who had succeeded in emancipating himself from Byzantine suzerainty. This province was called Rashka and extended around the Rivers Piva, Tara, and Lim, touching the basin of the River Ibar in the east and that of Vrbas in the west. But in the very beginning of its civil life there were dissensions amongst the leaders which facilitated the interference of the Bulgarian Tsar Siméon. Tchaslav, the djoupan of another Serbian tribe, though he possessed no rights to it, claimed the throne, and was supported by Siméon, who successfully invaded Rashka. The Bulgarians retained possession of the country for seven years (924-931), when Tchaslav succeeded in wresting from them a new state which comprised, together with Rashka, the territories of Zetta, Trebinye, Neretva and Houm. After his death, great disorder reigned in this principality.

In the course of the next century the Byzantine Empire, having again brought the now enfeebled Bulgaria within its rule, also overpowered Rashka, whose Grand Djoupan fled. The ruler of Zetta, Stephen Voïslav (1034–1051), son of Dragomir, djoupan of Trebinye, took the opportunity of declaring himself independent of his suzerain the Grand Djoupan of Rashka, and appropriated Zahoumlye (Herzegovina) and some other regions. His son Michaylo (1053–1081) succeeded further in bringing Rashka under his authority, and obtained the title of king (*rex Sclavorum*) from Pope Gregory VII in the year 1077. Under the rule of King Bodin, the son of Michaylo, the Serbia of Tchaslav was restored; furthermore Bosnia was added to his state. But after Bodin's death new disorder ensued, caused mainly by the struggles amongst the several pretenders to the throne.

Internecine Strife

Internecine strife is an unfortunate feature to be noticed throughout Serbian history, and constantly we see energy wasted in futile dissensions among various members of ruling families, who criminally and fatally neglected national interests, in pursuit by legitimate or illegitimate means of their personal ambitions. This has at all times hindered the Serbian nation from becoming a powerful political unit, although efforts were made by many of the rulers to realize this policy.

In 1169 a dynasty destined to rule Serbia for more than two centuries (1169–1372) within ever-changing political boundaries, was founded by the celebrated

Grand Djoupan Stephan Nemanya (1169-1196) who was created Duke (grand djoupan) of Serbia by the Byzantine Emperor after he had instigated a revolution, the result of which was favourable to his pretensions. By his bravery and wisdom he succeeded not only in uniting under his rule the provinces held by his predecessors, but also in adding those which never had been Serbian before, and he placed Ban Koulin, an ally, upon the throne of Bosnia. Furthermore he strengthened the orthodox religion in his state by building numerous churches and monasteries, and by banishing the heretic Bogoumils.[2] Feeling the weakness of advanced age, and wishing to give fresh proof of his religious faith to his people, the aged Nemanya abdicated in 1196, in favour of his able second son Stevan, and withdrew into a monastery. On his accession in the year 1217 Stevan assumed the title of King of Serbia.

When the crusaders vanquished Constantinople, Sava, Stevan's youngest brother, obtained from the Greek patriarch the autonomy of the Serbian Church (1219), and became the first Serbian archbishop.

Stevan was succeeded by his son Radoslav (1223-1233), who was dethroned by his brother Vladislav (1233-1242), who was removed from the throne by his third brother Ourosh the Great (1242-1276). Ourosh increased his territory and established the reputation of Serbia abroad. In his turn, he was dethroned by his son Dragoutln (1276-1281), who, owing to the failure of a campaign against the Greeks, retired from the throne in favour of a younger brother Miloutin (1281-1321), reserving, however, for himself a province in the north of the State. Soon afterward Dragoutin received from his mother-in-law, the queen of Hungary, the lands between the Rivers Danube Sava and Drina, and assumed the title of King of Sirmia. Dragoutin, while still alive, yielded his throne and a part of his lands to Miloutin, and another part remained under the suzerainty of the King of Hungary. Miloutin is considered one of the most remarkable descendants of Nemanya. After his death the usual discord obtained concerning the succession to the throne. Order was re-established by Miloutin's son, Stevan Detchanski (1321–1331), who defeated the Bulgarians in the famous battle of Velbouzd, and brought the whole of Bulgaria under his sway. Bulgaria remained a province of Serbia until the Ottoman hordes overpowered both.

Doushan the Powerful

Stevan Detchanski was dethroned by his son Doushan the Powerful (1331–1355), the most notable and most glorious of all Serbian sovereigns. He aimed to establish his rule over the entire Balkan Peninsula, and having succeeded in overpowering nearly the whole of the Byzantine Empire, except Constantinople, he proclaimed himself, in agreement with the *Vlastela* (Assembly of Nobles), Tsar of Serbia. He elevated the Serbian archbishopric to the dignity of the patriarchate. He subdued the whole of Albania and a part of Greece, while Bulgaria obeyed him almost as a vassal state. His premature death (some historians assert that he was poisoned by his own ministers) did not permit him to realize the whole of his great plan for Serbia, and under the rule of his younger son Ourosh (1355–1371) nearly all his magnificent work was undone owing to the incessant and insatiable greed of the powerful nobles, who thus paved the way for the Ottoman invasion.

Among those who rebelled against the new Tsar was King Voukashin. Together with his brother and other lords, he held almost independently the whole territory adjoining Prizrend to the south of the mountain Shar.[3]

King Voukashin and his brother were defeated in a battle with the Turks on the banks of the River Maritza (1371), and all Serbian lands to the south of Skoplye (Üsküb) were occupied by the Turks.

The Royal Prince Marko

The same year Tsar Ourosh died, and Marko, the eldest son of King Voukashin, the national hero of whom we shall hear much in this book, proclaimed himself King of the Serbians, but the Vlastela and the clergy did not recognize his accession. They elected (A.D. 1371) Knez[4] (later Tsar) Lazar, a relative of Tsar Doushan the Powerful, to be the ruler of Serbia, and Marko, from his principality of Prilip, as a vassal of the Sultan, aided the Turks in their campaigns against the Christians. In the year 1399 he met his death in the battle of Rovina, in Roumania, and he is said to have pronounced these memorable words: "May God grant the victory to the Christians, even if I have to perish amongst the first!" The Serbian people, as we shall see, believe that he did not die, but lives even to-day.

Knez Lazar ruled from 1371 to 1389, and during his reign he made an alliance with Ban[5] Tvrtko of Bosnia against the Turks. Ban Tvrtko proclaimed himself King of Bosnia, and endeavoured to extend his power in Hungary, whilst Knez Lazar, with the help of a number of Serbian princes, prepared for a great war against the Turks. But Sultan Amourath, informed of Lazar's intentions, suddenly attacked the Serbians on June 15 1389, on the field of Kossovo. The battle was furious on both sides, and at noon the position of the Serbians promised ultimate success to their arms.

The Treachery of Brankovitch.

There was, however, treachery in the Serbian camp. Vook (Wolf) Brankovitch, one of the great lords, to whom was entrusted one wing of the Serbian army, had long been jealous of his sovereign. Some historians state that he had arranged with Sultan Amourath to betray his master, in return for the promise of the imperial crown of Serbia, subject to the Sultan's overlordship. At a critical moment in the battle, the traitor turned his horse and fled from the field, followed by 12,000 of his troops, who believed this to be a stratagem intended to deceive the Turks. This was a great blow to the Serbians, and when, later in the day the Turks were reinforced by fresh troops under the command of the Sultan's son, Bajazet, the Turkish victory was complete. Knez Lazar was taken prisoner and beheaded, and the Sultan himself perished by the hand of a Serbian voïvode,[6] Milosh Obilitch.

Notwithstanding the disaster, in which Brankovitch also perished, the Serbian state did not succumb to the Turks, thanks to the wisdom and bravery of Lazar's son, Stevan Lazarevitch (1389-1427). His nephew, Dyourady Brankovitch (1427-1456), also fought heroically, but was compelled, inch by inch, to cede his state to the Turks.

The Final Success of the Turks

After the death of Dyourady the Serbian nobles could not agree concerning his successor, and in the disorder that ensued the Turks were able to complete their conquest of Serbia, which they finally achieved by 1459. Their statesmen now set themselves the task of inducing the Serbian peasantry in Bosnia, by promises of future prosperity, to take the oath of allegiance to the Sultan, and in this they were successful during the reign of the King of Bosnia, Stevan Tomashevitch, who endeavoured in vain to secure help from the Pope. The subjugation of Bosnia was an accomplished fact by 1463, and Herzegovina followed by 1482. An Albanian chief of Serbian origin, George Kastriotovitch-Skander-Beg (1443-1468), successfully fought, with great heroism, for the liberty of Albania. Eventually, however, the Turks made themselves master of the country as well as of all Serbian lands, with the exception of Montenegro, which they never could subdue, owing partly to the incomparable heroism of the bravest Serbians—who objected to live under Turkish rule—and partly to the mountainous nature of the country. Many noble Serbian families found a safe refuge in that land of the free; many more went to Ragusa as well as to the Christian Princes of Valahia and Moldavia. The cruel and tyrannous nature of Turkish rule forced thousands of families to emigrate to Hungary, and the descendants of these people may be found to-day in Batchka, Banat, Sirmia and Croatia. Those who remained in Serbia were either forced to embrace Islam or to live as *raya* (slaves), for the Turkish *spahis* (land-lords) not only oppressed the Christian population, but confiscated the land hitherto belonging to the natives of the soil.

The Miseries of Turkish Rule

We should be lengthening this retrospect unduly if we were to describe in full the miserable position of the vanquished Christians, and so we must conclude by giving merely an outline of the modern period.

When it happens that a certain thing, or state of things, becomes too sharp, or *acute*, a change of some sort must necessarily take place. As the Turkish atrocities reached their culmination at the end of the XVIIth century, the Serbians, following the example of their brothers in Hungary and Montenegro, gathered around a leader who was sent apparently by Providence to save them from the shameful oppression of their Asiatic lords. That leader, a gifted Serbian, George Petrovitch—designated by the Turks Karageorge ('Black George')—gathered around him other Serbian notables, and a general insurrection occurred in 1804. The Serbians fought successfully, and established the independence of that part of Serbia comprised in the pashalik of Belgrade and some neighbouring territory. This was accomplished only by dint of great sacrifices and through the characteristic courage of Serbian warriors, and it was fated to endure for less than ten years.

Serbia again Subjugated

When Europe (and more particularly Russia) was engaged in the war against Napoleon, the Turks found in the pre-occupation of the Great Powers the opportunity to retrieve their losses and Serbia was again subjugated in 1813. George Petrovitch and other Serbian leaders left the country to seek aid, first in Austria, and later in Russia. In their absence, Milosh Obrenovitch, one of Karageorge Petrovitch's lieutenants, made a fresh attempt to liberate the Serbian people from the Turkish yoke, and in 1815 was successful in re-establishing the autonomy of the Belgrade pashalik. During the progress of his operations, George Petrovitch returned to Serbia and was cruelly assassinated by order of Milosh who then proclaimed himself hereditary prince and was approved as such by the Sublime Porte in October 1815. Milosh was a great opponent of Russian policy and he incurred the hostility of that power and was forced to abdicate in 1839 in favour of his son Michel (Serbian 'Mihaylo'). Michel was an excellent diplomat, and had previously incorporated within the independent state of Serbia several districts without shedding blood. He was succeeded by Alexandre Karageorgevitch (1842–1860) son of Karageorge Petrovitch. Under the prudent rule of that prince, Serbia obtained some of the features of a modern constitution and a foundation was laid for further and rapid development. But an unfortunate foreign policy, the corruption existing among the high dignitaries of the state and especially the treachery of Milosh's apparent friends, who hoped to supplant him, forced that enlightened prince to abandon the throne and to leave his country. The Skoupshtina (National Assembly) restored Milosh but the same year the prince died and was succeeded once again by his son Michel (1860-1868). At the assassination of this prince his young cousin, Milan (1868-1889), ruled with the aid, during his minority, of three regents, in conformity of a Constitution voted in 1869.

The principal events during the rule of Milan were: the war against Turkey (1876-1878) and the annexation of four new districts; the acknowledgment of Serbian independence by the famous Treaty of Berlin; the proclamation of Serbia as a kingdom in 1882; the unfortunate war against Bulgaria, which was instigated by Austria, and the promulgation of a new Constitution, which, slightly modified, is still in force.

After the abdication of King Milan, his unworthy son, Alexander, ascended the throne. Despite the vigorous advices of his friends and the severe admonishments of his personal friend M. Chedo Miyatovich, he married his former mistress, Draga Mashin, under whose influence he entered upon a period of tyranny almost Neronian in type. He went so far as to endeavour to abolish the Constitution, thus completely alienating his people and playing into the hands of his personal enemies, who finally murdered him (1903).

King Peter I

The Skoupshtina now elected the son of Alexander Karageorgevitch, the present King Peter I Karageorgevitch, whose glorious rule will be marked with golden letters in modern Serbian history, for it is to him that Christendom owes the formation of the league whereby the Turk was all but driven from Europe in 1913. But, alas! the Serbians have only about one-half of their lands free, the rest of their brethren being still under the foreign yoke.

Brief as is this retrospect it will suffice to show the circumstances and conditions from which sprung the Serbian national poetry with which we shall be largely concerned in the following pages. The legends have their roots in disasters due as much to the self-seeking of Serbian leaders as to foreign oppressors; but national calamities have not repressed the passionate striving of a high-souled people for freedom, and these dearly loved hero tales of the Balkans express the ideals which have inspired the Serbian race in its long agony, and which will continue to sustain the common people in whatever further disappointments they may be fated to suffer ere they gain the place among the great nations which their persistence and suffering must surely win in the end.

1The English language is the only one which, instead of the correct forms 'Serbian,' 'Serbia,' uses the solecism 'Servia,' etc. Suggesting a false derivation from the Latin root which furnished the English words 'serf,' 'servant,' 'servitude,' this corrupted form is, of course, extremely offensive to the people to whom it is applied and should be abandoned.

2Protestants of the Greek Orthodox Church who later settled in Bosnia.

3See the poem: "Tsar Ourosh and his Nobles, or, The Royal Prince Marko tells whose the Empire will be."

4This title corresponds to 'prince.'

5'Ban' is the original title of the rulers of Bosnia.

6*Voïvode* originally meant 'leader of an army' or 'General.' As a title of nobility it corresponds with the English 'Duke,' which, derived from the Latin, *dux*, possesses the same root meaning.

Chapter II: Superstitious Beliefs & National Customs

General Characteristics

The Serbians inhabiting the present kingdom of Serbia, having been mixed with the ancient indigenous population of the Balkan Peninsula, have not conserved their true national type. They have mostly brown visages and dark hair; very rarely are blonde or other complexions to be seen. Boshnyaks (Serbians inhabiting Bosnia) are considered to be the most typical Serbians, they having most strongly retained the national characteristics of the pure Southern-Slavonic race. The average Serbian has a rather lively temperament; he is highly sensitive and very emotional. His enthusiasm is quickly roused, but most emotions with him are, as a rule, of short duration. However, he is extremely active and sometimes persistent. Truly patriotic, he is always ready to sacrifice his life and property for national interests, which he understands particularly well, thanks to his intimate knowledge of the ancient history of his people, transmitted to him from generation to generation through the pleasing medium of popular epic poetry composed in very simple decasyllabic blank verse—entirely Serbian in its origin. He is extremely courageous and always ready for war. Although patriarchal and conservative in everything national, he is ready and willing to accept new ideas. But he has remained behind other countries in agricultural and industrial pursuits. Very submissive in his *Zadrooga*[1] and obedient to his superiors, he is often despotic when elevated to power. The history of all the

Southern Slavs pictures a series of violations, depositions, political upheavals, achieved sometimes by the most cruel means and acts of treachery; all mainly due to the innate and hitherto inexpugnable faults characteristic of the race, such as jealousy and an inordinate desire for power. These faults, of course, have been most apparent in the nobles, hence the decay of the ancient aristocracy throughout the Balkans.

Paganism and Religion

There is available but slender material concerning the pre-Christian history of the Southern-Slavonic races, and their worship of Nature has not been adequately studied. Immediately after the Slavonic immigration into the Balkan Peninsula during the seventh and eighth centuries, Christianity, which was already deeply rooted in the Byzantines, easily destroyed the ancient faith. The last survivors of paganism lived in the western part of the peninsula, in the regions round the river Neretva, and these were converted to Christianity during the reign of Basil I. A number of Croatians had been converted to Christianity as early even as the seventh century, and had established an episcopate at Agram (Zagreb). In the course of some thousand years Græco-Oriental myths and legends, ancient Illyrian and Roman propaganda and Christian legends and apocryphal writings exercised so great an influence upon the ancient religions of the Southern-Slavonic peoples that it is impossible to unravel from the tangled skein of such evidence as is available a purely Southern-Slavonic mythology.

The God Peroon

Of Peroon, the Russian God of Thunder, by whom the Russian pagans used to swear in their treaties and conventions concluded with the Byzantines during the tenth century, only a few insignificant traces remain. There is a village named 'Peroon' near Spalato; a small number of persons in Montenegro bear the name;[2] and it is preserved also in the name of a plant, 'Peroonika' (*iris*), which is dedicated to the god. There is hardly a cottage-garden in the Serbian villages where one does not see the iris growing by the side of the house-leek (*Tchuvar-Koutchye*). The Serbians say that the god lives still in the person of St. Elias (Elijah), and Serbian peasants believe that this saint possesses the power of controlling lightning and thunder. They also believe that St. Elias has a sister 'Ognyena Maria' (Mary the Fiery One), who frequently acts as his counsellor.

The God Volos

From the Russian God of Cattle, 'Volos,' the city 'Veless' has obtained its name; also a village in the western part of Serbia, and there is a small village on the lower Danube called 'Velessnitza.' But the closest derivative appears in the Serbian word 'Vo,' or 'Voll' (in the singular) 'Volovi' (in the plural) which means 'Ox.'

The Sun God

Other phenomena of Nature were also personified and venerated as gods. The Sun god, 'Daybog' (in Russian

'Daszbog,' meaning literally 'Give, O God!'), whose idols are found in the group of idols in Kief, and whose name reappears as a proper name of persons in Russia, Moldavia and Poland, is to the Serbians the personification of sunshine, life, prosperity and, indeed, of everything good. But there have been found no remains of idols representing the god 'Daybog' among the Southern-Slavonic nations, as with the Russians, who made figures of him in wood, with head of silver and moustache of gold.

The Veele

The Serbian legends preserve to this day interesting traces of the worship of those pagan gods and of minor deities—which still occupy a considerable place in the national superstition. The "νύμφαι" and "ποταμὶ" mentioned by the Greek historian Procope, as inferior female divinities inhabiting groves, forests, fountains, springs or lakes, seem to have been retained in the Serbian popular *Veela* (or *Vila*—in the singular; *Veele* or *Vile*—in the plural). There are several fountains called "Vilin Izvor" in Montenegro (*e.g.* on Mount Kom), as also in the district of Rudnik in Serbia. During the Renaissance the Serbian poets of Ragusa and other cities of Dalmatia made frequent reference to the *nymphs*, *dryads*, and *oreads* beloved by them as "veele." The Serbian bards or troubadours from the early fourteenth century to our day have ever glorified and sung of the veele, describing them as very beautiful and eternally young, robed in the whitest and finest gauze, with shimmering golden hair flowing down over snow-white bosoms. Veele were said to have the most sweet voices and were sometimes armed with bows and arrows. Their melodious songs were often heard on the borders of the lakes or in the meadows hidden deep in the forests, or on high mountain-peaks beyond the clouds. They also loved to dance, and their rings are called 'Vrzino (or *Vilino*) Kollo.' In Mount Kom in Montenegro, there is one of these rings which measures about twenty metres across and is called 'Vilino Kollo.' The Treaty of Berlin mentions another situated between Vranya and Küstandil, through which ran the Serbo-Bulgarian frontier. When veele were dancing nobody dare disturb them, for they could be very hostile to men. Like the Greek nymphs, veele could also be amicably disposed; and on occasions they assisted the heroes. They could become the sisters of men and of women, and could even marry and have off-springs. But they were not by any means invulnerable. Prince Marko, the favourite hero of the Serbians, was endowed with superhuman strength by a veela who also presented him with a most wonderful courser, 'Sharatz,' which was, indeed, almost human. A veela also became his *possestrima* (Spiritual sister, or 'sister-in-God') and when Marko was in urgent need of help, she would descend from the clouds and assist him. But she refused to aid him if he fought in duels on Sundays. On one occasion[3] Marko all but slew the Veela Raviyoyla who wounded his *pobratim* (brother-in-God) Voïvode Milosh. The veele were wise in the use of herbs, and knew the properties of every flower and berry, therefore Raviyoyla could heal the wounds of Milosh, and his pierced heart was "sounder than ever before." They believed in God and St. John, and abhorred the Turk. The veele also possessed the power of clairvoyance, and Prince Marko's 'sister-in-God' prophesied his death and that of Sharatz.[4] Veele had power to control tempests and other phenomena of nature; they could change themselves into snakes or swans. When they were offended they could be very cruel; they could kill or take away the senses of any who threatened them with violence; they would lead men into deep waters or raze in a night magnificent buildings and fortresses.[5]

He is instantly pursued by a dense fog

To veele was attributed also the power of deciding the destiny of newly born children. On the seventh night after the birth of a child the Serbian peasant woman watches carefully for the *Oossood*, a veela who will pronounce the destiny of her infant, and it is the mother only who can hear the voice of the fairy.

Predestination and Immortality

The Serbians believe firmly in predestination, and they say that "there is no death without the appointed day" (*Nema smrti bez soodyena dana*). They believe universally in the immortality of the soul, of which even otherwise inanimate objects, such as forests, lakes, mountains, sometimes partake. After the death of a man, the soul delays its departure to the higher or lower spheres until the expiration of a certain period (usually forty days), during which time it floats in the air, and can perhaps enter into the body of some animal or insect.

Good and Evil Spirits

Spirits are usually good; in Montenegro the people believe that each house has its Guardian-Spirit, whom they call *syen* or *syenovik*. Such syens can enter into the body of a man, a dog, a snake, or even a hen. In the like manner every forest, lake, and mountain has each its syen, which is called by a Turkish word *djin*. So, for example, the djin of the mountain Riyetchki Kom, near the northern side of the lake of Scutari, does not allow passers-by to touch a branch or a leaf in the perpetually green woods on the mountain side, and if any traveller should gather as much as a flower or a leaf he is instantly pursued by a dense fog and perceives miraculous and terrifying visions in the air. The Albanians dread similar spirits of the woods in the region round Lurya, where they do not dare touch even the dry branches of fallen firs and larches. This recalls the worship of sacred bushes common among the ancient Lithuanians.

Besides the good spirits there appear evil spirits (*byess*), demons, and devils (*dyavo*), whom the Christians considered as pagan gods, and other evil spirits (*zli doossi*) too, who exist in the bodies of dead or of living men. These last are called *vookodlaks* or *Vlkodlaks* (i.e. *vook*, meaning 'wolf,' and *dlaka*, meaning 'hair'), and, according to the popular belief, they cause solar and lunar eclipses. This recalls the old Norse belief that the sun and moon were continually pursued by hungry wolves, a similar attempt to explain the same natural phenomena. Even to-day Serbian peasants believe that eclipses of the sun and moon are caused by their becoming the prey of a hungry dragon, who tries to swallow them. In other parts of Serbia it is generally believed that such dragons are female beings. These mischievous and very powerful creatures are credited with the destruction of cornfields and vineyards, for they are responsible for the havoc wrought by the hail-carrying clouds. When the peasants observe a partial eclipse of the moon or the sun, believing that a hailstorm is imminent, they gather in the village streets, and all—men, women, and children—beat pots and pans together, fire pistols, and ring bells in order to frighten away the threatening monster.

In Montenegro, Herzegovina, and Bocca Cattaro the people believe that the soul of a sleeping man is wafted by the winds to the summit of a mountain, and, when a number of such has assembled, they become fierce giants who uproot trees to use as clubs and hurl rocks and stones at one another. Their hissing and groans are heard especially during the nights in spring and autumn. Those struggling crowds are not composed merely of human souls, but include the spirits of many animals, such as oxen, dogs, and even cocks, but oxen especially join in the struggles.

Witches

Female evil spirits are generally called *veshtitze* (singular, *veshtitza*, derived obviously from the ancient Bohemian word *ved*, which means 'to know'), and are supposed to be old women possessed by an evil spirit, irreconcilably hostile to men, to other women, and most of all to children. They correspond more or less to the English conception of 'witches.' When an old woman goes to sleep, her soul leaves her body and wanders about till it enters the body of a hen or, more frequently, that of a black moth. Flying about, it enters those houses where there are a number of children, for its favourite food is the heart of an infant. From time to time veshtitze meet to take their supper together in the branches of some tree. An old woman having the attributes of a witch may join such meetings after having complied with the rules prescribed by the experienced veshtitze, and this is usually done by pronouncing certain stereotyped phrases. The peasants endeavour to discover such creatures, and, if they succeed in finding out a witch, a jury is hastily formed and is given full power to sentence her to death. One of the most certain methods used to discover whether the object of suspicion is really a witch or not, is to throw the victim into the water, for if she floats she is surely a witch. In this case she is usually burnt to death. This test was not unknown in England.

Vampires

The belief in the existence of vampires is universal throughout the Balkans, and indeed it is not uncommon in certain parts of western Europe. Some assert that this superstition must be connected with the belief generally held in the Orthodox Church that the bodies of those who have died while under excommunication by the Church are incorruptible, and such bodies, being taken possession of by evil spirits, appear before men in lonely places and murder them. In Montenegro vampires are called *lampirs* or *tenatz*, and it is thought that they suck the blood of sleeping men, and also of cattle and other animals, returning to their graves after their nocturnal excursions changed into mice. In order to discover the grave where the vampire is, the Montenegrins take out a black horse, without blemish, and lead it to the cemetery. The suspected corpse is dug up, pierced with stakes and burnt. The authorities, of course, are opposed to such superstitious practices, but some communities have threatened to abandon their dwellings, and thus leave whole villages deserted, unless allowed to ensure their safety in their own way. The code of the Emperor Doushan the Powerful provides that a village in which bodies of dead persons have been exhumed and burnt shall be punished as severely as if a murder had been committed; and that a *resnik*, that is, the priest who officiates at a ceremony of that kind, shall be anathematized. Militchevitch, a famous Serbian ethnographist, relates an incident where a resnik, as late as the beginning of the nineteenth century, read prayers out of the apocrypha of Peroon when an exorcism was required. The revolting custom has been completely suppressed in Serbia. In Montenegro the Archbishop Peter II. endeavoured to uproot it, but without entire success. In Bosnia, Istria and Bulgaria it is also sometimes heard of. The belief in vampires is a superstition widely spread throughout Roumania, Albania and Greece.[6]

Nature Worship

Even in our own day there are traces of sun and moon worship, and many Serbian and Bulgarian poems celebrate the marriage of the sun and the moon, and sing *Danitza* (the morning star) and *Sedmoro Bratye* ('The Seven Brothers'—evidently The Pleiades).[7] Every man has his own star, which appears in the firmament at the moment of his birth and is extinguished when he dies. Fire and lightning are also worshipped. It is common belief that the earth rests on water, that the water reposes on a fire and that that fire again is upon another fire, which is called *Zmayevska Vatra* ('Fire of the Dragons').

Similarly the worship of animals has been preserved to our times. The Serbians consider the bear to be no less than a man who has been punished and turned into an animal. This they believe because the bear can walk upright as a man does. The Montenegrins consider the jackal (*canis aureus*) a semi-human being, because its howls at night sound like the wails of a child. The roedeer (*capreolus caprea*) is supposed to be guarded by veele, and therefore she so often escapes the hunter. In some parts of Serbia and throughout Montenegro it is a sin to kill a fox, or a bee.

The worship of certain snakes is common throughout the Balkans. In Montenegro the people believe that a black snake lives in a hole under every house, and if anybody should kill it, the head of the house is sure to die. Certain water-snakes with fiery heads were also considered of the same importance as the evil dragons (or hydra) who, at one time, threatened ships sailing on the Lake of Scutari. One of these hydras is still supposed to live in the Lake of Rikavatz, in the deserted mountains of Eastern Montenegro, from the bottom of which the hidden monster rises out of the water from time to time, and returns heralded by great peals of thunder and flashes of lightning.

But the Southern Slavs do not represent the dragon as the Hellenes did, that is to say as a monster in the form of a huge lizard or serpent, with crested head, wings and great strong claws, for they know this outward form is merely used as a misleading mask. In his true character a dragon is a handsome youth, possessing superhuman strength and courage, and he is usually represented as in love with some beautiful princess or empress.[8]

Enchanters

Among celebrants of the various pagan rites, there is mention of *tcharobnitzi* (enchanters), who are known to have lived also in Russia, where, during the eleventh century, they sapped the new Christianity. The Slavonic translation of the Gospel recognized by the Church in the ninth century applies the name 'tcharobnitzi' to the three Holy Kings.

To this same category belong the *resnitzi* who, as is apparent in the Emperor Doushan's Code referred to previously, used to burn the bodies of the dead. *Resnik*, which appears as a proper name in Serbia, Bosnia and Croatia, means, according to all evidence, "the one who is searching for truth."

Sacrificial Rites

From translations of the Greek legends of the saints, the exact terminology of the sacrificial ceremonies and the places where they had been made is well known. Procopius mentions oxen as the animals generally offered for sacrifice, but we find that calves, goats, and sheep, in addition to oxen, were used by the Polapic Slavs and Lithuanians, and that, according to Byzantine authorities, the Russians used even birds as well. In Montenegro, on the occasion of raising a new building, a ram or a cock is usually slaughtered in order that a corner-stone may be besprinkled with its blood, and, at the ceremony of inaugurating a new fountain, a goat is killed. Tradition tells of how Prince Ivan Tzrnoyevitch once shot in front of a cavern an uncommonly big wild goat that, being quite wet, shook water from its coat so that instantly a river began to flow thence. This stream is called even now the River of Tzrnoyevitch. The story reminds one of the goats' horns and bodies of goats which are seen on the altar dedicated to the Illyrian god, Bind, near a fountain in the province of Yapod.

It is a fact that Russians and Polapic Slavs used to offer human sacrifices. Mention of such sacrifices among the Southern Slavs is found only in the cycle of myths relating to certain buildings, which, it was superstitiously believed, could be completed only if a living human being were buried or immured. Such legends exist among the Serbians and Montenegrins concerning the building of the fortress Skadar (Scutari) and the bridge near Vishegrad; with the Bulgarians in reference to building the fort Lidga-Hyssar, near Plovdiv, and the *Kadi-Köpri* (Turkish for 'the bridge of the judge') on the river Struma; and again among modern Greeks in their history of the bridge on the river Arta, and the Roumanians of the church 'Curtea de Ardyesh.' It seems very likely that certain enigmatic bas-reliefs, representing oval human faces with just the eyes, nose and mouth, which are found concealed under the cemented surface of the walls of old buildings have some connexion with the sacrificial practice referred to. There are three such heads in the fortress of Prince Dyouragy Brankovitch at Smederevo (Semendria), not far from Belgrade, on the inner side of the middle donjon fronting the Danube, and two others in the monastery Rila on the exterior wall close to the Doupitchka Kapiya.

Funeral Customs

During the siege of Constantinople in the year 626, the Southern Slavs burnt the bodies of their dead. The Russians did the same during the battles near

Silistria, 971, and subsequently commemorative services were held in all parts of Russia, and the remains of the dead were buried.

The Slavs of north Russia used to keep the ashes of the dead in a small vessel, which they would place on a pillar by the side of a public road; that custom persisted with the Vyatitchs of southern Russia as late as 1100.

These funeral customs have been retained longest by the Lithuanians; the last recorded instance of a pagan burial was when Keystut, brother of the Grand Duke Olgerd, was interred in the year 1382, that is to say, he was burnt together with his horses and arms, falcons and hounds.

There are in existence upright stones, mostly heavy slabs of stone, many of them broken, or square blocks and even columns, which were called in the Middle Ages *kami*, or *bileg*, and now *stetyak* or *mramor*. Such stones are to be found in large numbers close together; for example, there are over 6000 in the province of Vlassenitza, and some 22,000 in the whole of Herzegovina; some can be seen also in Dalmatia, for instance, in Kanovli, and in Montenegro, at Nikshitch; in Serbia, however, they are found only in Podrigne. These stones are usually decorated with figures, which appear to be primitive imitations of the work of Roman sculptors: arcades on columns, plant designs, trees, swords and shields, figures of warriors carrying their bows, horsemen, deer, bears, wild-boars, and falcons; there are also oblong representations of male and female figures dancing together and playing games.

The symbol of the Cross indicates the presence of Christianity. Inscriptions appear only after the eleventh century. But many tombstones plainly had their origin in the Middle Ages. Some tombs, situated far from villages, are described by man's personal name in the chronicles relating to the demarcations of territories, for example, Bolestino Groblye (the cemetery of Bolestino) near Ipek; Druzetin Grob (the tomb of Druzet). In Konavla, near Ragusa, there was in the year 1420 a certain point where important cross-roads met, known as 'Obugonov Grob.' Even in our day there is a tombstone here without inscription, called 'Obugagn Greb.' It is the grave of the Governor Obuganitch, a descendant of the family of Lyoubibratitch, famous in the fourteenth century.

Classic and Mediæval Influence

When paganism had disappeared, the Southern-Slavonic legends received many elements from the Greeks and Romans. There are references to the Emperors Trajan and Diocletian as well as to mythical personages. In the Balkans, Trajan is often confused with the Greek king Midas. In the year 1433 Chevalier Bertrandon de la Broquière heard from the Greeks at Trajanople that this city had been built by the Emperor Trajan, who had goat's ears. The historian Tzetzes also mentions that emperor's goat's ears ὠτία τράγου. In Serbian legends the Emperor Trajan seems also to be confused with Dædalus, for he is given war-wings in addition to the ears.

To the cycle of mediæval myths we owe also the *djins* (giants) who dwelt in caverns, and who are known by the Turkish name *div*—originally Persian. Notable of the *divs* were those having only one eye—who may be called a variety of cyclops—mentioned also in Bulgarian, Croatian and Slovenian mythology. On the shores of the river Moratcha, in Montenegro, there is a meadow called 'Psoglavlya Livada' with a cavern in which such creatures are said to have lived at one time.

The Spread of Christianity

When the pagan Slavs occupied the Roman provinces, the Christian region was limited to parts of the Byzantine provinces. In Dalmatia after the fall of Salona, the archbishopric of Salona was transferred to Spalato (Splyet), but in the papal bulls of the ninth century it continued always to be styled *Salonitana ecclesia*, and it claimed jurisdiction over the entire lands as far as the Danube.

According to Constantine Porphyrogenete, the Serbians adopted the Christian faith at two different periods, first during the reign of the Emperor Heraclius, who had requested the Pope to send a number of priests to convert those peoples to the Christian faith. It is well known, however, that the Slavs in Dalmatia even during the reign of Pope John IV (640–642) remained pagans. No doubt Christianity spread gradually from the Roman cities of Dalmatia to the various Slav provinces. The Croatians already belonged to the Roman Church at the time when its priests were converting the Serbians to Christianity between the years 642 and 731, *i.e.*, after the death of Pope John IV and before Leon of Isauria had broken off his relations with Rome.

The second conversion of those of the Southern Slavs who had remained pagans was effected, about 879, by the Emperor Basil I.

At first the Christian faith spread amongst the Southern Slavs only superficially, because the people could not understand Latin prayers and ecclesiastical books. It took root much more firmly and rapidly when the ancient Slavonic language was used in the church services.

Owing to the differences arising over icons and the form their worship should take, enthusiasm for the conversion of the pagans by the Latin Church considerably lessened. In the Byzantine provinces, however, there was no need for a special effort to be made to the people, for the Slavs came in constant contact with the Greek Christians, whose beliefs they adopted spontaneously.

From the Slavonic appellations of places appearing in certain official lists, one can see that new episcopates were established exclusively for the Slavs by the Greek Church. The bishops conducted their services in Greek, but the priests and monks, who were born Slavs, preached and instructed the people in their own languages. Thus they prepared the ground for the great Slav apostles.

The Slav apostles of Salonica, Cyrillos and his elder brother Methodius, were very learned men and philosophers. The principal of the two, Cyrillos, was a priest and the librarian of the Patriarchate; in addition he was a professor of philosophy in the University of the Imperial Palace at Constantinople, and he was much esteemed on account of his ecclesiastical erudition. Their great work began in 862 with the mission to the Emperor Michel III., with which the Moravian Princes Rastislav and Svetopluk entrusted them.

The Moravians were already converted to Christianity, but they wished to have teachers among them acquainted with the Slav language. Before the brothers started on their journey, Cyrillos composed the Slav alphabet and translated the Gospel.

Thus the Serbians obtained these Holy Books written in a language familiar to them, and the doctrines of the great Master gradually, but steadily, ousted the old, primitive religion which had taken the form of pure Naturalism. But the worship of Nature could not completely disappear, and has not, even to our day, vanished from the popular creed of the Balkans. The folk-lore of those nations embodies an abundance of religious and superstitious sentiment and rites handed down from pre-Christian times, for after many years' struggle paganism was only partially abolished by the ritual of the Latin and afterwards of the Greek Christian Church, to which all Serbians, including the natives of Montenegro, Macedonia and parts of Bosnia, belong.

Superstition

The foundations of the Christian faith were never laid properly in the Balkans owing to the lack of cultured priests, and this reason, and the fact that the people love to cling to their old traditions, probably accounts for religion having never taken a very deep hold on them. Even to this day superstition is often stronger than religion, or sometimes replaces it altogether. The whole daily life of the Southern Slav is interwoven with all kinds of superstition. He is superstitious about the manner in which he rises in the morning and as to what he sees first; for instance, if he sees a monk, he is sure to have an unfortunate day; when he builds a house, a 'lucky spot' must be found for its foundation. At night he is superstitious about the way he lies down; he listens to hear if the cocks crow in time, and if the dogs bark much, and how they are barking. He pays great attention to the moment when thunder is first heard, what kind of rain falls, how the stars shine—whether or not they shine at all, and looks anxiously to see if the moon has a halo, and if the sun shines through a cloud. All these things are portents and omens to his superstitious mind, and they play a considerable part in all his actions. When he intends to join a hunting expedition, for example, he decides from them whether there will be game or not; he believes that he is sure to shoot something if his wife, or sister (or any other good-natured person) jumps over his gun before he calls up his dogs. Especially there are numberless superstitions connected with husbandry, for some of which fairly plausible explanations could be given; for others, however, explanations are hopelessly unavailing, and the reasons for their origin are totally forgotten. Nevertheless, all superstitions are zealously observed because, the people say, "it is well to do so," or "our ancestors always did so and were happy, why should we not do the same?"

The planting of fruit-trees and the growing of fruit must be aided by charms, and numerous feasts are organized to secure a fruitful year, or to prevent floods, hail, drought, frost, and other disasters. But undoubtedly the greatest number of superstitions exist regarding the daily customs, most of which refer to birth, marriage and death. Charms are used to discover a future bridegroom or bride; to make a young man fall in love with a maid or *vice versâ*; also, if it seems desirable, to make them hate each other. Sorcery is resorted to to ensure the fulfilment of the bride's wishes with regard to children; their number and sex are decided upon, their health is ensured in advance, favourable conditions are arranged for their appearance. Death can come, it is believed, only when the Archangel Michael removes a soul from its body, and that can only happen on the appointed day.

The young man shakes a tree three times

The chief national customs of the Southern Slavs are involved in a mass of superstition. As the Serbians are the most representative of the Balkan Slavs, we shall consider a few of their customs in order to show

how little of the true spirit of religion is to be found in some of their religious observances.

Marriage

When a child is born in a Serbian family, the friends congratulate the parents and wish for them: "that they may live to see the green wreaths," which means living to see their child married. Marriages are most frequent in autumn, especially towards Christmas, and more rare in summer. When parents intend to find a bridegroom for their daughter or a bride for their son, they generally consider the question thoroughly for a whole year beforehand. They take their daughter or son to various social gatherings, in order that they may meet one suited to become the husband of their daughter or the wife of their son. When a daughter is informed of her parents' decision she must hasten her preparations: she must see that the *bochtchaluks*9 (wedding presents) which she has to distribute among the wedding guests (*svati* or *svatovi*) be finished soon. These presents are articles mostly made by her own hands, such as socks, stockings, shirts, towels, and rugs. Usually the house is put into good order and perhaps enlarged before the marriage, and when all the preparations are ready the rumour of her approaching marriage is allowed to spread through the village. As marriages are usually settled by the parents, love-matches, unfortunately, are rare, and elopements are regarded as phenomenal. There are, however, cases where young people are not docile to the will of their parents with regard to marriage. If a girl has fallen in love with a young man, she may have recourse, besides usual ways and methods, to professional enchantresses. Among the devices recommended by these friends of lovers are the following: The maiden looks through the muzzle of a roast sucking-pig (which has been killed for the Christmas festivities) at her beloved, whereupon he is sure to grow madly in love with her; her lover is bound to die of love for her if she sees him through a hole made in a cherry or certain other fruit; she is equally sure to gain his affection if she can succeed in finding the trace of his right foot-print and turns the earth under it. These and many other kinds of sorcery are usually practised on or about St. George's Day (23rd of April, O.S.).

Young men, too, have recourse on occasion to witchcraft when they desire the love of some obdurate maiden. For instance, if at midnight on a certain Friday the young man goes to the courtyard of the dwelling of the lady of his heart and there shakes a tree three times, uttering as many times her Christian name, she is absolutely certain to answer his call and to reciprocate his love. Another equally infallible method is for him to catch a certain fish and to let it die near his heart; then to roast its flesh until it is burnt to a cinder, then to pound this, and to place the powder secretly in water or some other beverage. If the girl can be induced to taste of it, she is as a matter of course constrained to love him. These expedients recall the famous exploit of the French troubadour Pierre Vidal undertaken to win the love of his beautiful patroness Donna Azalais de Baux. A magical recipe for success in love, taken from an Arabic monument, was given to the poet by Hugues de Baux, a mischievous young knight and brother-in-law of the fair Donna Azalais; the credulous Vidal was induced to ride on a pig one moonlight night three times round the castle of his lady-love, all unconscious that his waggish friend had brought all the inmates to a terrace to witness his ridiculous exhibition.

Marriage Negotiations

When parents have chosen their son's bride they send to her parents a fully qualified delegate (*navodagjya*) to inquire whether or not they would consent to give their daughter to the young man. As marriages are rarely concluded without the aid of these delegates there are numerous persons who make it their regular profession to negotiate marriages, and they receive a sum of money when their offices are successful. In addition to this fee the navodagjya receives from the future bride at least one pair of socks. If the father of the girl is not agreeable to the proposal, he generally does not give a decisive reply, but finds some pretext, stating, for example, that his daughter is still too young, or that she is not quite ready with her preparations for marriage; but if the young man appears to be eligible and the father is willing to give his consent, he generally answers that he would like to see his daughter married to such an excellent man, provided the couple be fond of each other. Then a meeting is arranged, although in fact this is merely a matter of form, since the final decision must come from the parents themselves, irrespective of the mutual feelings of the prospective husband and wife. The parents ask the young people if they like one another; usually an affirmative answer is given, whereupon all present embrace each other, and presents are exchanged, both between the parents and between the future husband and bride. This event is often celebrated by the firing of pistols and guns, in order to make it known all over the village that marriage festivities are soon to follow. Soon after the ceremony, which may be called a preliminary betrothal, the parents of the bridegroom, together with the young man and a few most intimate friends, pay an official visit to the house of the bride. The visit usually takes place in the evening, and, after the bridegroom has given the bride a ring, festivities begin and last until the next morning. A few days later the bride and the bridegroom go to church, accompanied by a few friends, and the priest asks them some stereotyped questions, such as: "Do you wish to marry of your own free will?" to which they are, so to speak, compelled to answer "Yes."

The Wedding Procession

A week before the wedding-day both families prepare their houses for numerous guests, whom they will entertain most hospitably for several days. Until very recent times, if the bride lived in some distant village the wedding procession had to travel for several days to fetch her, and, in the absence of good roads for carriages, the entire party had to ride on horseback. The wedding party includes the *dever*[10] (that is, leader of the bride), who remains in constant attendance upon the bride throughout the ceremonies, being, in a sense, her guardian; the *koom* (principal witness, who in due course becomes a sort of sponsor or godfather to the children); and the *stari-svat*, who is the second witness of the wedding ceremony. Throughout the wedding ceremonies the koom has to stand behind the bridegroom and the stari-svat behind the bride. The stari-svat is also a kind of master of the ceremonies on the wedding-day; he keeps order among the guests and presides at the nuptial banquets. With the dever come also his parents, and the koom and stari-svat must bring one servant each, to attend them during the ceremony. These two witnesses must provide themselves with two large wax candles, generally adorned with transparent silk lace and flowers, which they must present to the bride in addition to many other gifts.

Before the procession sets out, the young people fire pistols, sing, and dance, whilst the elders sit and take refreshment. The appearance of the bridegroom in his bridal garments, and wearing flowers in his hat, is the signal for the traditional nuptial songs from a chorus of girls. When the carriages are ready to start they sing the following:

> "A falcon flew from the castle
> Bearing a letter under its wing,
> Drops the letter on the father's knee
> See! Father! The letter tells you
> That thy son will travel far,
> Beyond many running rivers,
> Through many verdant forests,
> Till he brings you a daughter[-in-law]."

The *Tzigan* (Gipsy) band begins its joyful melodies; the bridegroom, the standard-bearer, and other young people mount their horses, all gaily bedecked with flowers, and the procession starts for the bride's house, the equestrians riding, generally, two and two, firing pistols and singing. The procession is always led by a frolicsome youth who carries a *tchoutoura* (a flat wooden vessel) containing red wine. It is his duty to offer this to every person the wedding party may meet on the road, and he is privileged to make, during the wedding festival, jokes and witticisms at the expense of everybody. He enjoys the licence of a court jester for that day, and nobody must resent his witticisms, which are, at times, indelicate and coarse.

A few steps behind the tchoutoura-bearer ride the *voivode* (general, or leader), whose office it is to support the former in his sallies, and the standard-bearer, who carries the national flag; after them, in one of the carriages profusely decorated with flowers, ride the bridesmaids, who are selected from among the relatives of the bridegroom. With other presents the maidens carry the wedding dress and flowers which the bridegroom's father has bought for his future daughter-in-law. Immediately following the bridesmaids rides the bridegroom between the koom and the stari-svat. Then come other relatives and guests, two and two in procession. At times these wedding processions offer a very impressive sight.

The Arrival

When the wedding procession approaches the house of the bride, its arrival is announced by firing off pistols and guns, whereupon a number of girls appear and sing various songs expressive of sorrow at the bride's departure from her old home. In some parts of Serbia there still survives a strange old custom; the bride's father requires that certain conditions should be fulfilled before the gates of the courtyard are opened for the procession. For example, he sends a good wrestler to challenge any or every man of the bridegroom's party, and one of the wedding guests must overpower the challenger before the gates are opened. Of course, the wrestling bout is not serious, as a rule. Another condition, obtaining in ether parts, is that the newcomers are not be to admitted before one of them, by firing his pistol, has destroyed a pot or other terra-cotta vessel fastened at the top of the chimney.

When such, or other, conditions have been successfully negotiated, the wedding party is admitted to the house and led to tables loaded with roast lamb or pork, cakes, fruit, wine and brandy. The bride's father places the father of the bridegroom in the seat of honour, and immediately next to him the stari-svat, then the koom and then the bridegroom. When the guests are seated, a large flat cake (*pogatcha*) is placed before the bridegroom's father, and he lays upon it some gold coins; it may be a whole chain made of golden ducats, which the bride is to wear later round her neck. His example is followed immediately by the stari-svat, the koom, and all the other guests. Finally the bride's father brings the dowry which he has determined to give to his daughter and lays it on the cake. All the money thus collected is handed over to the stari-svat, who will give it in due course to the bride. Next the bridesmaids take the wedding dress to the bride's apartment, where they adorn her with great care and ceremony. Her toilet finished, one of her brothers, or, in the absence of a brother, one of her nearest male relatives, takes her by the hand and leads her to the assembled family and friends. The moment she appears, the wedding guests greet her with a lively fire from their pistols, and the bridesmaids conduct her to the bridegroom, to whom she presents a wreath of flowers. She is then led to the stari-svat and the koom, whose hands she kisses. That ordeal concluded, she goes into the house, where, in front of the hearth, sit her parents on low wooden chairs. There she prostrates herself, kissing the floor in front of the fire. This is obviously a relic of fire-worship; now, however, symbolical of the veneration of the centre of family life. When she rises, the maiden kisses the hands of her father and mother, who, embracing her, give her their blessing. Now her brother, or relative—as the case may be—escorts her back to the bridegroom's party and there delivers her formally to the dever, who from that moment takes charge of her, in the first place presenting to her the gifts he has brought.

The Return from Church

After they have feasted the guests mount their horses and, firing tirelessly their pistols, set out with the bride for the nearest church. When the religious ceremony is over the wedding party returns to the bridegroom's home, and the bride has to alight from her horse (or carriage) upon a sack of oats. While the others enter the courtyard through the principal gate, the bride usually selects some other entrance, for she fears lest she may be bewitched. Immediately she enters, the members of the bridegroom's family bring to her a vessel filled with various kinds of corn, which she pours out on the ground "in order that the year may be fruitful." Next they bring her a male child whom she kisses and raises aloft three times. She then passes into the house holding under her arms loaves of bread, and in her hands bottles of red wine—emblems of wealth and prosperity.

Although the wedding guests have been well feasted at the bride's house, the journey has renewed their appetites, therefore they seat themselves at tables in the same order as we have already seen, and are regaled with a grand banquet. Throughout the meal, as at the previous one, the voivodes and the tchoutoura-bearer poke fun and satire at the expense of everybody. These mirthful effusions are, as we have already said, not generally in very good taste, but no one takes offence, and everybody laughs heartily, provided there be wit in the jokes. After this feast, during which the young people perform the national dances (*kollo*) and sing the traditional wedding songs, the dever brings the bride to the threshold of her apartment (*vayat*) and delivers her to the koom, who, in his turn, leads her in, places her hand in that of the bridegroom and leaves them alone. The guests, however, often remain in the house, until dawn, drinking and singing.

Slava (or Krsno Ime)

This custom is considered to be a survival of the times when the Serbians were first converted to Christianity. Every Serbian family has one day in the year, known as *slava*, generally some saint's day, when there are performed certain ceremonies partly of a religious and partly of a social character. The saint whom the head of the family celebrates as his patron, or tutelary saint, is also celebrated by his children and their descendants.

A few days before the celebration the priest comes to the house of every *svetchar*—the man who as the chief of the family celebrates the saint—in order to bless the water which has been prepared beforehand for that purpose in a special vessel; after this he besprinkles the heads of all the members of the family with the holy water, into which he has dipped a small sprig of basil. Then he proceeds from room to room performing the same ceremony in each.

In order to please their tutelary saint, all the members of the family fast for at least a week before the feast. On the eve of the saint's day a taper is lit before the saint's image, and remains burning for two days. One or two days before the festival the women prepare a *kolatch* (a special cake made of wheat-flour) which measures about fifteen inches in diameter, and is about three inches thick. Its surface is divided into quarters by being marked with a cross, each quarter bearing a shield with the letters I.N.R.I. In the centre there is a circle in which is a *poskurnik* (monogram of these initials). Besides the kolatch, another cake of white wheat well boiled and mixed with powdered sugar, chopped nuts, and almonds, is made. This is called *kolyivo* (literally "something which has been killed with the knife"). This is obviously a relic of the pagan times when kolyivo was the name given to animals sacrificed on the altar. When the Serbians were converted to the Christian faith, they were told that the Christian God and His saints did not call for animal, and still less for human sacrifice, and that boiled wheat might serve as a substitute. And it is interesting to find that kolyivo is prepared only for those saints whom the people believe to be dead, and not for those who are believed to be still living, such as St. Elias (Elijah), the patron Saint of Thunder, or the "Thunderer," the Archangel Michael and certain others, for it is emphatically a symbolic offering for the dead.

The Slava Eve Reception

On the eve of the Slava day enough food is prepared to last for the two following days, and toward sunset, all the tables are well loaded with refreshments in readiness for the arrival of numerous guests. Friends and relations are invited to come by a messenger especially sent out from the house. There are several stereotyped forms of this invitation, one of which is the following: "My father (or my uncle, as the case may be) has sent me to bring you his greetings and to invite you to our house this evening to drink a glass of brandy. We wish to share with you the blessings bestowed upon us by God, and our patron-saint. We entreat you to come!" At these words the messenger hands to the invited guest a tchoutoura filled with red wine and decorated with flowers, out of which the guest is obliged to take a little. He then makes the sign of the Cross, and says: "I thank you, and may your Slava be a happy and prosperous one!" After tasting the wine, he continues: "We will do our best to come. It is simple to comply with your wish, since we are invited to share such an honour." He invariably pronounces these words whether he really intends to accept the invitation or not.

In the meantime, while the messenger was away inviting guests, the women of the household have been making all the preparations necessary for their reception. Each guest, as he reaches the threshold exclaims: "O master of the house, art thou willing to receive guests?" Hearing this the Svetchar rushes to meet the guest and greets him in these words: "Certainly I am, and may there be many more good guests such as thou art!" Then the guest enters, embraces the Svetchar and says: "I wish thee a most pleasant evening and a happy Slava!" And then as a matter of course the host answers: "I thank thee, and welcome thee to my house!" In the same manner the other guests are greeted. When they have all arrived, the host invites them to wash their hands—for no Serbian peasant would ever sit down to take food without first doing so. Then the host shows to each one his place at the table, always strictly observing precedence due to seniority.

The girls of the house first pass round brandy to the assembled guests and this, at least in the winter, has generally been warmed, and honey or sugar has been added. While that is being served all the guests stand, and in silence wait reverently for the ceremonies of the Slava to begin.

The host places in the middle of the table a large wax candle, which he does not light until he has made the sign of the Cross three times. Next he takes an earthen vessel containing a few embers, places in it a few small pieces of incense and then lets the fragrance ascend to the icon, which is, according to custom, occupying the place of honour in the room, then still holding the censer he stops for a few moments before each guest. That ceremony being ended, and if there be no priest present, the host himself invites his guests to say their prayers to themselves. A great many Serbian peasants are gifted with the power of offering extempore prayers and they are always in request at these ceremonies. The host passes the censer to his wife, whose duty it is to see that the fumes of the incense reach into every part of the house. Next the host breaks silence with the following prayer: "Let us pray, O brethren, most reverently to the Almighty Lord, our God, and to the Holy Trinity! O Lord,

Thou omnipotent and gracious Creator of Heaven and Earth, deliver us, we pray Thee, from all unforeseen evil! O, St. George! (here he adds the name of the saint whose festival they are celebrating), our holy patron-saint, protect us and plead for us with the Lord, our God, we here gathered together do pray Thee. Ye Holy Apostles, ye, the four Evangelists and pillars upon whom rest the Heavens and the Earth, we, being sinners, do conjure ye to intercede for us," and so on. When his prayer is finished, the guests make the sign of the Cross several times and then supper begins.

Slava Toasts

During the first two or three courses, the guests continue to drink brandy, and wine is not served until they have partaken of meat. At the drinking of the first glass of wine the oldest guest or whoever enjoys the highest dignity of position (generally it is the village priest or the mayor) proposes the first toast, of which—as well as of all the subsequent ones—it may be said that tradition has ordered the exact programme to be followed in all these proceedings, and even prescribed the very words to be used. In some parts of Serbia the host himself proposes the first toast to the most distinguished of his guests, addressing him with: "I beg to thank you, as well as all your brethren, for the honour which you graciously show me in coming to my Slava! Let us drink the first glass to the glory of the gracious God! Where wine is drunk in His name, may prosperity always be!" The principal guest accepts the toast, makes the sign of the Cross and answers in such words as the following: "I thank you, most kind and hospitable host!

May your Slava bring you prosperity, let us drink this second glass 'for the better hour.'" The third toast is generally "To the glory of the Holy Trinity!" (In Serbian: *Tretya-sretya, sve u slavu Svete Troyitze!*)

In some parts of Serbia there are commonly seven or even more toasts to be drunk, but this custom shows, fortunately, a tendency to disappear.

The Ceremony at Church

Next morning all the members of the family rise very early in order to restore order in the house, and the Svetchar goes to the nearest church, taking with him the kolyivo, the kolatch, some wine, incense and a wax candle. All these things he places in front of the altar where they must remain during the morning service, after which the officiating priest cuts the Slava cake from underneath so that his cuts correspond with the lines of the cross shown on the upper surface. Then he breaks the cake and turns it in a circle with the help of the Svetchar, while they pronounce certain prayers together. This ceremony ended, the host takes one half of the cake home and leaves the other half to the priest. If it happens that the church is far away, and time does not allow the host to absent himself long from home, the Slava cake may be cut in halves by him in his own house with the help of his male guests, chanting all the while certain formal prayers: and standing in a circle they hold the cake so that a thumb of each guest should be placed on the top of the cake, whilst they each support it with four fingers.

The Slava Feast

Toward noon, a few minutes before the sun reaches his zenith, a part of the Slava cake is placed upon the table together with a lighted wax candle. To this midday meal many more guests are usually invited than had attended the supper on the previous evening; furthermore, on this day even a stranger—whatever his religion may be—has the right to enter the house and to claim hospitality. For instance, the Royal Prince Marko had many friends amongst the Turks, and they would invariably come to him as guests on his Slava day. All the guests rise together, cross themselves with great reverence, and, in perfect silence, with glasses filled, they await the address to be made by the Svetchar. Again three, or perhaps more, toasts are proposed and accepted, and, of course, as many times are the glasses again emptied and re-filled before the 'midday' meal is even begun. Eating and drinking, in all cases, "to the glory of God, the Holy Trinity, to the Holy Slava" and so forth continue till late at night, when the guests remember that it is time to go home. Many, however, remain in the house all night and for the next day. Some devotees of good wine used actually to remain, on occasions, for three whole consecutive days and nights. This very extreme devotion to the saints has been practised more especially at Nish, and in that neighbourhood, and has furnished the celebrated Serbian novelist Stefan Strematz with abundant material for one of the finest, as it is undoubtedly one of the wittiest, novels that have been written in Serbian.

Christmas Eve

Another festival, which the Serbians, like other nations, conduct with many rites and customs of unmistakably pagan origin and which fills the hearts of all with joy, is Christmas. It is a saying of the Serbian people that "there is no day without light—neither is there any real joy without Christmas."

The Serbian peasant is, as a general rule, an early riser, but on Christmas Eve (*Badgni dan*) everybody is up earlier than usual, for it is a day when each member of the household has his hands full of work to be done. Two or more of the young men are sent out from every house to the nearest forest[11] to cut, and bring home, a young oak tree, which is called *Badgnak*. (The etymology of this word is obscure, but it is probably the name, or derived from the name, of a pagan god.) When the young man who is to cut the tree has selected it, he kneels down, and murmuring words of greeting and uttering a special prayer, he throws at it a handful of wheat or corn; then he makes the sign of the Cross three times and begins carefully to cut in such a direction that the tree must necessarily fall toward the East, and at just about the moment when the sun first shows himself above the horizon. He has also to see that the tree does not touch, in falling to earth, the branches of any tree near it, otherwise the prosperity of his house would most surely be disturbed during the ensuing year. The trunk of the tree is now cut into three logs, one of which is rather longer than the others.

Toward evening, when everything is ready and all the members of the family are assembled in the kitchen, the chief room in the dwelling, a large fire is lit, and the head of the family solemnly carries in the Badgnak, and, placing it on the fire, so that the thicker end is left about twelve inches beyond the hearth, he pronounces in a loud voice his good wishes for the prosperity of the house and all within it. In the same way he brings in the other parts of the Badgnak, and, when all are in a blaze, the young shepherds embrace across the largest log, for they believe that by doing so they will ensure the attachment of the sheep to their lambs, of the cows to their calves, and of all other animals to their young.

At this point of the proceedings the oldest member of the family brings in a bundle of straw and hands it over to the housewife, to whom he wishes at the same time "a good evening and a happy Badgni dan." She then throws a handful of corn at him, thanks him for the straw and starts walking about the kitchen and the adjoining rooms, scattering straw on the floor and imitating the clucking of hens, while the children gleefully follow her and imitate the sounds made by young chicks.

The children gleefully follow her

This finished, the mother has next to bring a yellow wax candle and an earthen vessel filled with burning coal. The father again reverently makes the sign of the Cross, lights the candle and places some incense on the embers. Meanwhile the rest of the family have already formed themselves into a semi-circle, with the men standing on the right and the women on the left. The father now proceeds to say prayers aloud, walking from one end of the semi-circle to the other and stopping in front of each person for a short space of time that the fumes of smoking incense, in the censer, held in his right hand, should rise to the face of every one in turn. The prayers which they utter on these occasions last for about fifteen or twenty minutes, and vary in nearly every district.

After the prayers they all sit down to supper, which is laid, not upon a table, but on the floor, for it is considered a good orthodox custom to lay sacks over the stone or clay of which the floor is formed, and to use cushions instead of chairs, on Christmas Eve. During supper, at which no meat is served, the father of the family enthusiastically toasts the Badgnak, expressing at the same time his wishes for their common prosperity for the new year, and pours a glass of wine over the protruding end of the log. In many parts of Serbia all the peasants—men, women, and even small children—fast for the forty-five days immediately before Christmas. They abstain from meat, eggs, and milk-food, and eat simply vegetables and fruit.

When the supper is over the whole family retires to bed, except one of the young men, who remains near the fire to see that the Badgnak does not burn off completely, and that the fire is not extinguished.

Christmas Day

It is generally believed that the rites and customs concerning this Church festival, which we Serbians call in our own language *Bojitch*, meaning 'the little God,' is nothing but the modified worship of the pagan god Dabog (or Daybog), to whom we have already referred, or perhaps represents several forms of that worship. Our pagan ancestors used to sacrifice a pig to their Sun-god, and in our day there is not a single house throughout Serbia in which "roast pork" is not served on Christmas Day as a matter of course. The men and boys of each household rise very early in the morning that day to make a big fire in the courtyard, and to roast a sucking-pig on a spit, for which all preparations are made on Badgni dan. The moment each little pig is placed at the fire there is a vigorous firing of pistols or rifles to greet it, showing by the sound of shot after shot that the whole village is astir. As nearly all the houses in a village practise the same custom most zealously, and as naturally every youth considers it a part of his duty to fire a pistol, the neighbouring hills echo again and again as if persistent skirmishing were going on.

Still early in the morning one of the maidens goes to the public well to fetch some drinking water, and when she reaches the well she greets it, wishing it a happy Christmas, throwing at the same time into it a handful of corn and a bunch, or perhaps merely a sprig, of basil. She throws the corn in the hope that the crops may be as abundant as water, and the basil is to keep the water always limpid and pure. The first cupful of the water she draws is used to make a cake (*Thesnitza*) to be broken at the midday meal into as many pieces as there are members of the household. A silver coin has been put into the dough, and the person who finds it in his piece of cake is considered as the favourite of fortune for the year to come.

During the morning every house expects a visitor (*polaznik*), who is usually a young boy from a neighbouring house. When the polaznik enters the house he breaks off a small branch of the Badgnak's smouldering end, and while he is greeting the head of the house with 'Christ is born!' and all the others are answering him with a cry of 'In truth He is born!' the mother throws at him a handful of wheat. He then approaches the hearth, and strikes the Badgnak with his own piece of tree repeatedly, so that thousands of sparks fly up into the chimney, and he pronounces his good wishes: "May the holy Christmas bring to this house as many sheep, as many horses, as many cows, as many beehives, [and so forth,] as there are sparks in this fire!" Then he places on the Badgnak either a silver or a gold coin, which the head of the family keeps to give to the blacksmith to smelt in with the steel when making his new plough—for, as he believes, this cannot fail to make the ground more fertile and all go well. The polaznik is, of course, made to stay and share the meal with them, and afterwards he is presented with a special cake also containing a coin, sometimes a gold one, sometimes silver.

After the repast all the youths go out of doors for sports, especially for sleighing, while the older people gather together around a *gooslar* (a national bard), and take much, even endless, delight in listening to his recitals of their ancient ballads.

The Dodola Rite

The disasters which Serbian peasants most fear are of two kinds—drought and very violent storms. In pagan times there was a goddess who, it is believed, ruled the waters and the rain. When the Serbians were first converted to Christianity, the power of controlling the ocean, rivers, and storms, and the sailing of ships at sea, was attributed to St. Nicholas, and the Dalmatians, seagoing men, still pray only to him; whereas in the heart of Serbia, where the peasants have no conception of what large navigable rivers are, still less of what seas and lakes are like, recourse is taken to the favourite goddess *Doda* or *Dodola* whenever there is an unduly long spell of dry weather.

The Dodola rite is a peculiar one. A maiden, generally a Gipsy, is divested of her usual garments and then thickly wrapped round with grass and flowers so that she is almost concealed beneath them. She wears a wide wreath of willow branches interwoven with wild flowers around her waist and hips, and in such fantastic attire she has to go from house to house in the village dancing, while each housewife pours over her a pailful of water, and her companions chant a prayer having the refrain, *Oy Dodo, oy Dodole*, after every single line:

> Fall, O rain! and gentlest dew!
>   Oy, Dodo! Oy, Dodole!
> Refresh our pasture-lands and fields!
>   Oy, Dodo! Oy, Dodole!

In each verse that follows mention is made of a cereal or other plant, imploring Doda that rain may soon be shed upon it. Then the cottage women give them presents, either food or money, and the maidens sing other songs for them, always in the same rhythm, give their thanks, offer good wishes, and are gone.

Whitsuntide

During the Whitsuntide festivities, about fifteen young girls, mostly Christian Gipsies, one of whom personates the Standard-bearer, another the King, and another the Queen (*kralyitza*), veiled and attended by a number of Maids of Honour, pass from door to door through the village, singing and dancing. Their songs relate to such subjects as marriage, the choice of a husband or wife, the happiness of wedded life, the blessing of having children. After each verse of their songs follows a refrain, *Lado, oy, Lado-leh!* which is probably the name of the ancient Slavonic Deity of Love.

Palm Sunday

"In winter, just before Lent, the great festival in honour of the Dead is celebrated, at which every one solemnizes the memory of departed relations and friends, and no sooner does Palm Sunday arrive than the people join in commemorating the renovation of life.

"On the preceding Saturday the maidens assemble on a hill, and recite poems on the resurrection of Lazarus; and on Sunday, before sunrise, they meet at the place where they draw water and dance their country dance (*kolllo*), chanting a song, which relates how the water becomes dull by the antlers of a stag, and bright by his eye."[12]

St. George's Day

On St. George's Day, April 23rd (*Dyourdyev Dan*), long before dawn, all the members of a Serbian family rise and take a bath in the water, in which a number of herbs and flowers—each possessing its own peculiar signification—have been cast before sunset the preceding day. He who fails to get up in good time, and whom the sun surprises in bed, is said to have fallen in disgrace with St. George, and he will consequently have little or no luck in any of his undertakings for the next twelve months. This rite is taken as a sign that the Serbian peasants yield to the many influences of newly awakened nature.

It will be seen by anyone who studies the matter that each season in turn prompts the Serbians, as it must prompt any simple primitive people, to observe rites pointing to the mysterious relation in which man finds that he stands to nature.

---

[1] The male members of a Serbian family continue to live after marriage in the paternal home. If the house is too small to accommodate the young couple, an annexe is built. The home may be frequently enlarged in this way, and as many as eighty members of a family have been known to reside together. Such family associations are called 'zadrooga.'

[2] One of the principal characters in King Nicholas's drama *The Empress of the Balkans* is a warrior called 'Peroon.'

[3] See "Prince Marko and the Veela," page 102.

[4] See "The Death of Marko," page 117.

[5] See "The Building of Skadar," page 198.

[6] Monk Marcus of Seres, Ζήτησις περί βουλχολάχων, ed. Lambros; Νέος Ἑλληνομν'ημων, I (1904), 336–352.

7'Pleiades' are otherwise known under the name of Sedam Vlashitya.

8See "The Tsarina Militza and the Zmay of Yastrebatz." page 129.

9A Serbian word of Turkish origin.

10This personage is usually a brother or very intimate friend of the bridegroom. He corresponds somewhat to the 'best man' at an English wedding, but his functions are more important, as will be seen.

11Forests have been considered until recently as the common property of all. Even in our day every peasant is at liberty to cut a Badgnak-tree in any forest he chooses, though it may be the property of strangers.

12Quoted from the historian Leopold von Ranke.

Chapter III: Serbian National Epic Poetry

The Importance of the Ballads

That the Serbian people—as a distinct Slav and Christian nationality—did not succumb altogether to the Ottoman oppressor; that through nearly five centuries of subjection to the Turk the Southern Slavs retained a deep consciousness of their national ideals, is due in a very large measure to the Serbian national poetry, which has kept alive in the hearts of the Balkan Christians deep hatred of the Turk, and has given birth, among the oppressed Slavs, to the sentiment of a common misfortune and led to the possibility of a collective effort which issued in the defeat of the Turk on the battlefields of Koumanovo, Monastir, Prilip, Prizrend, Kirk-Kilisse, and Scutari.

Who has written those poems? We might as well ask, who is the author of the *Iliad* and the *Odyssey*? If *Homer* be the collective pseudonym of an entire cycle of Hellenic national bards, 'The Serbian people' is that of the national bards who chanted those Serbian epic poems during the centuries, and to whom it was nothing that their names should be attached to them. The task of the learned Diascevastes of Pisistrate's epoch, which they performed with such ability in the old Hellade, has been done in Serbia by a self-taught peasant, the famous Vouk Stephanovitch-Karadgitch, in the beginning of the nineteenth century. Vouk's first collection of Serbian national poems, which he wrote down as he heard them from the lips of the *gousslari* (i.e. Serbian national bards), was published for the first time at Vienna in 1814, and was not only eagerly read throughout Serbia and in the literary circles of Austria and Germany, but also in other parts of Europe. Goethe himself translated one of the ballads, and his example was quickly followed by others.

Those poems—as may be seen from the examples given in this volume—dwell upon the glory of the Serbian mediæval empire, lost on the fatal field of Kossovo (1389). When the Turks conquered the Serbian lands and drove away the flower of the Serbian aristocracy, these men took refuge in the monasteries and villages, where the Turkish horsemen never came. There they remained through centuries undisturbed, inspired by the eloquence of the Serbian monks, who considered it their sacred duty to preserve for the nation behind their old walls the memory of ancient kings and tzars and of the glorious past in which they flourished.

Professional bards went from one village to another, chanting in an easy decasyllabic verse the exploits of Serbian heroes and *Haïdooks* (knight-brigands), who were the only check upon the Turkish atrocities. The bards carried news of political and other interesting events, often correct, sometimes more or less distorted, and the gifted Serbians—for gifted they were and still are—did not find it difficult to remember, and to repeat to others, the stories thus brought to them in poetic form. As the rhythm of the poems is easy, and as the national ballads have become interwoven with the spirit of every true Serbian, it is not rare that a peasant who has heard a poem but once can not only repeat it as he heard it, but also improvise passages; nay, he can at times even compose entire original ballads on the spur of inspirational moments.

In Serbian Hungary there are schools in which the blind learn these national ballads, and go from one fair to another to recite them before the peasants who come from all Serbian lands. But this is not the true method. In the mountains of Serbia, Montenegro, Bosnia and Herzegovina there is no occasion to learn them mechanically: they are familiar to all from infancy. When, in the winter evening, the members of a Serbian family assemble around the fire, and the women are engaged with their spinning, poems are recited by those who happen to know them best.

The Goussle

The ballads are recited invariably to the accompaniment of a primitive instrument with a single string, called a *goussle*, which is to be met with in almost every house. The popular Serbian poet, Peter Petrovitch, in his masterpiece, *Gorsky Viyenatz* ('The Mountain Wreath') uttered the following lines, which have become proverbial:
> Dye se goussle u kutyi ne tchuyu
> Tu su mrtva i kutya i lyoudi.
> (The house in which the goussle is not heard
> Is dead, as well as the people in it.)

The old men, with grown-up sons, who are excused from hard labour, recite to their grandchildren, who yield themselves with delight to the rhythmic verse through which they receive their first knowledge of the past.

Even the abbots of the monasteries do not deem it derogatory to recite those ballads and to accompany their voices by the monotonous notes of the goussle. But the performance has more of the character of a recitation than of singing: the string is struck only at the end of each verse. In some parts of Serbia, however, each syllable is accentuated by a stroke of the bow, and the final syllable is somewhat prolonged.

The heroic decasyllabic lines have invariably five trochees, with the fixed cæsura after the second foot; and almost every line is in itself a complete sentence.

There is hardly a tavern or inn in any Serbian village where one could see an assembly of peasants without a gousslar, around whom all are gathered, listening with delight to his recitals. At the festivals near the cloisters, where the peasants meet together in great numbers, professional gousslars recite the heroic songs and emphasize the pathetic passages in such an expressive manner that there is hardly a listener whose cheeks are not bedewed with copious tears. The music is extremely simple, but its simplicity is a powerful and majestic contrast to the exuberance of romance manifested in the exploits and deeds of some favourite hero—as, for example, the Royal Prince Marko.

There are many bold hyperboles in those national songs, and little wonder if they are discredited by Western critics, especially in the ballads concerning the exploits of the beloved Marko—who "throws his heavy mace aloft as high as the clouds and catches it again in his right hand, without dismounting from his trusty courser Sharatz." Now and then an English reader may find passages which may seem somewhat coarse, but he must bear in mind that the ballads have usually been composed and transmitted from generation to generation by simple and illiterate peasants. Most of those concerning the Royal Prince Marko date from the early fourteenth century, when the customs, even in Western Europe, were different from those prevailing now. My translations have, however, been carefully revised by Mrs. C. H. Farnam, who has taken a great interest in this book, and has endeavoured to do no injustice to the rugged originals. Having passed some time in Serbia—as many noble English ladies have done—nursing the wounded heroes of the Balkan War, of 1912-13, and softening their pain with unspeakable tenderness and devotion, she was attracted by the natural, innate sense of honesty and the bravery which her cultivated mind discovered in those simple Serbians and her interest has since extended to their history and literature.

It is worthy of consideration that the history of the Serbian and other Southern Slavonic nations, developed by its poetry—if not even replaced by it altogether—has through it been converted into a national property, and is thus preserved in the memory of the entire people so vividly that a Western traveller must be surprised when he hears even the most ignorant Serbian peasant relate to him something at least of the old kings and tsars of the glorious dynasty of Nemagnitch, and of the feats and deeds of national heroes of all epochs.

Chapter IV: Kralyevitch Marko; or, the Royal Prince Marko

The Marko Legends

Marko was, as we have already seen, the son of King Voukashin; and his mother was Queen Helen, whom the Serbian troubadours called by the pleasing and poetic name Yevrossima (Euphrosyne) in their songs and poems.

According to the popular tradition, the Prince was born in the castle of Skadar (Scutari), and his mother, being the sister of that most glorious and adventurous knight Momchilo, fortunately transmitted much of the heroism, and many of the other virtues, characteristic of her own family, to her son.

But there is also another tradition, equally popular, which maintains that Marko was the child of a *veela* (fairy-queen) and a *zmay* (dragon). The fact that his father was a dragon is believed, by those who accept this tradition, to explain and in every way to account for, Marko's tremendous strength and his astonishing powers of endurance.

Truly Prince Marko possessed a striking and extraordinarily attractive personality: he so vividly impressed the minds of the Serbian people, people of all ranks and localities, that he has always been, remains to this day, and promises ever to remain, our most beloved hero. Indeed there is no Serbian to be found, even in the most remote districts, who has not a great love for Kralyevitch Marko, and who cannot tell his story.

This Prince's brave deeds and all his exploits have luckily been immortalized by the national bards, who are never weary of describing him in their ballads and legends as a lover of justice, the hater of all oppression, and the avenger of every wrong. He is always represented as the possessor of great physical strength: his principal weapon was his heavy war-club (it weighed one hundred pounds—sixty pounds of steel, thirty pounds of silver, and the remainder was pure gold) and it must be borne in mind that the swords and clubs wielded by the merely human hands of his antagonists can never kill him; they never injure him, for they scarcely ever even touch this hero. Marko is always thought to have had much of the supernatural in him.

Marko, who was often rough and ready in his behaviour, and more especially so to the Turks, whose very Sultan, indeed, he mightily terrified with the tales he told of his many bloodthirsty and warlike deeds, was invariably a most dutiful, loving and tender-hearted son to his mother: and there were occasions when he willingly consulted her, and followed the advice she gave him.

Prince Marko was fearless: It was said that "he feared no one but God"; and it was his rule to be courteous to all women. In Serbia it was the usual custom to drink a great deal of wine, the red wine of which we so often hear, and this custom was one which Marko upheld: but it is always said, and universally believed, that he was never drunk.

The ballads also sing of King Voukashin. Voukashin had been the Councillor of State during the reign of Doushan the Powerful. The capital of the Empire was Prizrend, and Marko was brought up then at the Court, by his father Voukashin. According to the generally accepted belief it was Marko who, a little later on, attended the Emperor as secretary and councillor of State, and was entrusted by Doushan, on the approach of death, with his young son Ourosh.

The Bad Faith of Voukashin

One ballad relates that the Emperor Doushan had bequeathed the crown to Voukashin and stipulated in his will that that monarch should reign for seven years, and at the end of that time he should give up the rule to the Tsarevitch Ourosh. King Voukashin not only prolonged his haughty rule to sixteen years, but absolutely refused to yield the sceptre even then, and moreover proclaimed himself sovereign Tsar. The ballad further depicts the incessant struggles which were in the end to cause the downfall of the Serbian mediæval State. And so tradition, earnestly sympathizing with the just anger felt by the people against the rebels, and their lamentation over the lost tsardom, charges Voukashin with all the blame and responsibility—curses him as a usurper and a traitor, and execrates him for his cunning and inconsistency: whilst on the other hand tradition ever extols and glorifies his son Marko as the faithful defender of Prince Ourosh, as the great avenger of national wrongs, and praises him at all times for his good heart, his generous foresight in politics and private affairs, his humanity, and above all his readiness to perish in the cause of justice.

The Horse Sharatz

The story of Marko cannot be told without some account of Sharatz, his much-loved piebald steed, from whom he was never parted.

Sharatz was undoubtedly unique. There are several versions of the story as to how Marko became possessed of him: Some of the bards assert that Sharatz was given to Marko by the same veela who had from the first endowed him with his marvellous strength; but there are others who affirm that Marko once bought a foal suffering from leprosy, and that the Prince tended him himself and completely cured him, taught him to drink wine, and finally made him the fine horse that he became.

And there are others again who say that at one time, in his youth, Marko served a master for three years, and that for his sole reward he asked permission to choose a horse from among those then grazing in the meadow. His master gladly consented, and Marko, according to his custom, tested each horse in turn, by taking it by the tail and whirling it round and round.

At last, when he came to a certain piebald foal he seized it by the tail: but this animal did not stir, and Marko, with all his vast strength, could not make it move one step. Marko chose that foal, and it became his beloved Sharatz. The Serbians of Veles still call a great plain near

Demir-Kapi 'Markova Livada' (Marko's meadow). Sharatz means 'piebald,' and it is said that the skin of Marko's horse was more like the hide of an ox in appearance than like the skin of an ordinary horse. The Prince called him by various endearing names, such as Sharin or Sharo, and was devoted to him for the hundred and sixty years they were together.

This wonderful beast was the strongest and swiftest horse ever known, and he often overtook the flying veela. He was so well trained that he knew the very moment when to kneel down to save his master from an adversary's lance; he knew just how to rear and strike the adversary's charger with his fore-feet. When his spirit was thoroughly roused Sharatz would spring up to the height of three lengths of a lance and to the distance of four lance-lengths forward; beneath his hoofs glittering sparks shone forth, and the very earth he trod would crack and stones and fragments fly in all directions; and his nostrils exhaled a quivering blue flame, terrifying to all beholders. He often bit off the ears of enemies' horses and crushed and trampled to death numbers of Turkish soldiers. Marko might peacefully doze, and sometimes even go to sleep, when riding through the mountains; and all the time he was safe, for Sharatz would keep careful guard. Therefore the Prince would feed his steed, with bread and wine, from the vessels that he used himself and loved him more than he loved his own brother; and Sharatz shared, as he deserved to share, the glory of many a victory with his master. Marko never rode upon another horse, and together they were described as "a dragon mounted upon a dragon."

There are in existence about thirty-eight poems and perhaps twice as many prose-legends containing detailed descriptions of Marko's thrilling exploits, and there is hardly a Serb or a Bulgar anywhere to be found who cannot recite at least a few of them. In the Balkans-Turkish War, 1912–13, a *gouslar*, when not fighting, would take his *goussle*[1] and recite to his comrades heroic poems of which the greater number related to Marko. The intense veneration felt by Serbians for this beloved Prince proves an unfailing bond between them in their own country and in all parts of the world.

There are, naturally enough, various accounts of the death of Marko. The story that has most appealed to his countrymen and taken a specially firm hold of their poets' imaginations is that he never died. It is believed that he withdrew to a cave, near his castle at Prilip, which is still standing, to rest, and that he is there, now, asleep. From time to time he awakes and looks to see if his sword has yet come out of a rock into which he had thrust it to the very hilt. When the sword is out of the rock Marko will know that the time has come for him to appear among the Serbians once more, to re-establish the mediæval empire, lost at the battle of Kossovo.[2]

As for Sharatz, he is still feeding, but he has now nearly finished his portion of hay.

PRINCE MARKO TELLS WHOSE THE EMPIRE SHALL BE

Four *tabors*[3] met together on the beautiful field of Kossovo near the white church Samodrezja:[4] One tabor was headed by King Voukashin; the second by Despot Ouglesha;5 the third by Voïvode Goyko, and the fourth by Tsarevitch Ourosh.

The first three of these were disputing over the inheritance of the Empire and were ready to stab one another, so eager were they all to reign. They did not know who had been appointed the Tsar's successor and who was the rightful heir to the throne. King Voukashin announced: "The Empire was left to me!" Voïvode Goyko cried out: "Not so! The Empire is mine!" and Despot Ouglesha interposed angrily, "You are both wrong, for know that the Empire is *mine.*"

The youthful Tsarevitch remained silent, for he was not bold enough to proffer a single word in the presence of his haughty elders.

King Voukashin prepared a message and sent it by a faithful servant to the Archdeacon Nedelyko, at Prizrend, summoning him to come at once to the field of Kossovo and state without delay to whom the Empire had been left—for he must surely know, having received the last confession of the illustrious Tsar Doushan the Mighty and been in attendance upon him up to his death. Besides, it was known that the Archdeacon had the archives under his care, and could at least produce the Emperor's will. Despot Ouglesha also sent a missive to the Archdeacon by his swiftest messenger; a third was written by Voïvode Goyko, who dispatched it by his special courier, and a fourth was inscribed and sent off by Ourosh.

The messages were all dispatched secretly, but the couriers reached Prizrend and met at the gates of

Nedelyko's dwelling. But Nedelyko had gone, as Court Chaplain, to officiate at the morning service in the Cathedral. The men were enraged at the delay, and without even alighting from their horses, they rushed infuriated, into the sacred edifice, raised their whips and brutally struck the good Archdeacon, commanding him: "Behold, O Archdeacon Nedelyko! Hasten now, this very hour, to the plain of Kossovo. Thou must state to whom the Empire belongs, for thou hast received the confession from the illustrious Tsar and administered the last sacrament to him, and it is thou who hast the state records in thy care. Hasten, hasten, lest we, in our fierce impatience, do sever thy head from thy body!"

Archdeacon Nedelyko wept with grief and mortification and thus replied: "Begone, ye servants of the most mighty princes! Begone from the House of God! Suffer first that we end God's service, then will I make known into whose hands the Empire is to fall!"

The couriers then went out and awaited the coming of the Archdeacon. Presently the Archdeacon came to them and spake in this wise: "O my children, messengers from the King himself, and from the Princes! I received the last confession of our glorious Tsar, and gave him the sacrament; but about the Empire and affairs of state he spoke never a word, for we were concerned only with the sins that he had committed. Ye must go to the city of Prilip, for there is the castle of the Royal Prince Marko. Marko, as ye may remember, learned from me how to read and write; later he was secretary to the Emperor and he was then entrusted with the care of the records, and he will surely know to whom the empire was entrusted. Call Marko to the field of Kossovo to say who is now the Tsar. Marko will tell the truth, for he fears none but God!"

Marko is Summoned

The messenger set out at once, and, arriving at Prilip, they smote on the portals of the castle. The knocking was heard by Yevrossima, and she spoke thus to her son: "O Marko, my dearest son! who are they who knock at the gates below? They may be messengers from thy father!"

Marko commanded that the gates should be opened, and when the messengers entered they bowed with profoundest respect, and said: "May God always help thee, O noble Lord Marko!"

The Prince laid his hand upon their heads with kindness and said: "Be welcome, ye my dear children! Are the Serbian knights in good health? And is all well with the glorious Tsar and King!"

The couriers again made humble obeisance, saying: "O noble Lord, thou most Royal Prince Marko! All are well, though not, we fear, upon friendly terms together! The King, thy father, and other princes are seriously contending for the Empire upon Kossovo, that vast field which is near the church Samodrezja; they are ready to stab each other at any moment with their blades, for they know not to whom the Empire rightly belongs. Thou art now called upon, O noble Prince, to proclaim the heir to the Imperial crown."

The bard goes on to narrate how Marko went to Yevrossima and asked her advice, and although it was well known that Marko himself loved the truth, his good mother implored him with the following words: "O Marko, thy mother's only son! May the food on which thou wert nourished be not cursed! Speak not falsely either to please thy father, or to satisfy the ambitions of thine uncles, but tell, I beg of thee, the truth before God lest thou shouldest lose thy soul. It were better that thou shouldst perish than sin against thy soul!"

Marko took the ancient documents, mounted Sharatz and rode forthwith to the plain of Kossovo. As he approached his father's tent King Voukashin saw him and exclaimed: "Oh, how fortunate am I! Here is my son Marko; he will say that the Empire was left to me, for of course he knows that it will pass from father to son!"

Marko heard this, but said not one single word, neither would he turn his head towards the King's tent.

When Despot Ouglesha saw Marko, he spoke in this wise: "Oh, what a lucky thing for me! here is my nephew Marko; he is certain to say the Empire is mine! Say, O Marko, the Empire is mine! We would reign together, you and I, like brothers!" Marko still kept silent and did not even turn his head in the direction of his uncle's tent.

As Voïvode Goyko perceived his coming, he exclaimed: "Oh, here is a stroke of good fortune for me! here is my dear nephew Marko: he is sure to say that the Empire was left to me. When Marko was a little child I used to caress him fondly, for he was dear to me as a golden apple, and always most precious. Whenever I rode out on horseback I always used to take Marko with me. O

Marko! dear Marko, thou must say that the Empire is mine! It will be virtually thou who shalt reign as Tsar, and I shall be at thy right hand, at all times ready, as thy counsellor!" Marko, still without a word, and completely ignoring Voïvode Goyko, went straight on to the tent where Tsarevitch Ourosh was, and there he alighted from his Sharatz.

When the young Ourosh saw him, he sprang from his silken couch, and exclaimed: "Hurrah! Behold my godfather Marko! Now he is going to tell us who the true Tsar is!" They embraced each other, inquired after each other's health, and seated themselves upon the couch from which Ourosh had just risen.

Marko tells the Truth

Some time elapsed and the sun had set, the night passed, morning dawned, and church bells called all to morning prayers, and after the service the King, the Princes and great Lords went out into the churchyard, where they took their places at tables, and ate sweet-meats and drank brandy. Marko at last opened the ancient documents, and said aloud: "O my father, thou King Voukashin! Art thou not content with thy Kingdom? May it be turned into a desert if thou art not. Oh! that thou shouldst wish to seize another's Empire! And thou, my uncle, Despot Ouglesha! Art thou not satisfied within thine own territory? Is it indeed too small for thee that thou must struggle for the Empire that belongs to another? May it also turn into a desert! And thou, my uncle, thou Voïvode Goyko! Is thy Dukedom not vast enough for thee? May it likewise become a desert if it is not! Oh that thou too shouldst strive for another's Tsardom? Do ye not all see and understand? If ye fail to see may God not see ye! It is clearly stated in the records that the Empire was left to Ourosh. From father shall it pass to son. To this youth now belongs the Imperial Crown of his ancestors. It was Ourosh whom our late Tsar, on his dying day, named as his successor!" When King Voukashin heard this, he sprang to his feet, drew out his golden yatagan and would have pierced his son with it. The Prince, pursued by his father, fled, for, indeed, it would have been unseemly for Marko to fight with and perhaps mortally strike his own father. Marko ran round the church Samodrezja, his father closely following, till they had run round the building three times, and then, when Voukashin was on the point of getting within reach of his son, all at once a mysterious voice from within the church uttered these words: "Run into the church, O, thou Royal Prince Marko! Seest thou not that otherwise thou shalt perish by thy father's hand, because thou hast spoken the truth so dear to God?" The doors suddenly opened of themselves and Marko passed inside; then they closed and interposed themselves between the two men. King Voukashin began to strike violently upon the doors with his short hanging sword until he noticed that there were drops of blood trickling down the beam, whereupon he was seized with remorse and sighed in lowly penance, saying: "Alas! Unfortunate man that I am! O, thou infinite and divine God! Hear me! I have killed my son Marko!" But the mysterious voice from the church answered: "Behold! Voukashin thou most mighty King! Lo, thou hast not even wounded thy son Marko, but thou hast injured the angel of the true God!"

Voukashin was on the point of getting within reach of his son

At these words the King grew again enraged with Marko and cursed him in these words: "O Marko, my only son, may God kill thee! Mayest thou never be entombed! Mayest thou have no son to come after thee! May thy family end with thee! And, worse than all, may thy soul depart not from thy body before thou hast served as vassal to the Turk!" In these bitter words the King cursed Marko, but the new Tsar, Ourosh, blessed him, saying: "O my beloved god-father, Marko! May God ever support thee! May thy word be always respected and accepted by all just men for ever in the *divan*![6] May thy bright sabre prosper in all battles and combats! May there never be a hero to overpower thee! May it please God that thy name shall at all times be remembered with honour, for so long as the sun and the moon continue to shine."

PRINCE MARKO AND A MOORISH CHIEFTAIN

A great and powerful Moorish chieftain had built for himself a magnificent castle, rising to the height of twenty storeys. The place he had chosen for the castle was by the sea, and when it was quite completed he had panes of the most beautiful glass put in for windows; he hung all the rooms and halls with the richest silks and velvets and then soliloquized thus: "O my *koula*,[7] why have I erected thee? for there is no one but I who is there to tread, with gentle footsteps, upon these fine rugs, and behold from these windows the blue and shining sea. I have no mother, no sister, and I have not yet found a wife. But I will assuredly go at once and seek the Sultan's daughter in marriage. The Sultan must either give me his daughter or meet me in single combat." As soon as the Moor, gazing at his castle, had uttered these words, he wrote a most emphatic letter to the Sultan at Istamboul,[8] the contents of which ran thus: "O Sire, I have built a beautiful castle near the shore of the azure sea, but as yet it has no mistress, for I have no wife. I ask thee, therefore, to bestow upon me thy beloved daughter! In truth, I demand this; for if thou dost not give thy daughter to me, then prepare thyself at once to meet me face to face with thy sword. To this fight I now challenge thee!"

The letter reached the Sultan and he read it through. Immediately he sought for one who would accept the challenge in his stead, promising untold gold to the knight who would show himself willing to meet the Moor. Many a bold man went forth to fight the Moor, but not one ever returned to Istamboul.

Alas! the Sultan soon found himself in a most embarrassing position for all his best fighters had lost their lives at the hand of the haughty Moor. But even this misfortune was not the worst. The Moor prepared himself in all his splendour, not omitting his finest sabre; then he proceeded to saddle his steed Bedevia, securely fastening the seven belts and put on her a golden curb. On one side of the saddle he fastened his tent, and this he balanced on the other side with his heaviest club. He sprang like lightning on to his charger, and holding before him, defiantly, his sharpest lance, he rode straight to Istamboul.

The instant he reached the walls of the fort, he spread his tent, struck his lance well into the earth, bound his Bedevia to the lance and forthwith imposed on the inhabitants a daily tax, consisting of: one sheep, one batch of white loaves, one keg of pure brandy, two barrels of red wine, and a beautiful maiden. Each maiden, after being his slave and attending on him for twenty-four hours, he would sell in Talia for large sums of money. This imposition went on for three months, for none could stop it. But even yet there was a greater evil to be met.

The Entrance of the Moor

The inhabitants of Istamboul were terrorized one day when the haughty Moor mounted upon his dashing steed entered the city. He went to the Palace, and cried loudly: "Lo! Sultan, wilt thou now, once and for ever, give me thy daughter?" As he received no answer he struck the walls of the Palace with his club so violently that the shattered glass poured down from the windows like rain. When the Sultan saw that the Moor might easily destroy the Palace and even the whole city in this way, he was greatly alarmed, for he knew that there was no alternative open to him in this horrible predicament but to give up his only daughter. Although overwhelmed with shame, therefore, he promised to do this. Pleased with his success, the Moor asked for fifteen days' delay before his marriage took place that he might go back to his castle and make the necessary preparations.

When the Sultan's daughter heard of her father's desperate resolution, she shrieked and exclaimed bitterly: "Alas! Behold my sorrow, O almighty *Allah*! For whom have I been taught to prize my beauty? For a Moor? Can it be true that a Moor shall imprint a kiss upon my visage?"

The Sultana's Dream

That night the Sultana had a strange dream, in which the figure of a man appeared before her, saying: "There is within the Empire of Serbia a vast plain Kossovo; in that plain there is a city Prilip; and in that city dwells the Royal Prince Marko who is known among all men as a truly great hero."

And the man went on to advise the Sultana to send, without delay, a message to Prince Marko and beg him to become her son-in-God, and at the same time to offer him immense fortune, for he was without doubt the only one living likely to vanquish the terrible Moor and save her daughter from a shameful fate. The next morning she sped to the Sultan's apartments and told him of her dream. The Sultan immediately wrote a *firman*[9] and sent it to Prince Marko at Prilip, beseeching him to journey with all speed to Istamboul and accept the challenge of the Moor, and if he should succeed in saving the Princess the Sultan would give him three *tovars*[10] of pure golden ducats.

When Marko read the firman, he said to the Sultan's young courier, a native of Tartary: "In the name of God go back, thou Sultan's messenger, and greet thy master—my father-in-God—tell him that I dare not face the Moor. Do we not, all of us, know that he is invincible? If he should cleave my head asunder, of what avail would three tovars, or three thousand tovars, of gold be to me?"

The young Tartar brought back Marko's answer which caused the Sultana so much grief, that she determined to send a letter to him herself, once more beseeching him to accept the challenge and this time increasing the reward to five tovars of pure gold. But Marko, though generally so chivalrous and courteous to all women, remained inexorable, replying that he would not meet the Moor in combat even if he were to be presented with all the treasure the Sultan possessed; for he did not dare.

The Princess appeals to Marko

When the broken-hearted bride heard that this answer had come from Marko she sprang to her feet, took a pen and some paper, struck her rosy cheek with the pen and with her own blood traced the following: "Hail, my dear brother-in-God, O, thou Royal Prince Marko! Be a true brother to me! May God and Saint John be our witnesses! I implore thee, do not suffer me to become the wife of the Moor! I promise thee seven tovars of pure gold, seven *boshtchaluks*, which have been neither woven nor spun, but are embroidered with pure gold. Moreover, I shall give thee a golden plate decorated with a golden snake, whose raised head is holding in its mouth a priceless gem, from which is shed a light of such brilliance, that by it alone you can see at the darkest hour of midnight as well as you can at noon. In addition to these I shall present thee with a finely tempered sabre; this sabre has three hilts, all of pure gold, and in each of them is set a precious stone. The sabre alone is worth three cities. I shall affix to this weapon the Sultan's seal so that the Grand Vizir may never put thee to death without first receiving his Majesty's special command."

When he had read this missive, Marko reflected thus: "Alas! O my dear sister-in-God! It would be but to my great misfortune if I came to serve thee, and to my still greater misfortune if I stayed away. For, although I fear neither the Sultan nor the Sultana, I do in all truth fear God and Saint John, by whom thou hast adjured me! Therefore I now resolve to come and, if necessary, to face certain death!"

Marko prepares to succour the Princess

Having sent away the Princess' messenger without telling him what he had resolved to do, Marko entered his castle and put on his cloak and a cap, made of wolves' skins; next he girded on his sabre, selected his most piercing lance, and went to the stables. For greater safety he fastened the seven belts under the saddle of his Sharatz with his own hands; he then attached a leathern bottle filled with red wine on one side of his saddle and his weightiest war-club on the other. Now he was ready and threw himself upon Sharatz and rode off to Istamboul.

Upon reaching his destination he did not go to pay his respects either to the Sultan or to the Grand Vizir, but quietly took up his abode in a new inn. That same evening, soon after sun-set, he led his horse to a lake near by to be refreshed: but to his master's surprise Sharatz would not even taste the water, but kept turning his head first to the right, then to the left, till Marko noticed the approach of a Turkish maiden covered with a long gold-embroidered veil. When she reached the edge of the water she bowed profoundly toward the lake and said aloud: "God bless thee, O beauteous green lake! God bless thee, for thou art to be my home for ever more! Within thy bosom am I henceforth to dwell; I am now to die, O beauteous lake;

rather would I choose such a fate than become the bride of the cruel Moor!"

Marko greets the Princess

Marko went nearer to the maiden and spoke thus: "O, thou unhappy Turkish maiden! What is thy trouble? What is it that has made thee wish to drown thyself?"

She answered: "Leave me in peace, thou ugly *dervish*,11 why dost thou ask me, when there is nought that thou canst do to help me?"

Then the maiden related the story of her coming marriage with the Moorish chieftain, of the messages sent to Marko, and finally she bitterly cursed that Prince for the hardness of his heart.

Thereupon Marko said: "O, curse me not, dear sister-in-God! Marko is here and is now speaking to thee himself!"

Hearing these words the maiden turned toward the famous knight, embraced him and earnestly pleaded: "For God's sake, O my brother Marko! Suffer not the Moor to wed me!"

Marko was greatly affected, and declared: "O dear sister-in-God! I swear that so long as my head remains upon my shoulders, I shall never let the Moor have thee! Do not tell others that thou hast seen me here, but request the Sultan and thy mother to have supper prepared and sent to the inn for me, and, above all things, beg them to send me plenty of wine. Meanwhile I shall await the Moor's coming at the inn. When the Moor arrives at the Palace, thy parents should welcome him graciously, and they should go so far as to yield thee to him in order to avoid a quarrel. And I know exactly the spot where I shall be able to rescue thee, if it may so please the true God, and if my customary good luck, and my strength, do not desert me."

The Prince returned to the inn, and the maiden hastened back to the Palace.

When the Sultan and the Sultana knew that Marko had come to their aid, they were much comforted, and immediately ordered a sumptuous repast to be sent to him, especially good red wine in abundance.

Now all the shops in Istamboul were closed, and there was silence everywhere as Marko sat drinking the delicious wine in peace. The landlord of the inn came presently to close his doors and windows, and, questioned by Marko as to why the citizens were all shutting up their dwellings so early that day, he answered: "By my faith, you are indeed a stranger here! The Moorish chieftain has asked for our Sultan's daughter in marriage, and as, to our shame, she is to be yielded to him, he is coming to the Palace to fetch her this day. Therefore, owing to our terror of the Moor, we are forced to close our shops." But Marko did not allow the man to close the door of the inn, for he wished to see the Moor and his gorgeous train pass by.

The Moor in Istamboul

At that very moment, as they were speaking, Marko could hear from the city the clangour caused by the Moorish chieftain and his black followers, numbering at least five hundred, and all in glittering armour. The Moor had roused his Bedevia, and she trotted in such a lively manner that the stones, which she threw up with her hoofs, whizzed through the air in all directions, and broke windows and doors in all the shops she passed! When the cavalcade came up to the inn, the Moor thought: "Allah! I am struck with wonder and astonishment! The windows and doors of all the shops and houses throughout the entire city of Istamboul are closed from the great fear the people have of me, except, I see, the doors of this inn. There must either be nobody within, or if there is anybody inside, he is assuredly a great fool; or perhaps he is a stranger, and has not yet been told how terrible I am." The Moor and his retinue passed that night in tents before the Palace.

Next morning the Sultan himself presented his daughter to the Moorish chieftain, together with all the wedding gifts, which were known to weigh twelve tovars. As the wedding procession passed the inn where Marko waited, the Moor again noticed the open door, but this time he urged Bedevia right up to it to see who might be there.

Sharatz and Bedevia

Marko was seated at his ease in the most comfortable room the inn could boast, leisurely drinking his favourite red wine; he was not drinking from an ordinary goblet, but from a bowl which held twelve litres; and each time he filled the bowl he would drink only one half of its contents, giving, according to his habit, the other half to his Sharatz. The Moor was on the point of attacking Marko, when Sharatz barred his way and kicked viciously at Bedevia. The Moor, meeting such unexpected resistance, promptly turned to rejoin the procession. Then Marko rose to his feet, and, turning his cloak and cap inside out, so that to the first glance of those who saw him he presented the terrifying appearance of a wolf, inspected his weapons and Sharatz's belts carefully, and dashed on his charger after the procession. He felled horsemen right and left, till he reached the dever and the second witness, and killed them both. The Moorish chieftain was immediately told of the stranger who had forced his way into the midst of the procession, and of those whom he had killed, also that he did not look like other knights, being clad in wolves' skins.

Marko and the Moor

The Moor astride his Bedevia, wheeled round and addressed Marko thus: "Ill fortune is indeed overtaking thee to-day, O stranger! Thou must have been driven here by Satan to disturb my guests and even kill my dever and second witness; thou must be either a fool, knowing nothing of to-day's events, or thou must be extremely fierce and hast gone mad; but maybe thou art merely tired of life? By my faith, I shall draw in the reins of my Bedevia, and shall spring over thy body seven times; then shall I strike off thy head!" Thereupon Marko answered: "Cease these lies, O Moor! If God, and my usual luck, do but attend me now, thou shalt not even spring near to me; still less can I imagine thee carrying out thy intention of springing over my body!" But, behold! The Moor drew in his Bedevia, spurred her violently forward and indeed he would have sprung over Marko, had not Sharatz been the well-trained fighter that he was, and in a trice he reared so as to receive the adversary against his forefeet and swiftly bit off Bedevia's right ear, from which blood gushed forth profusely and streamed down over her neck and chest. In this way Marko and the Moor struggled for four hours. Neither would give way, and when finally the Moor saw that Marko was overpowering him, he wheeled his steed Bedevia round and fled along the main street of Istamboul, Marko after him. But the Moor's Bedevia was swift as a veela of the forest, and would certainly have escaped from Sharatz if Marko had not suddenly recollected his club, and flung it after his adversary, striking him between his shoulders. The Moor fell from his horse and the Prince severed his head from his body. Next he captured Bedevia, returned to the street where he had left the bride, and found, to his astonishment, that she with her twelve tovars of presents, was alone, awaiting him, for all the wedding-guests and the retinue of the Moorish chieftain had fled at full gallop. Marko escorted the Princess back to the Sultan, and cast the head of the Moorish chieftain at his feet.

The hero now took his leave and started at once on his journey back to Prilip, and the following morning he received the seven tovars of gold which had been promised to him, the many precious gifts which the Princess had described, and last of all a message thanking him for the marvellous deeds he had done, and telling him that the vast stores of gold belonging to his father-in-God, the Sultan, would for ever be at his disposal.

PRINCE MARKO ABOLISHES THE WEDDING TAX

Early one morning the Royal Prince Marko rode across the plain of Kossovo. When he reached the river a maiden from Kossovo met him, and Marko greeted her in the usual Serbian custom: "May God aid thee, O maiden of Kossovo!"

The maiden bowed very profoundly, and answered: "Hail! thou unknown hero!"

Marko, after having looked for a while at her, said: "Dear sister, thou maiden of Kossovo, thou art beauteous, though thou mightest well be a little younger! Thou art tall, strong and graceful; thy cheeks look healthful and thou hast a pleasing and dignified appearance. But, alas! dear sister, thy hair is grey and becomes thee not. Who caused thy sorrow? Tell me, is it thyself, thy mother or thy aged father."

The maiden shed many bitter tears, and amidst her sobs answered Marko thus: "O dear brother, thou unknown knight! I am not the cause of mine own misfortune, and it is neither my mother nor yet my father who has brought great trouble upon me; but I have lost all happiness through the evil-doing of a Moor who dwells beyond the sea. He has taken possession of the whole field of Kossovo and has imposed, among other extortions, a terrible tax of thirty ducats to be paid by all brides, and thirty-four ducats by all bridegrooms. My brothers are poor and have not the money necessary to pay my tax, therefore I am unable to wed my sweetheart and have thus lost all happiness. Merciful God, should I not go and take my life?"

Thereupon Prince Marko said: "Dear sister, thou maiden of Kossovo! Do not trifle with thy life; abandon every such idea, else thou shalt bring sin upon thy soul! Tell me, where is the castle where the Moorish Lord may be found? I think I have something to say to him!"

To this the maiden answered: "O my brother, thou unknown knight! Why dost thou inquire about his castle? How I wish it could be razed to the ground! Thou hast, perhaps, found a maiden according to thy heart and thou goest now to pay the wedding tax, or art thou the only son of thy dear mother? I fear for thee, O brother, for thou mayest perish there, and what then would thy sorrowful and lonely mother do?"

Marko plunged his hand into his pocket, took out a purse and handed it to the maiden saying: "O sister! take these thirty ducats, go home and await in peace for what may befall thee;12 only kindly point out to me the castle of the Moor, for I am going to pay him thy wedding tax!"

Thereupon the maiden, glowing with unexpected happiness spoke thus: "It is not a castle, but tents (and may they be cursed!). Seest thou not upon the plain where flutters that silken flag? There is the Moor's own pavilion; around it grows a pleasant garden which he has dared to decorate with the heads of seventy-seven Christian heroes, and he has forty servants, who are, day and night, on guard near by."

Marko visits the Moor

Upon hearing these words Marko took leave of the maiden and rode toward the tents. He urged his steed so violently that under his hoofs living fire shone, and from his nostrils appeared a bright blue flame. Mad with anger Marko rode fiercely across the camp and, with tears streaming from his eyes which were fixed upon the plain of Kossovo he exclaimed: "Alas, O plain of Kossovo! Oh! to think that thou shouldst have remained to see this day! And, after the reign of our great Emperor,[13] that thou shouldst be here to witness the tyranny of a Moor! Can I endure such shame and sorrow: Oh! that the Moors should be allowed to ravage thee! Now shall I either avenge thee, or perish!"

The sentinels observed Marko's arrival and went to inform their Lord: "O Master, thou Moor! A strange and fierce hero, riding a piebald steed, is approaching; and it is plain that he intends to attack us."

But the Moor answered indifferently: "O my children, ye forty true servants of mine! That hero will not attack us. He is undoubtedly bringing his wedding tax and, because he regrets the amount of money he has to give up, he is impatiently urging on his charger. You had better go forth and welcome him; take his steed and his weapons from him and show him to my tent. I do not care for his treasure, but I am quite willing to cleave his head and seize his courser, which would suit me well!"

The servants went forth to obey, but when they saw Marko near, they were so terrified that they did not dare face him, but fled to hide themselves behind their chieftain, concealing their yataghans under their cloaks at the sight of Marko.

As the fierce Prince came up, he alighted in front of the opening of the tent and spoke aside to his trusty courser: "Walk about alone, my Sharo," said he, "for I am going into this tent to see the Moor; go not too far from this spot, as should evil happen I may have need of thee!" Then Marko entered the pavilion.

The Moorish chieftain sat enjoying cool wine which was poured out for him by a Christian woman and a maiden. The princely Marko saluted the Moor: "May God help thee, my Lord!" The Moorish chieftain answered: "Hail, thou unknown knight! Be seated, that we may drink wine together ere thou dost tell me why thou hast come hither!"

Prince Marko answered: "I have no time to drink with thee; but I have come with the intention of seeing thee. I have found a maiden after my own heart, my guests and their horses await me a little way down the road, while I came to pay thee my wedding tax. I shall at once give thee the gold so that nothing may hinder my happiness. Tell me now, what must I pay?"

The Moor answered in a very friendly manner: "Well, thou oughtest to have known that long ago: it was thirty ducats for brides and thirty-four for bridegrooms; but as thou appearest to be a distinguished knight, it would not hurt either of us if thou gavest me a round hundred ducats!"

Prince Marko took out of his pocket three ducats and laid them before the haughty Moor, saying: "Believe me

I have no more money; I should be grateful if thou wouldest wait till I reach my bride's house, for there we shall certainly receive many rich presents. I shall give thee all the presents and will retain the bride only for myself!"

Marko pays for All

Thereupon the mighty Moor shouted out, bitterly enraged: "I allow no credit, thou wretch! Thou art bold enough to laugh at me!" Then he sprang to his feet, raised his club and struck Marko's shoulders three or four times.

Marko smiling, said: "Heroic Moor, dost thou strike in earnest or dost thou merely strike in jest?"

The Moor, continuing the assault, hissed: "I beat thee in earnest!"

Marko smiled again, and remarked: "Oh, then, I pity thee! Since thou art striking with serious intent, know then that I too have a club. Now I shall smite thee as many times as thou hast struck me, no more than that! Let us make it a fair fight!" With this, Marko raised his mace and smote the Moor with such force that his head fell from his shoulders!

At this Marko burst into laughter: "Merciful God, mayest thou be thanked! How quickly the Moorish hero's head was cleft asunder! It now lies just as if it had never been upon his shoulders!"

He now unsheathed his sword, and caught the Moor's bodyguard, cleaving also their heads one after the other, except four of their number, whom he left to tell the tale to all who wished to hear the truth. Then he took down the heads of the Christian heroes and carefully buried them, that wolves and vultures might not devour them. He next instructed the four remaining servants to run across the field of Kossovo, north, east, south, and west, and to proclaim to all that maids and youths were henceforth free to marry without paying the hated tax, for had not the Royal Prince Marko come and paid once for all?

When the oppressed Christians learned the news, they all, young and old, joined in the joyful cry: "May God grant Royal Prince Marko long life! For Marko has freed our land of a monster! We pray to God that his soul may be purified of all sin."

PRINCE MARKO AND BOGDAN THE BULLY

Early one morning three Serbian knights rode out from Kossovo; one was Prince Marko of Prilip; the second was Relya of Bazar, and the third was Milosh of Potzerye. They were bound for the seashore, and their way lay through the vineyards of Bogdan the Bully. Relya of Bazar was a joyous young knight, and he encouraged his steed to prance gaily through the vineyard, whereby he broke some of the tall vines loaded with sweet grapes.

Marko admonished his friend thus: "Thou hadst better leave these vineyards alone, O my Relya! If thou only knewest whose they are thou wouldst keep thy courser under careful control: for they belong to Bogdan the Bully. Once I, myself, was riding through these very vineyards, and as I was young then, I also made my Sharatz prance along, as thou art doing. But, alas! I was seen by Bogdan riding on his slender mare Bedevia. I knew that I was at fault and, as the true God does not support guilty men, I dared not face him, but fled up the rocky coast. He pursued me, and if I had not had my trusty Sharatz he would indeed have caught me. But thanks to Sharatz I at last got farther and farther from him. When Bogdan saw that at the rate I was fleeting he could never reach me, he swiftly threw his club after me and just touched my back with its handle, so that I fell forward over on the ears of my Sharatz and regained my seat only by a great effort. However, I did escape him. This happened some seven years ago, since when I have not come this way until to-day."

"But thanks to Sharatz I got farther and farther from him"

As Marko said this, the three knights noticed in the distance a cloud of dust, in the midst of which they recognized Bogdan with twelve attendants on horseback. Marko exclaimed: "Hark ye, my two brothers-in-God! Here he is! and he will surely kill all three of us if we do not make our escape."

To this Milosh of Potzerye answered: "O my brother-in-God, thou Royal Prince Marko! The whole people believe that there are no greater heroes living than we three Serbian knights; it would be far better for us all to perish than shamefully to flee!"

When Marko heard this, he said: "Listen to me, my brothers-in-God! Since that is so, let us divide the enemy. Will ye face Bogdan alone or his twelve knights?"

Milosh and Relya chose to fight Bogdan alone, leaving Marko to meet the twelve followers. This division was quite agreeable to Marko, and it was hardly arranged than Bogdan came up at the head of his troop. He was immediately engaged by Milosh and Relya, while Marko turned his attention to the twelve attendants. Swinging his heavy mace he urged Sharatz against his foes, and in a very short time all were hurled to the ground. Marko then alighted from his horse, bound their hands behind them, and drove them through the vineyards.

He had gone but a little distance when he saw Bogdan driving toward him his two friends, their arms bound in the same manner as those of Bogdan's followers. At this Marko was seized with fear and looked around for a means of escape. The next moment he remembered that the three brothers-in-God had sworn faithfulness one to another, and that they were pledged at all times to help one another. So tightening Sharatz's reins he drew his helmet over his forehead, furiously unsheathed his trusty sabre, and cast one fierce, dark glance at Bogdan.

The Bully fears to meet Marko

When the Bully saw the terrific fury and determination in Marko's eyes his legs shook beneath him, and he turned his mare away, not daring to meet Marko face to face. He could not, however, hope to escape the vengeance of the Prince, and so after a short silence he called out: "Come, O Marko, let us be reconciled. Wilt thou release my twelve attendants? If thou art willing to do that I shall in turn set free thy brothers-in-God."

Marko agreed to this, and alighting from Sharatz, he unhooked from his saddle a skin of wine, and they all sat down to refresh themselves with the cool wine and to partake of freshly gathered grapes. When they had rested, the three friends mounted their horses and prepared to depart. As they were about to ride off Marko thus addressed Bogdan: "Mayest thou prosper with God's help, O Bogdan! And may we meet again some day in good health and once more drink together!"

To this Bogdan replied: "Farewell! and may God ever help thee, O thou Royal Prince Marko! But may my eyes never again behold thee! Seeing how thou hast terrified me this day, I do not think that I shall wish ever to meet thee again!"

PRINCE MARKO AND GENERAL VOUTCHA

Hark! Is it thunder or is it an earthquake? Neither, but guns are roaring from fort Varadin: General Voutcha is feasting in triumph, for he has captured three Serbian heroes; the first is Milosh of Potzerye, the second is Milan of Toplitza, and the third is Ivan Kosantchitch. The General has thrown them into the deepest dungeons of his castle, noisome holes where stagnant water lies knee-deep and the bones of warriors lie piled as high as the shoulders of a hero.

Milosh of Potzerye is of noble lineage, unaccustomed to privation and suffering, and he bitterly laments and deplores his fate, as he peers anxiously through the grating of the massive door into the dark passage by which alone succour might come. And, indeed, after three days he saw a messenger, to whom he called: "O, my brother-in-God! Bring me that whereon I may inscribe a missive!"

The man was pleased to be called a brother-in-God of such a famous hero and swiftly brought a roll to Milosh, who inscribed on it the following words: "To the Royal Prince Marko of Prilip: O brother-in-God, thou princely Marko! Either thou dost not want to hear more of me or thou hast ceased to care for me! Fate has been hard, and I have fallen, O brother, into the hands of a foe. The Magyar Voutcha has captured me and my two brothers-in-arms. We have been immured in this vile dungeon for three whole days, and it is impossible that we should remain for another three days and live. Therefore, if thou wouldst see us again, rescue us, O brother, either by heroic deeds or by ransom!" Milosh scratched his cheek and sealed the missive with his blood; he then handed it to the man, together with twelve ducats, and implored him to hasten with it to Prilip. The messenger rode with all speed, arriving at the city of Prilip on a Sunday morning. Prince Marko was coming out of church when the courier dashed up to him with the missive. As the Prince read of the terrible straits in which his friends found themselves tears ran down his cheeks, and he swore that he would save his noble brothers-in-God.

The bard here describes Marko's preparations in much the same manner as in the ballad, "Prince Marko and the Moorish Chieftain." Next he tells of the journey from Prilip to Varadin, but not without exaggerating as a matter of course, the wonderful alertness of Sharatz, who, on this occasion, swam across the Danube.

The Arrival of Marko

Arrived on the plain before the castle of Varadin, Marko spread his tent, unhooked his skin of wine, the contents of which he drank from a bowl 'containing twelve *okas*' (about forty-eight pints), never forgetting to have half the quantity of wine each time he filled the bowl, for his beloved Sharatz. This action was observed by a fair Magyar lady, the wife of General Voutcha's son Velimir, and being alarmed at seeing such a strange hero, she was suddenly seized with a fever ('which will torture her for three years') and hastened to tell the General what she had seen, and described to him every detail of Marko's attire.

But General Voutcha, feigning indifference, comforted his beloved daughter-in-law, promising that he would capture him as easily as he had captured the three knights already lying in his dungeons. Voutcha called his son, whom he ordered to take three hundred horsemen, and seize the haughty stranger immediately.

Marko sitting and enjoying his wine, did not see the approach of Velimir, but the faithful Sharatz began striking the earth with his right forefoot, thus warning his unobservant master. Marko understood, turned his head, and saw that a whole squadron was surrounding him; so he drank one more bowl of wine, threw the vessel on the grass, sprang on to his horse and fiercely attacked the army, 'as a falcon attacks the timid pigeons.' One portion he cut to pieces, the second he ran down with his Sharatz, and the third he drowned in the Danube.

But Velimir nearly escaped him, thanks to his own speedy charger. When Marko saw that Sharatz, tired out, could not possibly come up with Velimir's horse, he remembered his mace, which he now hurled so skilfully that the heavy handle only touched the youth with sufficient force to fling him to the earth. Marko was by his side immediately and he had Velimir securely bound, whereupon he threw him down on to the soft, green grass, and went on drinking more of his wine.

Velimir's wife had witnessed the whole of the proceedings, and she now ran swiftly to the General, who was furious at the intelligence and ordered all the siege-guns to be fired. Then he collected three thousand warriors and mounting his mare he led this host against Marko.

The Magyars completely surrounded the hero, but Marko saw nothing of it as he went on sipping his wine. Sharatz, however, was watchful and came to the side of his master, who, realizing his critical position, sprang to the saddle and, more furious than before, rushed fiercely at the Magyars, with his sabre in his right hand, his lance in his left, and Sharatz's reins held firmly in his teeth. Those whom he struck with his sabre, he cut in two; those he touched with his lance, were thrown over his head.

Marko captures General Voutcha

After three or four encounters Marko had killed so many Magyars that those who were left, filled with horror, fled in disorder. Marko next captured General Voutcha in the same manner as he had his son, and after tying his hands, bound him to his Sharatz's saddle and carried him off to where Velimir lay groaning. Making the two of them fast to the General's mare, he proceeded to Prilip and cast them prisoners into a dungeon.

A few days later he received a letter from Voutcha's wife, beseeching him not to destroy Velimir and his father, and offering him vast sums of gold as ransom. And Marko sent the following answer: "Behold! thou faithful consort of General Voutcha! If thou desireth that I should release my prisoners, thou hast but to release my old friends Milan of Toplitza and Ivan Kosantchitch and give to each three tovars of gold to compensate for the time he has wasted in prison; and thou must also give me a like sum, for I have had to overwork my good Sharatz. And there is still my friend Milosh of Potzerye within your castle, but I authorize him to settle his own affairs with you in person, for I agree to whatsoever he may arrange."

The wife of the General lost no time in sending the required quantity of gold. Then she took the keys of the dungeons, and released the heroes; sent for a number of barbers to shave their beards, and to attend to their hair and nails. She next ordered a large quantity of the finest wines and most costly dishes to be served to the noble Serbians, and after the feast, she narrated to them Marko's wonderful deeds, beseeching Milosh of Potzerye to use all his influence and persuade the princely Marko to have mercy on her husband and her son. Thereupon Milosh promised that her wish should be gratified, and that she had no need to fear. Only he requested her to give him: first, the best horse from General Voutcha's stables, the one that Voutcha rode once a year to go in state to the church at Tekiye; secondly, the gilded coach, harnessed with twelve Arabian coursers used by General Voutcha when travelling to Vienna on his visits to the Emperor, for in that carriage Milosh wished to drive home the aged hero, Milan of Toplitza. And finally he asked that his friend Toplitza might be allowed to wear the fine attire which the General wore on Easter day. To all this Voutcha's wife agreed and, moreover, she gave each of the friends one thousand ducats in order that they might not be short of wine on their journey to Prilip.

Marko greeted the knights in a warm brotherly manner, and then released General Voutcha and his son Velimir, ordering a powerful convoy to escort them to Varadin. When the noble Serbian voïvodes had enjoyed Marko's hospitality for several days (consuming during that time a formidable quantity of his red wine) they embraced and kissed each other on the cheek; the friends, in addition, kissing Marko's uncovered hand. Then each proceeded in peace to his own domains.

PRINCE MARKO'S WEDDING PROCESSION

One evening as Prince Marko sat at meat with his aged mother, she requested him to seek a maiden of his heart, that she might enjoy the companionship and support of a daughter-in-law. Thereupon Marko answered: "May God be my witness, O mother dear! I have journeyed through nine kingdoms and through the whole Turkish empire, and whenever I found the maiden I wished to make my bride, I never found that thou wert of the same mind with me. Sometimes it was that thou didst not feel friendly toward her family; and when I chanced to find a family to thy liking there was never the maiden thou didst desire for me! Howbeit, when I was wandering through Bulgaria I once reined my Sharatz near a well, and lo! there I saw a maiden so fair and gentle, that all at once it seemed to me as if the grass near where we stood were turning round us again and again. Later I learned that this maiden was the daughter of King Shishman of Bulgaria: assuredly this would be the very maiden for me and a family which would please thee! If thou approvest, therefore, I will at once go and ask her in marriage."

Marko's mother, delighted with this choice of her son, hastened to prepare the usual presents that very night, for she feared her son might change his mind before the morrow. Next morning, however, Marko ordered Sharatz to be saddled, and slinging the necessary skin of wine on one side of the saddle and his war-club on the other, he took leave of his mother and rode straight to the castle of King Shishman.

The Bulgarian sovereign saw Marko while he was still a long way off, and walked forth to greet him. When he was quite close, Marko alighted from Sharatz, stretched out his arms and the two embraced, each inquiring after the state of the other's health. The King then led Marko into the castle while Sharatz was taken by the grooms to the royal stables.

A little later, in the course of the gorgeous banquet which had been immediately arranged in honour of the princely guest, Marko sprang to his feet, bowed deeply before the King and asked his daughter's hand in marriage. The King was so pleased to have such a noble and valiant son-in-law that he consented without hesitation. Marko expended three tovars of gold on the ring to be worn by his future bride, for her wedding-robe and other presents. Next he asked if he might return to Prilip to gather his wedding guests and friends, and as he was on the point of leaving the Palace, the Queen specially advised the Prince not to select as the bride's leader one whom he could not trust implicitly, but rather to choose his own brother or at least a cousin, for, said she, a stranger might possibly prove a rival, so charming and beauteous was her daughter.

When Marko came near to Prilip, his mother walked forth to greet him, and, after embracing him warmly on both cheeks and giving him her fair hands to kiss, she inquired if he had had a prosperous journey and had become betrothed to the Princess. Marko narrated all that had happened, and did not forget to repeat the

Queen's words at parting, complaining of his great misfortune in that his brothers were dead, neither had he a cousin. His mother, filled with joy, advised Marko not to lament because of that, but to send at once a message to the Doge of Venice, inviting him to come with a company of five hundred and to act as koom; also to send to Styepan Zemlyitch, asking him to join the wedding party with five hundred followers and to be the bride's leader.

Marko thought the counsel good and dispatched couriers forthwith, as his mother advised. The Doge soon appeared with his five hundred horsemen and Styepan Zemlyitch likewise. Marko welcomed them cordially and hospitably, and there was no lack of good red wine.

The company now proceeded to the court of the Bulgarian King, who received them most heartily and feasted them for three days. On the fourth day the wedding party prepared to return for it was evident that if the guests were to remain for another three days the King would have no wine left. Shishman presented all with royal gifts: to some he gave silks, to others costly shirts, to others again golden dishes and plates; to the bride's leader was presented a special shirt embroidered in gold. When the bride was mounted, her royal father presented her to the bride's leader with these words: "Here are now, in thy keeping, the bride and her horse till thou arrivest at Marko's castle; once there thou shalt give Marko the bride, but her courser thou mayst retain for thyself!"

The Wedding Procession

The procession rode on through the Bulgarian woodland and meadows, and as there is no happiness without some misfortune, a gust of wind blew aside for a moment the bride's veil. The Doge of Venice, riding close by her side, beheld the maiden's fair face and was so fascinated by her wondrous beauty that he fell violently in love with her. When the whole party of wedding guests halted for the night, he went unperceived to the tent of Styepan Zemlyitch, addressing him thus: "O thou bride's leader! Wilt thou yield to me thy charge that we may flee together: I will give thee a bootful of golden ducats!" Styepan Zemlyitch answered indignantly: "Keep silent, thou Doge of Venice! Mayest thou be turned to stone! Hast thou made up thy mind to perish!"

When they reached the halting-place on the second day, the Doge again went secretly to the tent of Styepan Zemlyitch and once more asked for the bride, but this time he offered two bootfuls of ducats. Again the bride's leader refused, saying: "Begone, O Doge! Lest thou shouldst have thy head cleft asunder! Has anybody ever heard of a koom taking his kooma from her bridegroom?"

The Unfaithful Koom

When the third night came, the Doge offered to the bride's leader three bootfuls of pure golden ducats. This enormous sum of money was too great a temptation for the bride's leader, and he gave up the bride to the Doge, who conducted her to his own tent.

Then he declared his love to the maiden, and in impassioned tones implored her to fly with him to Venice, where he could offer her all that heart could desire. But the Bulgarian maiden turned from him with loathing. "For pity's sake, O thou Doge of Venice!" said she, "the earth under us would surely crack to swallow us and the skies above us would burst asunder if a kooma should thus be false to her bridegroom."

But the Doge persisted: "Oh do not be so foolish, my sweet kooma! I have kissed and caressed many koomas, but never once did the earth open under us, or the heavens burst asunder. Come, let us embrace!" The maiden thought it well to dissemble, and she replied: "O my koom, thou Doge of Venice! My aged mother told me that I should have her curse if I ever kissed a bearded hero; and I swore to her that I should love only a shaven knight such as is the Royal Prince Marko."

Upon this the Doge called two barbers: one to shave his beard and the other to wash his face clean. As they were thus engaged the maiden stooped and gathered up, unnoticed, the Doge's beard and wrapped it in the folds of her silken robe.

The Doge now dismissed the barbers and endeavoured afresh to make love to the bride, who feigned coyness and said that she feared that they both would surely perish when Marko learned of what had taken place. But the Doge protested: "Oh do not be so foolish. I have five hundred followers with me! Marko's tent stands far away. Dost thou not see it in the distance? On its top is fixed a golden apple. In the apple are placed two large diamonds which shed a light so far and wide that the neighbouring tents need no candles at night."

The Escape of the Maiden

The maiden pretended that she wished to have a clear view of this wonder, and the Doge gallantly raised the hanging at the door that she might see more clearly. The next moment she was running swiftly as a deer toward Prince Marko's pavilion.

The Doge gallantly raised the hanging at the door

Marko was sleeping, and was greatly astonished when suddenly he was awakened by the entrance of his unexpected visitor. When he recognized in the maiden his future wife he addressed her angrily: "Thou maiden of low birth! Is it seemly that thou shouldst visit me contrary to all our Christian customs?"

The maiden bowed low and replied: "O my Lord, thou Royal Prince Marko! I am not a girl of low birth, but of most noble lineage. Thou hast brought with thee guests of most evil dispositions. Know then, that my leader Styepan Zemlyitch sold me, thy bride, to the Doge of Venice for three bootfuls of gold! If thou canst not believe this, look! Here is the Doge's beard!" and she unfastened her robe and took out the Doge's beard and showed it to him.

Marko's wrath was now directed against his perfidious friends, and at break of day, wrapping himself in his wolf-skin cloak, and taking his heavy mace, he went straight to the bride's leader and to the koom, saying: "Good morning to ye, O bride's leader and koom! Thou leader, where is thy sister-in-law? And thou, O koom, where is thy kooma?" Styepan Zemlyitch kept as silent as a stone, but the Doge said: "O thou Royal Prince Marko! There are such strange people about that one cannot even make a joke without being misunderstood!"

But Marko answered: "Ill is thy joke, O thou Doge of Venice! Where is thy beard? It is a very strange joke to shave one's beard!" The Doge would have answered, but before he could do so Prince Marko had unsheathed his sabre and cleft his head in twain.

Styepan Zemlyitch attempted to escape, but Marko rushed after him and struck him so neatly with his keen sabre that he fell to earth in two pieces.

This done, Marko returned to his tent, ordered the procession to advance, and arrived without mishap at Prilip.

PRINCE MARKO AND THE MOORISH PRINCESS

One day the mother of Prince Marko spoke thus to her son: "O, my darling son, thou Royal Prince Marko! Why dost thou erect so many churches and shrines? Either thou hast sinned gravely before God and thou art in lowly penance, or thou must have piled somewhere superabundant wealth?" Then Marko of Prilip answered her: "My beloved, aged mother! I will tell thee the truth. Once while I travelled through the Moorish country I rose early one morning in order to go and refresh my Sharatz at the well. When I arrived there I found twelve Moors who had come for the same purpose, and, as I, in my pride, would not await my turn, the twelve Moors opposed me because they had come first. At once we began to quarrel. I lifted my heavy club and felled one of the Moors, to the earth; his companions attacked me and I struck another to the ground; ten assailed me and I killed a third; nine engaged me and a fourth bit the dust; the other eight rushed on me and I knocked down the fifth; seven strove with me and I sent to eternity the sixth; but I had to face the remaining six, who overpowered me; they bound my arms to my back and carried me to their Sultan, who flung me in prison. There I dwelt for eight years knowing nothing of the seasons, save that in winter girls would play with snow-balls and sometimes fling them through my prison bars, wherefore I knew that it was winter; or maidens flung me bunches of basil, and thus I knew when it was early summer."

The Moorish Princess

"When the eighth year broke upon me, it was not my dungeon that distressed me so much as a Moorish maiden, the beloved daughter of the Sultan. She annoyed me by coming every morning and every evening and calling to me through my dungeon-window: 'Why shouldst thou perish in this prison, O Marko? Give me thy word that thou art willing to marry me and I will release thee, and thy Sharatz too, I would take with me, also, heaps of golden ducats; as much, O Mark, as thou canst ever wish to have.'

"At that time I was in very great misery and despair, O my mother, and so taking off my cap and placing it upon my knee I addressed it thus: 'By my firm faith! I shall never abandon thee; neither shall I ever forget thee, upon my soul! The sun itself has often changed, shining not in winter as in summer, but my promise shall be unbroken for ever!'

"The maiden believed, in pleasant delusion, that I had sworn faithfulness to her, and so at dusk one evening she opened the doors of my prison, led me along to my spirited Sharatz, having got ready for herself a fine noble charger. Both steeds bore on their backs bags filled with ducats. The Moorish maiden brought in addition my best tempered sabre and we sped swiftly through the Moorish lands.

"When darkness came upon us and I flung myself on the ground to slumber, the Moorish princess did likewise, and lo! she threw her arms around me. And I looked at her, O my mother, and I saw how black her face was and how white were her teeth! I shuddered with horror and hardly knowing what I did, I sprang to my feet, mounted my Sharatz, and galloped away madly, leaving her alone. The maiden called after me in anguish: 'O my brother-in-God, thou Royal Prince Marko! Leave me not thus!' But I would not stay my flight.

"I saw how black her face was and I shuddered with horror"

"Then and there, O my mother, I sinned before God! Then it was that I obtained gold in profusion, and

141

therefore is it that I have built numberless churches and shrines to expiate my sin!"

PRINCE MARKO AND THE VEELA

Prince Marko and Milosh of Potzerye rode early one morning across the beauteous mountain Mirotch, carrying their lances and trotting their steeds. They loved each other so dearly that they would now and then embrace. Suddenly Marko began to doze on his Sharatz, and tried to persuade his companion to sing something in order to keep him awake. Thereupon Milosh answered: "O dear brother-in-God, thou Royal Prince Marko! I would gladly sing a song for thee, but last night when I was with veela Raviyoyla, I drank far too much wine, and she threatened, in truth she promised, to pierce both my heart and my throat with arrows if she ever heard me sing again."

But Marko insisted: "Oh do sing, brother dear! Fear not the veela as long as I, Prince Marko, live; and as long as I have Sharatz and my six-edged club!"

So Milosh to please his pobratim, began to sing a beautiful song telling of their valiant and virtuous ancestors; how they had held kingdoms and ruled in succession over the much-honoured land of Macedonia; and how every one of those good sovereigns had erected a shrine or a church.

The song pleased Marko so much that, lulled by Milosh's melodious voice, he fell asleep. But it happened that the veela also heard the song, and began to sing in turn with

Milosh, doing all the time her very best to show him that she sang better than he did. Milosh really sang better, for he possessed a magnificent voice, and this fact much irritated the veela; she took two slim arrows, twanged her bow, and transfixed first Milosh's throat and then his heart.

Milosh uttered a piercing cry: "Alas, O my mother! Alas, Marko, my brother-in-God! The veela has shot me with her arrows! Did I not tell thee, O pobratim, that I must not sing on the mountain Mirotch?"

The Pursuit of the Veela

This lamentation awoke Marko at once. He leaped lightly from the saddle, tightly fastened his Sharatz's girths, embraced him, and thus whispered in his ear: "Lo, *Sharo*, thou on whom I depend for speed! Oh, thou must overtake, now, the veela Raviyoyla; and I shall shoe thy hoofs with pure silver and gild them with the finest gold; I shall cover thee with a silken cloak reaching to thy knees, and on it I shall fasten fine silk tassels to hang from thy knees to thy hoofs; thy mane shall I intertwine with threads of gold and adorn it with rare pearls. But, woe to thee if thou reachest not the veela! Both thy eyes shall I tear out; thy four legs shall I break; and I shall abandon thee here and thou shalt for ever creep from one fir-tree to another, exactly as I should do if I lost my dear brother Milosh!"

Then Marko sprang upon Sharatz, and rode swiftly after the veela. Raviyoyla was already flying over the mountain top, and when Sharatz caught sight of her he bounded fiercely forward, leaping to the height of three lances in the air, and covering the length of four lances at each bound. In a few moments Sharatz came up with the veela, who, greatly affrighted, flew upward to the clouds. But Marko pitilessly hurled his far-reaching club and struck her between the white shoulders, and she fell instantly to the earth. Marko struck her several times as she lay on the earth, exclaiming: "O Veela! May God requite thee! Why didst thou pierce my dear pobratim's throat and heart? Thou hadst better give him healing herbs, else thou shalt not carry thy head much longer upon thy shoulders!"

In a few moments Sharatz came up with the veela

The veela implored Marko to forgive her, and to become her brother-in-God. "For God's sake, O my brother Marko, and by the memory of St. John," she cried, "spare my life, and I will go through the mountain and gather herbs to heal thy pobratim's wounds!"

Marko was very easily moved by the mention of the divine's name, and he released the veela, who went at once, but never out of hearing and answering to Marko's frequent calls.

When the veela had collected herbs she brought them to Milosh and healed his wounds; his voice was not only quite restored, but it was finer than before and his heart was sounder. Then the brothers-in-God rode straight to the district of Poretch, where they crossed the River Timok, and soon arrived at the town of Bregovo, whence, after tarrying awhile, they departed to the district of Vidin. When the veela rejoined her sisters she admonished them, saying: "Hark, ye veelas, my sisters! Do not shoot any heroes in the mountains with your bows and arrows, so long as the Royal Prince Marko and his Sharatz are alive. Oh, what I, much to be pitied, have suffered at his hands to-day! I marvel, indeed, that I still live!"

PRINCE MARKO AND THE TURKISH HUNTSMEN

Amouradh, the grand Vizir once arranged a hunting party of twelve Turkish warriors to which he also invited Prince Marko. They hunted for three days and found nothing in the mountain-forest. But, behold! they suddenly discovered a green-bosomed lake upon which a team of wild ducks was swimming! The Vizir let loose his falcon and bade him pounce upon a gold-winged duck, but the duck did not even allow the falcon to see it, so swiftly it flew toward the clouds; as for the falcon it fell on the branches of a fir-tree.

Then Prince Marko spoke thus to the Vizir: "Am I permitted, O Vizir Amouradh, to release my falcon and try to secure the gold-winged duck?" "Surely you may, Prince Marko," answered the Vizir. Then the princely Marko let loose his falcon, and the bird ascended to the clouds, sprang upon the gold-winged prey, and bore it down to the foot of the green fir-tree.

When Amouradh's falcon saw this it became greatly excited and, according to its natural habit of seizing others' spoil, it turned violently upon its rival and tried to pluck the duck from its claws.

But Marko's falcon was exceedingly valiant, worthy of its master, and would yield its well-earned trophy to none but its master. So it turned sharply on Amouradh's falcon and vehemently tore at its proud feathers.

When the Vizir saw this, he too became excited and in great rage rushed to the combatants and flung Prince Marko's falcon fiercely against a fir-tree so that its right wing was broken. He then took horse with his followers and fled from the scene of his violence.

The noble falcon, as it lay upon the ground, wailed in its pain and Prince Marko ran quickly and caught it to his breast, for he loved it very dearly. Then very tenderly he bound its wounded pinion and addressed the bird with emotion: "Woe to me and to thee, my falcon, that ever we went hunting with the Turk without our dear

Serbians, for the Turk must ever violate the rights of others!"

After having bound his falcon's wing, Marko sprang upon Sharatz and sped through the forest swift as a veela. Soon he left the mountain behind and he observed the fleeing Turks in front of him. The Vizir turned in his saddle and saw Marko in the distance, wherefore he spoke thus to his twelve valiant companions: "Ye, my children, ye twelve valiant heroes! See ye yonder mountain-mist approaching, and in it the Royal Prince Marko? Hark! how fiercely he enrages his Sharatz! God alone knows, what will befall us!"

The Vengeance of Marko

He had barely uttered these words when Prince Marko came up flourishing his bright sabre. Instantly the twelve Turks dispersed like a flock of sparrows startled by a vulture. Marko made for the Vizir and with one thrust of his sabre cleft his head asunder. Next he pursued the twelve Turkish warriors, each of whom he cut in two, striking them through their Turkish sashes. Then he stood for a while in doubt: "Oh, what am I to do now? Ought I to go to the Sultan at Yedrenet or had I perhaps better return to my white castle at Prilip?" After long thought he decided that it would be far better to go to the Sultan and give an account of what had happened than to give an opportunity to his foes to calumniate him to the Padishah.

When Prince Marko arrived at Yedrenet he was at once received in divan by the Sultan.

A poet describes Marko's eyes as being as bright and fierce as those of a hungry wolf; and the Sultan was terrified by the lightning flashing from his eyes. He deemed it well to temporize and so spoke gently to the hero: "O my dear son Marko, why art thou so enraged to-day? Art thou, perchance, short of gold?"

Prince Marko narrated to the Sultan what had happened to his Vizir Amouradh, not omitting to mention one single incident. When he had heard the tale, the Sultan, convulsed with laughter, comforted Prince Marko: "May Blessings fall upon thee, my dearest son Marko!" said he. "If thou hadst not behaved thus, I would no longer call thee a son of mine; any Turk may become Vizir, but there is no hero to equal Marko!" With these words the Sultan plunged his hand in his silk-lined pocket, drew out a purse containing one thousand ducats and proffered it to Prince Marko, exclaiming: "Accept this as a gift from me, O my dearest son Marko, take some wine and go in peace!" Marko, nothing loth, accepted the purse and left the divan.

The Sultan, however, was not moved to this seeming generosity by friendliness to Marko; on the contrary he feared him exceedingly and was anxious only for his speedy departure.

PRINCE MARKO AND MOUSSA KESSEDJIYA[14]

"Moussa Arbanass[15] was one day drinking wine in a white tavern in Istamboul. Presently, when he had drunk a good deal he began to talk thus: 'It is just about nine years since I entered the service of the Sultan at Istamboul, yet he has never given me a horse, or arms, or even a velvet cloak! By my faith, I shall rebel! I shall go down to the coast, seize the harbours and all the roads leading to them: and then build myself a koula, around which I shall erect gibbets with iron hooks and hang his *hodjas* (priests) and *hadjis* (pilgrims) upon them.'"

The threats the Albanian made in his drunkenness he actually carried out when he became possessed of his senses. He turned rebel, seized the sea-ports and the main roads, captured and robbed the rich merchants, and hanged the Sultan's hodjas and hadjis. When the Sultan heard of all these misdeeds, he sent the Grand Vizir Tyouprilitch with three thousand men to undertake a campaign against Moussa. But, alas! no sooner had the Turkish army reached the sea-coast than Moussa dispersed it and took the Grand Vizir prisoner. Next he bound the Vizir hand and foot and sent him back thus ignominiously to his master at Istamboul.

Now the Sultan, in despair, published a proclamation all over his vast empire, promising untold riches to any knight who would vanquish the rebel. And many a brave knight went to fight the rebel, but, alas! not one ever returned to Istamboul to claim the promised gold! This humiliation threw the Sultan into unspeakable distress and anxiety.

At length the Grand Vizir Tyouprilitch came to him and said: "Sire, thou Glorious Sultan! If only we had now with us the Royal Prince Marko! He would surely overcome Moussa the Bully!"

The Sultan cast at his Vizir a reproachful glance, and, with tears in his eyes, said: "Oh, torture not my soul, by speaking of the princely knight Marko! His very bones must have rotted long before this day, for at least three years have flown since I threw him into my darkest dungeon, the door of which has remained fast bolted." Thereupon the Vizir asked: "Gracious master, what wouldst thou give to the man who could bring Marko into thy presence alive?" And the mighty Sultan answered: "I would give him the vizirate of Bosnia, with power there to remain for nine years without recall, and I would not demand from him even a *dinar* of the revenues and taxes which he might collect."

Marko is Sent for

Hearing this, the cunning Vizir hastened to the prison, opened the door of the dungeon, brought out the Royal Prince Marko and led him before the Sultan. Marko's hair had grown to the ground, one-half of it he had used to sleep upon, and with the other part he covered himself at night; his nails were so long that he could plough with them; the dampness and dirt in the dungeon had changed him so that he was as black as a black stone.

When the Sultan saw him, he exclaimed: "Dost thou still live, Marko?" "Yea, I am still alive, but hardly can I move my limbs," the hero answered.

And the Sultan went on to tell Marko about the evil doings of Moussa, and asked him: "Couldst thou undertake, O Marko, to go to the sea-coast and kill

Moussa Kessedjiya? If thou wouldst do this, I would gladly give thee as much gold as thou canst desire."

Thereupon Prince Marko answered: "Alas, O Sire! The dampness of the stone dungeon has ruined my bones and much hurt my eyes. How could I venture to fight a duel with Moussa? But, if thou wishest me to try that feat, place me in a good inn somewhere, supply me with plenty of wine and brandy, fat mutton and good white bread, that I may perhaps regain my strength. I shall then tell thee as soon as I feel myself able to fight a duel."

Hearing this, the Sultan summoned attendants to wash Marko, to cut his hair, to shave him and to trim his nails. Then he had him conducted with honour to the New Inn, where there was abundance of everything to satisfy his needs.

Marko remained in the inn for three months, zealously eating and drinking, and he had thus considerably restored his strength, when the Sultan asked him: "Dost thou yet feel thyself able to go and overcome Moussa, for my poor subjects are incessantly sending me complaints against that accursed brigand?" And Marko answered the Sultan thus: "Let a piece of perfectly dry wood of a medlar-tree, which has been cut off nine years be brought to me, that I may test my strength!" When the piece of wood was brought, Marko took it in his right hand and squeezed it so hard that it broke in three. "By my faith, Sire, it is not yet time for me to venture a duel with such a dangerous adversary as Moussa!"

So Marko remained in the New Inn for another month, eating, drinking, and resting, till he felt a little stronger. Then he asked again for a dry stick from a medlar-tree.

When the wood was brought to him, he squeezed it with his right hand till it broke in pieces, and this time two drops of water came from it. Then Marko said to the Sultan: "Sire, now I am ready to fight the duel."

Marko orders a Sword

From the palace Marko went straight to Novak, the famous maker of swords. "Make me a finer sword than any thou hast ever made before, O Novak!" said Marko, and he gave the smith thirty ducats and went back to the inn. There he stayed to drink red wine for the next few days, and then went again to the smith's. "Hast thou finished my sword, O Novak?" And the swordsmith brought forth the blade and gave it to Marko, who asked: "Is it good?" "There is the sword and here is the anvil; thou canst try on it the quality of thy sword!" answered Novak timidly. Thereupon Marko lifted his sword and struck the anvil with it so hard that he cut right through it. "O Novak, the swordsmith, tell me now, truthfully—and may God help thee—hast thou ever made a better sword?" And Novak answered: "Since thou didst call upon the name of the true God, I must tell thee truthfully that I did once make a better sword; yea, and it was for a better warrior. When Moussa turned rebel and went to the sea-coast, he ordered me to make him a sword, with which he cut right through the anvil as thou hast done, and through the trunk of an oak-tree upon which it was standing, as well."

"There is the sword and here is the anvil"

This enraged Marko. "Hold out thy hand, Novak, that I may pay thee for my sword!" No sooner had the man stretched forth his right arm, than Marko by a swift stroke cut it off from the shoulder. "Now, O Novak, from this day thou shalt not make either a better or a worse sword than mine! And take these hundred ducats as thy reward!"

Marko meets Moussa

Then Marko mounted his Sharatz and rode off to the sea, seeking and inquiring all the way for Moussa. One morning early he rode up the defile Katchanik, when suddenly he saw Moussa Kessedjiya, calmly seated on his black steed with his legs crossed, throwing his mace to the clouds and catching it again in his right hand. When the two knights met, Marko said to Moussa: "Knightly Moussa, move aside and leave the path free for my Sharatz to pass! Move aside or bow before me!"

To this Moussa answered: "Pass on quietly, Marko, do not start a quarrel. Better still, let us dismount and take refreshment together. I shall never move aside to make way for thee. I know well that thou wert born of a queen in a palace, and wert laid upon silken cushions. Doubtless thy mother wrapped thee in pure silk, and fastened the silk with golden thread, and gave thee honey and sugar; my mother was a poor, wild Albanian, and I was born on the cold rocks near the sheep she was tending, and she wrapped me in a rough, black cloth, tying it on to me with bramble twigs; she fed me on oatmeal—but above all things she always made me swear that I should never move aside for anybody."

Hearing this, Marko of Prilip aimed his lance at Moussa's breast, but the fierce Albanian received it on his warrior-mace, and it glanced off, whizzing high above his head. Then Moussa threw his own lance, aiming at Marko's breast, but the princely hero received it on his club and it broke in three. They next unsheathed their swords and attacked each other at close quarters. Marko gave a great stroke, but Moussa interposed his mace and the sword was shattered. Instantly Moussa raised his own sword to strike his adversary, but Marko, in the like manner, received it upon his club and the weapon snapped in two near its hilt. Then they began labouring each other with their maces until these broke too. They next dismounted and seized each other fiercely. The famous heroes were equally matched for once, the knightly Moussa against the princely Marko. Moussa could neither throw Marko down, nor could Marko overcome Moussa. For a whole summer's morning did they wrestle together. At about noon, white foam rose on Moussa's lips, and Marko's lips were covered with blood and foam. Then Moussa exclaimed: "Do throw me down, O Marko! or, if you cannot do it, let me throw you down!" Marko did all he could, but his attempts were vain. Seeing this, Moussa exerted his last remnants of strength and, lifting Marko from the ground, he threw him on to the grass and pressed his knees on his breast.

Marko, in great danger, exclaimed: "Where art thou now, my sister-in-God, thou Veela? Where art thou to-day, mayst thou live no longer! Now I see thine oath was false when thou didst sware to me that whenever I should be in distress, thou wouldst help me!"

The veela appeared from behind the clouds, saying: "O my brother, Royal Prince Marko! Hast thou forgotten my words: That thou shouldst never fight on Sunday? I cannot help thee, for it would not be fair that two should fight against one. Where are thy secret poniards?"

Moussa cast a glance to the clouds to see where the voice came from, and this was his undoing, for Marko seized the moment, drew out a secret blade, and with a sudden fierce stroke cut Moussa so that his body was opened from his waist to his neck.

Marko disengaged himself with difficulty from the embraces of the horrible Moussa, and as the body lay upon its back the Prince discovered through the gaping wound that his adversary had three rows of ribs and three hearts. One of the hearts had collapsed; another was still beating excitedly; on the third a serpent was just awaking, and as it saw Marko it hissed: "Praise God, O Royal Prince Marko, that I still slept while Moussa was alive—for a three hundred fold misfortune would surely otherwise have befallen thee!"

When Marko heard this, tears poured down his cheeks and he lamented: "Alas! Gracious God forgive me, I have killed a better knight than I am!"

Then he struck off Moussa's head with his sword, put it into Sharatz's nose-bag and returned triumphantly to Istamboul. When he flung the head of Moussa before the Sultan the monarch was so horrified that he sprang to his feet. "Do not fear the dead, O gracious Sultan! If thou art frightened by the sight of Moussa's head, what wouldst thou have done if thou hadst met him alive?"

The Sultan gave three tovars of gold to Marko, who returned to his castle at Prilip.

As for Moussa the Bully, he remained on the top of Katchanik Mountain.

THE DEATH OF PRINCE MARKO

In the early dawn of a Sabbath morning Prince Marko paced the sea-shore. Soon he came to a bridle path that led up the slopes of the Ourvinian mountain, and as he got near to the mountain top, his faithful Sharatz suddenly stumbled and began to shed tears. His moans fell sadly upon Marko's heart and he addressed his favourite thus: "Alas! dear Sharo, my most precious treasure! Lo! we have dwelt happily together these many summers as beloved companions; till now thou hast never stumbled, and to-day for the first time thine eyes do weep: God alone knows what fate awaits us, but I can see that my life or thine is in great peril and that one of us is surely doomed to die."

When Marko had spoken to his Sharatz thus, the veela from the Ourvinian mountain called to him: "My dear brother-in-God! O Royal Prince Marko! Knowest thou not, brother, why thy horse is stumbling? Thy Sharatz is grieving for thee, his master. Know that ere long ye must be divided!"

Marko answered: "O thou white veela! May thy throat cause thee pain for speaking thus: How in this world could I ever part from Sharatz, who through many a land and many a city hath borne me from dawn till sunset; better steed never trod our earth than Sharatz, and Marko never better hero. While my head is on my shoulders, never will I be severed from my beloved steed!"

And the veela called again: "O my brother, Royal Prince Marko, there is no force which can tear thy Sharatz from thee; thou canst not die from any hero's shining sabre, or battle-club, or lance of warrior; thou fearest no hero on earth—but, alas! thou must die, O Marko! Death, the ancient slayer, will smite thee. If thou wilt not believe me, hasten to the summit of the mountain, look to the right and to the left, and thou wilt presently see two tall fir-trees covered with fresh green leaves and towering high above the other trees of the forest. Between those fir-trees there is a spring; there alight, and bind thy Sharatz to one of the fir-trees; then bend thee down and the water will mirror thy face. Look and thou shalt see when death awaits thee!"

Marko learns his Fate

Marko followed the veela's instruction, and when he arrived upon the mountain top, he looked to the right and to the left, and truly, he saw the two tall straight fir-trees just as she described them, and he did everything she had counselled him to do. When he looked into the spring he saw his face reflected in the water, and lo! his fate was written on its surface!...

Then he shed many bitter tears, and spoke in this wise: "O thou treacherous world, once my fairy flower! Thou wert lovely—but I sojourned for too short a time with thee: yea for about three hundred years! The hour has come for me to depart!" Then he drew his sabre and hastened to Sharatz; with one stroke he smote off his head. Never should he be mounted by the Turk; never should a Turkish burden be placed upon his proud shoulders; never should he carry the *dyugoom*[16] from the well for the hated Moslem!

Marko now dug a grave for his faithful Sharatz and interred him with more honour than he had buried Andreas, his own brother. Then he broke his sabre in four that it might not fall into the hands of a Moslem, and that the Turk might not brandish it with something of his own power, lest the curse of Christendom should fall upon him. Marko next broke his lance in seven pieces throwing the fragments into the branches of the fir-tree. Then he took his terrible club in his right hand, and swiftly flung it from the Ourvinian mountain far into the dark sapphire sea, with the words: "When my club returns from the depths of the ocean, then shall come a hero as great as Marko!" When he had scattered thus all his weapons, he drew from his belt a golden tablet upon which he inscribed this message: "To him who passes over this mountain, and to him who seeks the spring by the fir-trees and finds Marko's body: know that Marko is dead. There are here three purses filled with golden ducats. One shall be Marko's gift to him who digs his grave: the second shall be used to adorn churches; the gold in the third shall be distributed among the blind and maimed, that they may wander in peace through the land and with hymns laud Marko's deeds and feats of glory!"

When Marko had thus written he bound the tablet to a branch that it might be seen by the passers-by. He spread his cloak on the grass beneath the fir-trees, made the sign of the holy cross, drew over his eyes his fur cap and laid himself down....

The Finding of Marko

The body of Marko lay beside the spring day after day till a whole week had passed. Meanwhile many a traveller passed over the broad path and saw the knightly Marko, but one and all believed him to be slumbering and kept a safe distance, fearing to disturb or awake the sleeping hero. Fortune is the leader of misfortune, as misfortune often leads to fortune: and it befell that Vasso the *igouman* (abbot) of Mount Athos, rode that way from the white church Vilindar attended by the youthful Issaya his deacon. When the igouman noticed Marko, he beckoned to Issaya. "O my son," he said, "be cautious, lest thou wake the hero, for Marko is furious when disturbed and may destroy us both." Then he looked anxiously round and saw the inscription which Marko had fixed above his head. He drew near cautiously and read the message. Then he dismounted hastily from his horse and seized Marko's hand—but the hero moved not! Tears rushed from the eyes of Vasso, and he lamented loudly the fate of Marko. After a time he took the three purses from the hero's girdle and hid them beneath his belt. Long he pondered as to where he should entomb Marko; at length he placed the hero's body on his horse and brought it to the shore. In due course he arrived safely with it at the white church Vilindar, and having sung the customary hymns and performed those rites which are fitting he interred Marko's body beneath the centre of the church.

He lamented loudly the fate of Marko

There the aged igouman buried Marko but he raised no monument over the tomb, lest foes should learn the whereabouts of the hero's grave and take vengeance on the dead.

[1] An instrument which emits droning monotonous sounds, and which resembles in many points the hurdy-gurdy. In olden times, in Serbia, this instrument was played by minstrels thirty years of age or more; younger men played the flute, violin, and a kind of bagpipes.

[2] In order to illustrate how firmly rooted is that belief throughout Serbia, the author quotes from his article (condensed): "How a Fourteenth Century Serbian Prince achieved a Miraculous Victory in the Late War," *The International Psychic Gazette*, May 1913.

"... When we arrived on the 15th of November last year, at Skoplye (Uskub), the Serbian officers gave a comparatively sumptuous banquet at their barracks in honour of Surgeon-General Bourke and the two units of the British Red Cross, on which occasion the aged General Mishitch related to us the following incident from the battle of Prilip, fought a few days previously.

"... Our infantry was ordered to make a forced march on the eve of that battle, which is unique in the history of warfare. They were to wait at the foot of the mount of Prilip on which stood the Castle of Marko for the effect of our artillery, which was superior both in numbers and quality to that of the Turks. They were especially cautioned against storming the fort before they received the order from their commander-in-chief. This was necessary, for our soldiers had won recently several battles at the point of the bayonet, and were convinced that there was nothing that would frighten the Turks more than the sight of the shining bayonets of the Serbian troops. They knew well that the mere exclamation of Bulgarians, *Na noge!* put the Turks to flight at Kirk-Klissé and Lülé Bourgass.

"During the early morning the infantry kept quiet, but at the first cannon-shots we noticed an effervescence among our troops, and soon afterward we heard them shouting frantically and saw them running like wolves straight to the castle of the Royal Prince Marko. I could hear the voice of our Captain Agatonovitch, commanding them to stop and await the General's order. When the immediate commanders saw that discipline proved futile, they essayed in vain to appeal to the soldiers' reason, assuring them of certain death if they would not await at least the effect of our artillery. Our warriors, deafened by the roaring of the Turkish siege-cannon and mitrailleuses, ran straight into the fire, and appeared to fall in dozens! The sight was horrible. I was unable to stop my soldiers. My blood froze, I closed my eyes. Disastrous defeat! Demoralisation of other troops! My own degradation was certain!

"In a little while our artillery ceased firing, lest they should kill their own comrades, who were now crossing bayonets with the Turkish infantry.

A few minutes later we saw the Serbian national colours fluttering on the donjon of Kralyevitch Marko's castle. The Turks were fleeing in greatest disorder. The Serbian victory was as complete as it was rapid!

"When we arrived on the scene a little later, a parade was ordered. After calling together the troops we found our loss had been comparatively insignificant. I praised my heroes for their brave conduct, but reproached them bitterly for their disobedience. At my last admonishing words, I heard from thousands of soldiers in majestic unison:

"'*Kralyevitch Marko commanded us all the time: FORWARD! Did you not see him on his Sharatz?*'

"It was clear to me that the tradition of Kralyevitch Marko was so deeply engraved on the hearts of those honest and heroic men that, in their vivid enthusiasm, they had seen the incarnation of their hero.

"I dismissed the troops and ordered double portions of food and wine to be given to all for a week. Every tenth man obtained a '*Medalya za Hrabrost*' (medal for courage)."

[3]*Tabor* is a Turkish word meaning an army, or a camp.

[4]Other bards mention 'Gratchanitza.'

[5]Despot was an honorary title of the Byzantine emperors, then of members of their families, and was later conferred as a title of office on vassal rulers and governors. The rank of Despot was next to that of the king.

[6]*Divan*, a Turkish word for "senate."

[7]*Koula* is a Serbo-Turkish word for "castle."

[8]*Istamboul* is the Turkish name for Constantinople.

[9]*Firman* is a Turkish word for an imperial "letter" or "decree."

[10]*Tovar* is a Serbian measure, representing what a normal horse can carry on its back. It is now an obsolete term.

[11]*Dervish* is an ecclesiastic official amongst the Mohammedans. When applied to the laity it is used as a term of reproach.

[12]Literally, "until thy good luck calls thee," and means in Serbia *until she marries*.

[13]This is a reference to Lazar, who fell at the battle of Kossovo.

14*Kessedjiya* means 'fighter' or 'bully,' and is the nickname of an Albanian *chevalier-brigand* Moussa, who defied for years the distant power of the Sultan. The incident described in the poem here referred to recounts—according to some Serbian historians—an event which actually took place in the beginning of the fourteenth century. There is hardly any inn or tavern in the villages of the Southern Slavs on the front wall of which one cannot see a rough fresco illustrating the duel between Marko and Moussa.

15*Arbanass* is another appellation for Albanian.

16*Dyugoom*, a water vessel made of copper and enamelled inside.

Chapter V: Banovitch Strahinya

Historical Data

The ballad relating to Banovitch Strahinya is one of the finest and most famous which the anonymous Serbian bards composed during the Middle Ages. The author was probably a dependent of the descendants of Banovitch, and utilized a few historical and biographical data, which he must have found among the manuscripts and other records belonging to his lord or in the other castles he visited from time to time.

Prince Ourosh (of the Nemanya dynasty) married Helen, a French princess of the house de Courtenay, and through her he kept up friendly relations with the French Court of Charles of Anjou in Naples, and he endeavoured to negotiate an alliance between Serbs and French for the overthrow and partition of the Byzantine Empire.

Some Serbian historians believe that Banovitch Strahinya was really the glorious Strashimir Balshitch-Nemanyitch (who reigned conjointly with his two brothers from 1360–1370 in Skadar, the capital of Northern Albania) and a descendant of the old Provençal family of des Baux.

In early local records the name Baux is latinized Balcius, and members of the family who attended the Court at Naples changed the name, in Italian fashion, into Balza. And it is supposed that these Italianized Seigneurs des Baux, who were permitted to marry into the Royal

House of Nemanyitch, and who settled in Serbian lands, then further changed their patronymic to Balsha or Balshitch—*itch*, or *ich*, or *ić* being the characteristic termination of most Serbian family names.

It may here be stated that Skadar was at that time still the capital of Zeta (the Montenegro of modern times). The valiant Nicholas I Petrovitch, the present King of Montenegro, and an indirect descendant out of Balshitch, was obliged by the Great Powers to evacuate the town after he had obtained possession of it by the heroism of his troops, and Serbian bards throughout the kingdom are now improvising ballads, in which they may transmit to future generations the story of the sad events of the present time, just as their ancestors recorded the exploits of Strahinya. But let us turn to the story of Banovitch as it was given in the old ballad.

The Falcon Banovitch

In the opening verses the bard describes the hero and eulogizes him as "a falcon without equal." He tells of the orders given by Banovitch to his servants and pages relative to the preparations to be made for himself, Dyogo his faithful steed, and the greyhound Caraman, his inseparable companion. He is not going to the hunt, however; he intends to visit the aged Youg Bogdan, and is clad in pure silk and velvet embroidered with fine gold. Bogdan, his beloved father-in-law, resides at his sumptuous castle in Kroushevatz. The old man rejoiced to see him, and his nine sons and their wives, as well as Bogdan's sons-in-law, of whom one was a direct descendant of King Nemanya, greeted him warmly.

As they were feasting, a letter was brought from Banovitch's mother, telling him that innumerable hordes of Turks had encamped on the field of Kossovo. Strahinya seized the letter and read in horror his mother's malediction: "Woe to thee and thy feasting in the accursed castle of thy wife's father!" The letter went on to say that a certain chieftain named Vlah-Ali, proud, haughty, and independent not only of Mehmed, the Grand Vizir, but of Sultan Amourath himself, had attacked, conquered, and pillaged his castle, captured his servants, and taken his wife away to his tent on a mountain near the field of Kossovo, where she was seemingly quite content to remain. Youg Bogdan, observing Strahinya's grief, asked him in alarm what was amiss, if he lacked anything in his castle, or if any one of his family had offended him. Banovitch thanked his father-in-law, and assured him that other misfortunes were troubling him, and he read the letter aloud. Banovitch then begged Youg Bogdan to allow his sons to accompany him to the field of Kossovo, as he had resolved to rescue his wife from the hands of the foe. But Youg Bogdan, thinking that it would be foolish for so few to go and face the many thousands of bloodthirsty Turks, disapproved altogether of this, and strongly advised Banovitch to abandon the idea. He even promised to find him a bride fairer and more worthy of him than his own faithless daughter. But Strahinya remained unshaken in his resolution, and convinced of his father-in-law's lack of chivalry, ran hurriedly to the stables, refusing in scorn the help of Bogdan's servants, saddled Dyogo, and indignant and sorrowful mounted forthwith. As he was riding out of the courtyard he suddenly remembered Caraman, so he whistled, and instantly Caraman ran to his master and comforted him.

Banovitch seeks the Turk

So over fields and over mountains, straight to Kossovo, Banovitch rode forth with courage and gladness, for his dog was even dearer to him than his steed. At Kossovo he saw the plain crowded with tents and soldiers, and as he looked he felt something like dread within him; nevertheless, he called on the name of the true God and taking the precaution of disguising himself as a Turk, he rode over the plain. For several days he sought, but alas! in vain, the tent of Vlah-Ali. At last from the banks of Sitnitza, he beheld a spacious green tent upon the pole of which a golden apple shone; before the entrance stood an Arab steed stamping sharply with his forefeet upon the ground. Strahinya thought that this must surely be the tent of Vlah-Ali, and he fiercely spurred on his Dyogo. Reaching the tent in a moment, spear in hand, he boldly drew aside the silken curtain which veiled the entrance. To his disappointment he saw that the only occupant of the pavilion was an old dervish with a white beard reaching to his knees. The old man was drinking wine, a thing forbidden to him by the laws of his order, and he returned the greeting of Strahinya, who spoke good Turkish, with a profound salaam. Then, to Strahinya's astonishment, the dervish said: "Hail! O Banovitch Strahinya, Lord of Little Banyska near Kossovo!" Banovitch was taken aback, but he tried to put a good face upon it and asked in apparent surprise: "Who is the man thou hast called Banovitch Strahinya?" The half-drunken dervish laughed aloud. "Thou canst not deceive me," said he, "I would instantly recognize thee, yea, even wert thou on the top of the mountain Goletch." Then he told Banovitch how that he had been a captive in his castle a few years previously, and had been treated most humanely, even receiving a daily measure of wine. Finally Banovitch had let him go to his estates to collect his ransom. Upon reaching his home he discovered that his estates had been appropriated by the Sultan, and his house and other possessions had been given to Pashas' daughters as dowries. All was dreariness and desolation; he had lost his fortune—and, he added bitterly, consequently all his friends—so he was reduced to ride to Yedrenet[1] to offer his services to the Sultan. The Vizir, he continued, told the Sultan that he looked as if he might quite likely be of use as a soldier, whereupon the Sultan had given him good clothes and better weapons and the Vizir added his name to the roll of warriors sworn to fight for the Sultan. "Now," he concluded, "I do not possess so much as even a dinar, give me, I pray thee, time for my fortunes to improve."

Strahinya was deeply touched by the dervish's misfortunes and, alighting from his steed, he embraced him and spoke to him in the following friendly manner: "Thou art my brother-in-God! I forgive thee gladly thy ransom, neither shall I ever ask even a dinar from thee, but thou canst repay me! I am now seeking the haughty Vlah-Ali, who demolished my castle and robbed me of my wife. Tell me, O aged dervish! Where shall I find my foe? I beseech thee as my brother-in-God, not to let the Turks know of my presence here, and not to suffer them to take me by guile." The dervish was glad to become brother-in-God of such a valiant hero as Strahinya, and he pledged his unalterable faith that, even if Strahinya should destroy half of the Sultan's army, he would never betray him; but at the same time, he tried to persuade Banovitch to give up all intention of attacking such an unconquerable and terrible foe, whose mere name was enough to strike terror into the heart of the best and bravest. He went on to describe the warlike character of the invincible rebel of the Padishah, and finished by assuring Banovitch that neither his sharp sword, nor his poisoned spear, nor his steed would avail to protect him, for the terrible Vlah-Ali would surely seize him alive in his iron grasp, break his limbs to pieces and pluck out his eyes.

Strahinya laughed aloud when he heard all this; "O my brother," said he, "thou aged dervish! Thou needest not warn me against one warrior, only do not bring upon me the Sultan's whole army! Since thou goest to water thy horses every evening and every morning at the River Sitnitza, thou must know where the fords are, and thou couldst save me from riding my steed into muddy depths!"

At this the dervish repeated his oath, and exclaimed:
Strahni-Bane, ti sokole Srpski!
Tvome Dyogu i tvome junashtvu
Svud su brodi, dyegody dodyesh vodi![2]

Banovitch crossed the river, and rode without haste to mount Goletch. He was still at the foot of the mountain when the morning sun shone out upon the field of Kossovo, making the tents and the soldiers' armour gleam.

The Faithless Wife

What was the mighty Vlah-Ali doing when dawn came? The Turk's custom was to seek slumber only at sunrise. "How very dear to him was his new slave, Strahinya's wife," recites the bard, "may be understood when I tell that he had closed his eyes with his head on her ivory shoulder." The faithless woman was not sleeping; through the door of the tent she gazed over the sleeping camp. Suddenly she roused her new lord and pointed in terror to the figure of an advancing horseman in whom she had recognized her true husband.

At first the Turk laughed at her fears and said that it was only an ambassador from the Sultan. "Verily," said he, composing himself again to rest, "Strahinya will not dare to come near the tent!"

Presently his companion again roused Vlah-Ali and told him that the horseman was no messenger from Amouradh, but her own husband, Banovitch Strahinya himself, and she warned Vlah-Ali that he was in peril of his life.

Upon this, the mighty Vlah-Ali leapt to his feet, girded on a long silken sash, fastened in it a sharp gleaming yataghan, quickly belted on his shining sabre, and was soon firmly seated in his saddle.

The Combat

A moment later Banovitch came up, and a fearful contest began between the two champions—heroes of almost equal renown, though not equal in strength. Strahinya addressed his opponent with reproachful and taunting words, and Vlah-Ali replied in equally offensive terms. But they did not fight only with words. Banovitch spurred Dyogo and furiously cast his spear, which the mighty Turk, stretching out his hands, caught and broke into pieces. "O Strahinya," he shouted derisively, "thou callest me a poltroon, indeed! Dost thou know to whom thou didst speak? Here is no woman of thy Serbian land whom thy threats might alarm; thou hast here to deal with the mighty Vlah-Ali who fears neither the Sultan nor his Grand Vizir, yea, not even the countless horde which they command! One and all, they are to me but a swarm of ants!" Speaking thus, he alertly reined in his sturdy horse and sent his spear whistling through the air. So straight it went to Strahinya's breast that he surely would have been stricken had the just God not helped him. Dyogo, accustomed to duels, knelt swiftly in the nick of time, so that the Turk's weapon flew over Banovitch's head and struck against a rock behind him, breaking into three pieces. Their spears being thus destroyed, the fierce warriors next grasped their heavy clubs, and rushed to close quarters. Their blows fell thick and fast until Vlah-Ali struck Strahinya so violently that he was stunned and fell forward upon Dyogo's neck. Again the true God stood by Strahinya; his beloved grey steed, trained for such a struggle, moved his head and his neck so cleverly that he threw his master back into the saddle. Strahinya, in his turn, now struck his adversary's shoulder with great force, but the mighty Turk sat unshaken, although by this time his horse's legs were sunk in the black earth up to the knees.

And so the battle went on until the combatants broke each other's clubs, when they took to their sharp sabres, hoping to decide the combat very soon. But lo! Banovitch's sabre was not a common one; two strong smiths had spent a week in shaping it and in smelting the finest of fine steel for its blade. The Turk made a swift slash at his foe, but Strahinya caught the gleaming steel on his own blade, and the sabre was instantly severed above the hilt. This pleased Banovitch greatly, and, fiercely pressing the Turk, he now tried to hack off his adversary's arms. But the heroes were well matched; Vlah-Ali guarded his head most deftly with the remaining stump of his sabre, and, bit by bit, he broke away his adversary's weapon, until once more the two were on equal terms. They now dismounted, and grasping each other firmly, they heaved and wrestled with all their strength.

Finally Strahinya, feeling that he was almost spent, called upon his wife to take the other part of the Turk's sabre and to settle the contest by striking either his head or that of Vlah-Ali. Thereupon Vlah-Ali called out: "My darling! O thou wife of Strahinya! Strike me not, but rather strike Banovitch as thou canst never again be dear to him; he will blame and scorn thee for ever and ever. But thou shalt be always most dear to me. I will escort thee to Yedrenet, thirty maids shall there be to wait upon thee: to carry thy robes and wide sleeves. With sweet-meats will I feed thee and will cover thee with golden ducats from head to foot!"

Women may easily be misled by fair words: and so the wife of Strahinya sprang forward and picked up a piece of the sharp blade, wrapping it carefully in fine silk, for she feared it might wound her hand. Then she ran swiftly to the fighting heroes, and taking all care not to hurt Ali, she violently struck the head of Banovitch, and cut through the golden crest and the white helmet. The blade but slightly gashed Strahinya's head, but down rushed the blood over his face fast and thick and all but blinded him.

At this bitter moment, Strahinya thought of his faithful Caraman and called to him twice. The dog rushed furiously at the faithless woman and held her fast,[3] whereupon she was much terrified and screaming loudly, she threw the blade afar and seized the dog by its ears. The Turk, alarmed and distracted, turned round to see what had happened. So encouraged was Strahinya at this new proof of his dog's intelligence and faithfulness, that new strength came to him and seizing the opportunity he threw his adversary on the ground and slew him with his teeth "as wolves slaughter lambs." Then he carried away his wife (whom the intelligent Caraman had left unhurt) to her father's castle.

The return of the Falcon

When Youg Bogdan and his sons saw Strahinya covered with blood, they were greatly astonished that there should be a Turk valiant enough to wound a hero such as Strahinya. But Strahinya narrated to them the shameful conduct of his wife, and the story made Youg Bogdan so incensed that he commanded his sons to pierce their sister with their swords. But the ever chivalrous Strahinya protested, exclaiming: "O my brothers-in-law, ye nine Yougovitch! Why, O brothers would ye cover yourselves with shame to-day? On whom would ye draw your blades? Since ye are, O brothers, so blood-thirsty and so courageous, where were all your knives and your bright sabres when I went to the field of Kossovo? Why did ye not accompany me then, and exhibit your bravery before the fierce Turks? Why did ye not then prove yourselves to be my friends? I will not let ye kill your sister; without your help I could have slain her myself.

She is but a frail and easily misguided woman! But I shall not kill her: on the contrary she will henceforth be dear to me as ever."

The bard ends his poem:
Pomalo ye takiyeh younaka,
Ka' shto beshe Strahinyityou Bane!

("Few are the heroes fit to be compared with Banovitch Strahinya!")

---

[1] Adrianople.

[2] The lines are considered to be the finest composed by any Serbian bard, and may be freely translated: "O Lord Strahinya, thou Serbian glorious falcon! Depending ever upon thy true steed Dyogo and upon thine own courage, wherever thou goest, there thou shalt find a way free of all danger."

[3] Here the bard in his naïve meditations on the psychology of women, states that the fair sex is always alarmed by true dogs.

Chapter VI: The Tsarina Militza and the Zmay[1] of Yastrebatz

Militza tells the Tsar

"O thou one and indivisible God! Mayest thou be glorified!".... Tsar Lazar sat at supper, and with him sat the Tsarina Militza, sorrowful and depressed. This unusual aspect of his beloved consort alarmed the Tsar, and he asked her tenderly: "O Militza, thou my Tsarina! If I put a question to thee, wouldst thou answer me with the truth? Why art thou so gloomy, so sorrowful and pale to-night? Is anything thou desirest lacking in our castle?" The Tsarina replied: "O Tsar Lazar, thou Serbian golden crown! Verily whensoever thou speakest to me I answer but the truth. Nothing is lacking in our palace; but truly a great misfortune has befallen me, for the Zmay of Yastrebatz is accustomed, ever since last year to come to my tower each night to embrace me." Tsar Lazar, astounded, said: "Listen to me, O Tsarina Militza! When thou hast retired to thine apartment in the white tower to-night and thy magic lover hath come, ask him if there be any besides God whom he fears, and if there is to be found on this earth a hero whom he deems superior to himself!"

Soon after supper the Tsar went to his narrow and many-storied *tchardack*,[2] and the Tsarina retired to her tower. And it was seen how the mountain Yastrebatz glowed suddenly as if on fire, and how out of the flames flew the Zmay straight over the level plain of Kroushevo to the Tsarina's tower.

When he entered the Tsarina's apartment he took off his fairy garment and looked tenderly upon the fair woman. The Tsarina affected to welcome her lover, and after a time she said: "I pray thee, O Zmay of Yastrebatz, since thou comest so daringly to my tower, tell me is there any besides God whom thou dreadest? and lives there in the whole world any hero whom thou deemest superior to thyself?" Thereupon the Zmay answered in surprise: "Keep silent, O Militza! (or mayest thou remain speechless for ever!) Surely thou askest me this question because thou hast been instructed by Lazar!"

But Militza swore to him, saying: "No, not so! May I perish if I speak not the truth! I ask thee because I see thou art such an excellent hero."

When the Zmay heard this he trusted to the false oath (less dangerous it would have been for him if a viper had bitten him!) and spoke in this wise: "O Militza, dearest Tsarina! Since thou askest me truly, truly shall I answer thee. On the whole of this earth I dread none but God; neither is there hero whom I fear, save only that on a plain called Sirmia there is a village known as Koopinovo, and in that village lives a Zmay-Despot Vook; him I fear, for I have known him ever since our foolish childhood. We often used to play together on the summit of the high mountain Yastrebatz, and Vook would always get the better of me in our contests. It is Vook only whom I dread, for he is the champion Zmay on this earth."

As the Zmay pronounced the last of these words, Danitza—the morning star—appeared on the horizon and the Zmay instantly took flight to his castle.

The Tsarina hastened to Lazar's tchardack and informed him of what she had learnt from the Zmay. Hearing the story the Tsar decided to write in 'slender characters' a message to Zmay-Despot Vook telling what he had learned beseeching him to come to Kroushevatz and kill his detested enemy the Zmay of Yastrebatz. For rendering that service Vook should receive three tovars of ducats and the kingdom of Sirmia to be his for life.

Vook as Champion

The message duly reached the hands of Zmay-Despot Vook, and, having perused it he considered for a while as to what he should do. He loved the friend of his childhood, but he could not condone his shameful conduct. Finally he decided to battle with the Zmay of Yastrebatz, so he saddled his black steed, presented to him by the veela, and that very night he reached the plain of Kroushevo; there he alighted; spread his tent in the wheat-fields of Lazar and drank cool wine.

Meantime the sun rose and as the Tsar slowly paced his balcony, he suddenly noticed a tent in his fields, and a strange and very wonderful knight within it. He immediately called the Tsarina and pointed out to her what he saw. Militza exclaimed that this must be none other than Zmay-Despot Vook, for he much resembled her magic lover the Zmay of Yastrebatz.

The Tsar immediately sent a messenger to the stranger bidding him come at once to the palace, where a noble feast awaited him. But Vook sent word that he desired to remain in his tent and he requested that the Tsarina should not close fast the doors of her apartments that night but should quietly await the coming of the Zmay of Yastrebatz and leave the issue to her new protector.

Upon receiving Vook's reply the Tsar ordered a fine repast to be prepared and taken to his tent, not omitting a large quantity of red wine.

The day passed uneventfully, and when night came the fair Militza retired. As usual Mount Yastrebatz burst into its customary light, and its lord flew from the flames straight to the Tsarina's tower and stole into her chamber, where he doffed his magic garment. Suddenly he heard the voice of Zmay-Despot Vook saying: "Thou who hath presumed to embrace the Serbian Tsarina, come forth this instant from the white tower!"

Greatly alarmed, the Zmay of Yastrebatz cursed the Tsarina thus: "Lo, Militza, may God destroy thee! Thou hast betrayed me to Lazar!"

Saying this he donned his magic garment and made haste to depart. Instead of as usual, directing his flight to his castle on Yastrebatz, he ascended straight into the clouds. Vook pursued him very closely and coming up with him at an extreme height, he struck him violently with his heavy club and broke both his wings. Down fell the Zmay of Yastrebatz, swift as a stone to the earth, where he lay writhing like a snake and moaning piteously—"May a similar misfortune befall every hero who entrusts his mistress with his secrets!" He had not a long time in which to indulge his bitter reflections for Vook was following and the instant he alighted he struck off the head of the Zmay. Then he went to Lazar and threw the head upon the ground before him. The Tsar was so terrified at the mere sight of the ghastly object that he was seized suddenly by a severe fever. But he gave the promised gold to Vook as well as an imperial decree empowering him to rule independently over Sirmia for the remainder of his life. Moreover, he promised that should Vook ever be without gold, he need but apply to the Tsar, and he should have his needs supplied. The bard ends: "And they long lived happily, always helping each other, as fellow-countrymen should do; and the glory of the hero became a tradition; we now remember the anniversary of the slaying of the Zmay of Yastrebatz as the happiest day in the year!"

---

[1] *Zmay* is the Serbian word for 'dragon,' but in this poem it is employed metaphorically to suggest the superhuman attributes supposed to be possessed by the heroes.

[2] *Tchardack* is a Turkish word and signifies: a tower provided with balconies.

Chapter VII: The Marriage of Maximus Tzrnoyevitch

The Ballad

This ballad from which the King of Montenegro—Nicholas Petrovitch—drew inspiration for his drama *The Empress of the Balkans* is undoubtedly the finest Serbian national poem ever composed and chanted in Montenegro. To render it satisfactorily in its poetic form into another language, compact as it is of intensely national characteristics, metaphors and other figures of speech, religious conceptions, customs and superstitions, would be impossible for even the greatest of our poets.

A French proverb says *quand on n'a pas ce que l'on aime, ou aime ce que l'on a*, and the hope may here be expressed that the philosophic English reader will make the best of the following prose version, such as it is, of a most interesting national poem.

The Story

Ivan Tzrnoyevitch[1] sailed across the Adriatic to Venice, in order to pay a visit to the doge and to ask his daughter in marriage for his son Maximus. He remained there three years, during which he spent three tovars of gold and upon his departure at the end of this period he arranged to return the following year with his son and with one thousand, or more, guests for the marriage festivities. The doge and his two sons, as well as a hundred of the doge's high dignitaries, accompanied Ivan to his galley and the Montenegrin prince repeated his promise to come again the next year with his guests and with his son, than whom, he averred, no finer hero or handsomer youth could be found in any gathering of one thousand Montenegrins or one thousand Venetians. The doge, exceedingly pleased to have for his son-in-law such a fine hero, embraced Ivan, saying: "I thank thee, my friend, for such words! How happy I am to have gained such a dear son-in-law, whose equal should in vain be sought among thousands! I shall love him more than the sight of my eyes; and shall prepare precious gifts for him: horses and falcons, helmets with golden crests and round him cloaks to wrap such as he may be proud to wear. But if he be not as handsome as thou hast said; woe to thee!"

After this Ivan sailed for Zablak. As he neared his castle he felt very happy and urged on his steed Zdral the sooner to reach home. His faithful consort perceived him from afar, and at once gave orders to the servants to make the necessary preparations for the arrival of their lord. She judged from the gay appearance of her husband that he must have succeeded in his mission.

When Ivan arrived in the courtyard of his castle, some of his servants helped him to alight from his steed, others took off his armour and arms, and his son Maximus brought him a silver settle that he might be seated and rest. Ivan turned to thank his son, but behold! A misfortune had befallen him! During his father's absence Maximus had been stricken with small-pox—that terrible scourge!—and his once handsome face was so pitted and seamed that it was now horrible to look upon. The bard assures us that it was hardly possible to find an uglier fellow than Maximus had become.

The prince immediately recollected his boast to the doge, that there could not be found amongst thousands a handsomer youth than his son, and he felt very sad; his long moustache drooped down on to his shoulders,[2] and, with eyes fixed on the ground he sat silent and gloomy. His consort saw with concern her husband's despondency and she endeavoured to raise his spirits. Gathering up the folds of her flowing robe and the ends of her long sleeves, she came close and, bending, kissed his hand. "Pray, my lord," she said, "why art thou so sad? Hast thou, perhaps, not been successful in thy mission? Hast thou not betrothed the doge's daughter to our son? Is she perhaps not fair enough to become thy daughter-in-law? Dost thou regret the three tovars of gold which thou hast spent?"

Thereupon Ivan roused himself and replied that it was quite another misfortune which was troubling him. He told how he had successfully betrothed the doge's daughter, and that she was so beautiful that even the veele could not be compared with her; that it was not the thought of the gold he had spent that tormented him—for his castle was heaped up with treasure, and the abstraction of three tovars of ducats had hardly affected the size of the store. No, the real cause of his misfortune was that he had promised the doge to give him for his son-in-law a youth who was the handsomest to be found amongst thousands, and that if he were to present his son Maximus as he now was, the doge would surely be angry and a war would ensue.

When the princess heard this, she reproached Ivan with having gone so far away for a bride, when he could have found in Montenegro itself a much finer maiden whose family would be worthy of an alliance with his own. Prince Ivan was persuaded that he had acted unwisely, and he decided to abandon the betrothal, and forbade his friends to congratulate him.

The Message from the Doge

Nine years elapsed, and it seemed that the betrothal had been forgotten by all, and that the doge's daughter, having heard nothing from Ivan, had surely wedded another prince. But one day a message from the doge arrived, in which he reproached the Montenegrin prince with having allowed nine years to pass without sending a word to his daughter—who, "from only a bud, had developed into a beauteous rose." He further requested Ivan to write to his still patient daughter, and to tell her plainly what he had decided with regard to the proposed marriage; for if he did not now deem his son worthy of such a precious maiden, he must at once tell her so, that a prince deserving of her might be found.

The prince was seized with great grief as he read the doge's message. What could he say or do? After pondering long he sought his princely consort and addressed her in this wise: "O my sweet-eyed darling! I pray you counsel me now what to do! Shall I despatch a message to the maiden and tell her that she is at liberty to seek another in marriage, or how otherwise shall I write?"

The princess was a wise woman, and she advised her husband prudently:[3] "O my lord, thou Tzrnoyevitch Ivo! Has ever any man been counselled by a wife? This has never been and never shall be. For we women have long hair, but little brains. But as thou hast asked for my opinion, I will venture to say that it would be a sin before God, and before the world a shame, to deprive a maiden of happiness by releasing her from a suitably arranged betrothal. Listen to me, dear lord! What an insignificant reason alarms thee! If the small-pox has damaged thy son's visage, thy distant friends should make allowance for such misfortune resulting from illness—for who is exempt? Furthermore, if thou dreadest a conflict when thou comest to Venice, I would remind thee that thou hast dungeons full of pure golden ducats; in thy cellars there is old wine in abundance; thy granaries are overfilled with wheat and other grain; consequently thou art well able to gather a great number of svats. Thou hast promised the doge to go thither with one thousand svats, but why shouldest thou not take two thousand chosen heroes and equerries with thee? When the Venetians see with how great a force thou journeyest, they will not dare to attack thee, even if thy son were blind. Therefore, gather the svats, and hasten to bring the bride. O my lord, lose no more time in vain musing." At these bold words, the prince expressed his great satisfaction in a burst of laughter. He immediately inscribed a missive and despatched it by a speedy courier. Its contents ran thus: "O my friend, thou Doge of Venice! Thou could'st hear, if thou didst but listen, the roaring of my thirty cannons, which I am about to fire from my fortress! O friend, do not lose a single moment, but send at once galleys to meet me, my son and all our svats. Farewell!" Ivan then sent to Milosh Obrenbegovitch, inviting him to be the stari-svat and to attend with as many chosen heroes as he could possibly find within the provinces of Antivari and Dulzigno. He wrote also to his cousin, Captain Yovan, inviting him to come to the wedding with as many of his friends as possible. Couriers were sent to other friends, who received Ivan's invitation gladly, and before long the plain of Zablak was studded with their innumerable tents. One morning Ivan noticed Captain Yovan, the bride's leader, pacing sadly the ramparts of the castle, and casting frequent glances at the spearmen, equerries and standards in the encampment below. Prince Ivan would not suffer anybody to be unhappy in the midst of his festive preparations, and so asked Captain Yovan the cause of his gloom. Yovan said, that if he might speak of what was lying upon his heart, he would counsel the prince to prepare a great feast for those numberless Montenegrins encamped before his castle, after which couriers should be sent throughout the camp telling all to return home that their fields should not be ruined by neglect. Thus the land would not be deprived of defenders against their persistent foe, the Turk, who might attack the country at any moment while they were away. Then Yovan went on to relate to the prince how the previous night he had seen in a dream the sky suddenly covered with dark clouds; from those clouds a thunderbolt had fallen upon his princely castle and razed every single stone of it to the ground; a fire had then broken out and consumed the beautiful capital Zablak. When the castle fell a tower had struck Maximus but without doing him serious hurt. "Nevertheless," continued Yovan, "if there be any truth in dreams, Maximus would either perish or be severely wounded in Venice, and if I should be offended by a Venetian, all my followers, five hundred men of Podgoritza, would die in my defence."

A tower had struck Maximus without doing him serious hurt

Prince Ivan laughed heartily when Yovan had ended, and said that his good friend owed his bad dreams to the fact that his pillows were either too high or too low. Then saying, "dreams are false, but God is true," he turned away to give orders to fire thirty guns from the fortress as the signal for departure.

When the cannon roared, especially the two famous guns *Krgno* and *Zelenko*, the whole valley quaked, the black mountains resounded and the water of Zetina was stirred to its depths. Some equerries were shaken from their steeds and those standing fell on their knees on the grass, for it is no light matter when siege-guns roar!

The Wedding Procession sets out

The svats started on the journey in the best of spirits; some urged and raced their coursers, others were drinking and singing gay wedding songs as they marched. In their midst rode Prince Ivan on his courser Zdral, with two proud falcons on his shoulders; on his right rode Maximus, and on his left Milosh Obrenbegovitch. Prince Ivan glanced often at his companions, and involuntarily drew a comparison between the two. All at once he ordered a halt and spake aloud, saying: "Listen, O my brothers, ye glorious svats! I have a plan to propose, and hope that you will think it good. We are on the point of embarking, O brothers, and will soon arrive in Venice. But look upon my son Maximus, how much spoilt is his appearance by horrible disease; he is unquestionably the ugliest of us all! Alas! when I was in Venice nine years ago I praised him as the handsomest youth to be found amongst one thousand Montenegrins; yea, even amongst one thousand Venetians. Therefore, O brothers, I am very sad this morning, and have no pleasure in the thought of meeting the doge. Hear that the Venetians may attack us, so great will be their disappointment. But behold! O ye my valiant svats! We have here with us a hero whose equal in manly beauty must be vainly sought amongst us, as also amongst the proud Venetians. I speak of Voïvode Milosh Obrenbegovitch. Let us, then, take off the plumed helmet from the head of my son and place it upon Milosh's head, and thus make him the bridegroom for the time being, until we have peacefully gained possession of the maiden!"

The svats were greatly impressed by Ivan's scheme, but they hesitated to speak, fearing to hurt the feelings of Maximus, who was a spirited youth and might resent the proposal. But Voïvode Milosh said graciously: "O Ivan, our lord! Why dost thou make vain appeal to the svats? Rather give me thy hand as a sign of firm faith that the plan does not in any way offend thy noble son. Swear to me by the true God that thou hast suggested this after an understanding with thy son, and I will in return pledge my honour that I shall obtain the bride for Maximus without a fight. You shall consent, however, to cede to me as my reward for playing a false part all the presents that may be given to me as the bridegroom, and I shall not be expected to divide them with anybody, but shall retain them all for myself!"

Ivan burst into laughter, and exclaimed: "O Milosh, thou Serbian Voïvode! As to the presents thou namest, I give thee my faith, firmer and harder than stone itself, that nobody shall seek to have a share in them with thee! Only secure the bride and honourably escort her till we reach our city of Zablak, and I promise to give thee two bootfuls of golden ducats, a golden cup to hold nine litres of wine, a mare 'Bedevia,' the mother of studs like my Zdral, and I shall girdle on thee a sabre worth thirty purses of golden ducats."

So they all agreed, and having placed the distinctive hat and ornaments of the bridegroom on the head of Voïvode Milosh they resumed their journey, and after some tossing upon the waters of the Adriatic they reached Venice without misadventure.

There came large numbers of people curious to see the Montenegrins and especially to discover for themselves if Maximus was really the fine and handsome prince that they had heard he was.

When the Venetian princes heard from their servants that their future brother-in-law was really as handsome as his father had described him nine years earlier, they came eagerly with outstretched arms to embrace and welcome him. They showed him the apartments in their palace which had been prepared for the princely guests, and all were lodged in comfort.

The wedding festivities lasted for three days and then came the hour of departure. At the sound of cannon the svats assembled in the great courtyard awaiting the commands of Prince Ivan, and his noble son. They felt uneasy when they saw the gate of the palace closed, and on each side of it two Moorish and two Venetian soldiers standing with drawn swords the blades of which, and even their own arms, were covered with blood. Their uneasiness became alarm when after some time they saw no sign of their prince and the bride and bridegroom. They were beginning to murmur loudly when suddenly they heard the sound of horses' hoofs on the marble pavement and they saw Voïvode Milosh trying to curb his destrier with his bit as he spurred him gently in order to make him bound and prance.

The Wedding Gifts

Behind Milosh rode his two brothers-in-law bringing gifts. The elder of them led a black steed without a single blemish, bearing a silver saddle adorned with heavy gold, upon which sat the fair bride holding a grey falcon. "Accept, O my dear and noble Maximus," said the prince, "this fair maiden, together with her black steed and her grey falcon as a token of our love, for thou art in truth the pride of thy brothers!"

Milosh bowed deeply over his horse's neck as he thanked the prince for his gracious words and accepted the bride with the gifts which she brought. The second brother now bestowed upon the bridegroom a sabre in a golden scabbard, saying: "Wear this, O brother, and be proud of it!" Next came the father of the bride. What a beautiful present he placed in his hands! A helmet in the crest of which shone a precious stone dazzling like the sun so that one could not look at it long. But the gift which was given to him by the mother of the bride was more magnificent than all! This gift was a shirt of pure gold, which was neither woven nor twined, but had been made entirely with fingers; in its collar, representing a viper ('and a viper will finally bite him') there was fixed a brilliant diamond shedding forth such a blaze of light that he would never need a candle when he went to visit his bride in her bed-chamber. All the svats were astonished at the magnificence of the present.

Now came the aged brother of the doge, Yesdimir, with his beard reaching to his waist, walking slowly and supporting himself with a golden staff. Bitter tears streamed from his eyes. He wept, it is true, with good reason. Seven wives he had had in turn during his long life, but no sons or daughters had been born to him. Therefore he bestowed all his affections upon his niece, whom he looked upon as a daughter, and who took in his heart the place of the children he had once hoped to be blessed with, and now that the beloved maiden was to depart to a far-away land he was greatly grieved. He had some 'wonder' folded under his arm, and as he approached the svats, he called the bridegroom by name. The latter appeared at once and the venerable lord laid upon the young man's shoulders a magnificent cloak which reached from his shoulders down to the grass. Indeed when Milosh remounted his horse, the cloak concealed not only himself, but also his steed down to its very hoofs. How precious it was! and oh! that it might never be the cause of anything but happiness to the hero! It was said that thirty purses of gold had been spent on its lining alone, and what a sum of money the cloth itself must have cost! Prince Maximus watched and saw with envious eyes how Voïvode Milosh received the presents which were intended for him, the real bridegroom. When the large gateways of the courtyard were opened, the svats, passing out in procession, received from the doge's servants each a piece of precious silk and a box containing various presents, and then they sailed away in galleys.

Soon they arrived on the field of Zablak, where they had met on starting out for their journey, and where they were now to separate. Prince Maximus had ridden a little ahead with his ten brothers-in-arms in order to hasten and communicate the joyful news to his mother and Voïvode Milosh, being aware that Prince Maximus was out of sight, spurred forward his courser and coming up with the bride and the dever, he boldly took the hand of the noble maiden. The bride, thinking in her innocence that he was Prince Maximus, removed her veil and stretched out her hands to the pretended bridegroom.

The Princess learns of the Deception

Those who were near feigned not to have noticed the incident, but Prince Ivan himself happened to see what had occurred and it troubled him, and he rode up and addressed the bride thus: "Touch him not with thy hands, O my dear daughter-in-law! or may they be struck with a palsy! Veil thine eyes! or may thy sight for ever fail thee! How canst thou act so in the presence of all the svats? Dost thou see that hero riding his black steed, and holding his lance? Dost thou see his shining shield and his face disfigured by small-pox? That is my son Maximus, whom I praised to thy father—when I asked your hand for him—saying that there was no handsomer youth than he to be found amongst thousands. But I was afraid to present my son with his ugly face to you and to your father, and so we had recourse to a stratagem and made Voïvode your groom temporarily in order to succeed in bringing thee away in peace. For acting so Milosh is entitled to all the presents which were assigned to the bridegroom!"

To the noble maiden her father-in-law's words came as a thunderbolt. She halted her horse and refused to go any farther, saying: "O my dear father-in-law, thou Prince Ivan! Thou hast caused thine own son's misfortune by having made Milosh the alleged bridegroom. Why hast thou done so? May the true God give thee thy deserts for that! What matters it if his face is pitted? All are subject to disease, and might have to suffer even worse consequences. If his face is damaged, his eyes are certainly bright and his heart is as sound as ever. If thou hadst considered thy son to be still too young to be my husband, thou shouldest have told me so, and I would have waited in my father's palace for another nine years—but even then I would certainly never have caused you to blush with shame before your own nobles in Zablak. Now thou hadst better give up the presents to their rightful owner, thy son Maximus, else I shall not go a step further, even if thou shouldest threaten to put out my eyes."

Hearing this firm speech, Prince Ivan was greatly disturbed, and he called friends and Voïvodes to counsel him as to what he should do. But none of them dared say one word, for they well remembered the arrangement made before sailing across the sea.

Milosh's Offer

Voïvode Milosh saw that no one would speak, and he spurred his steed and addressed Prince Ivan in this wise: "O Ivan, thou our lord! Where is thy firm faith? If it fails now, may you yourself live to be betrayed! Hast thou not given me thy word that the wedding gifts should be mine intact? But now you frame a plan to break thy faith! Since thou art so little to be depended on, I agree—for the sake of peace among our brothers and svats—to give up the first two presents: I return to your son the fair bride and her steed with all its gold and silver trappings. In justice, and according to impartial judgment, I should be fully entitled even to marry the fair maiden—for she was presented to me by all, her parents and her brothers—but I shall say no more about that, and simply cede to you these two presents, together with the grey falcon. Here! I return to your son even the golden scabbard and the bright sabre, but I shall never consent to yield the helmet, the cloak, and the golden shirt; for I am determined to carry them to my own land, and show them to my friends and brothers, who, I am certain, will be proud of them. I swear by my faith in the true God that I shall not give up these three presents."

All the svats, moved by Milosh's fairness, agreed to the offer, and thanked him for his noble sacrifice for the sake of peace, but they were strongly opposed by the bride, who could not reconcile herself to the loss of the precious gifts, and especially the golden shirt. So she called aloud for Prince Maximus. This alarmed Prince Ivan very much, and he tried to quieten the maiden in these words: "O my sweet daughter-in-law, thou Venetian maiden! Do not call my son, for we have done him great injustice. Prince Maximus has a high sense of honour and is a brave man. I dread a fight above everything, and our festivities may so easily turn into mourning. I possess in Zablak a dungeon full of golden treasure, which I shall present to thee, and thou canst do with it whatever pleases thee!"

But the maiden was not easy to persuade, and she once more called Prince Maximus, who came with all speed to the scene. "O Maximus, thou only son of thy mother!"

began his bride, "may she lose thee! May the warriors make a handbier of thy lance and with thy shield may they cover thy tomb! May thy visage blush with shame on the day of judgment, as it does to-day at the contest with Voïvode Milosh! Why didst thou agree to yield to another the presents which rightly belong to the bridegroom? I care nothing for all the other presents, let Milosh take them away, and may a torrent take him away with them! but I cannot suffer the loss of the golden shirt, which I made for thee myself, and which took me three years to make, with three maidens assisting me. I nearly lost my sight before I finished working at this shirt, and all the time I was thinking of thee. Thou hadst better recover the shirt from Voïvode Milosh at once, for I swear by the name of the true God that otherwise I will not take a step forward; but I shall rein back my steed, and, when I reach the sea-coast, I shall pluck a leaf of aloe and shall scratch my face with its thorns till blood flows; then I shall write and send a message by my falcon to my aged father, beseeching him to call to arms all his force, to come and conquer and pillage thy Zablak and repay thee thus with mourning for thy shameful conduct!"

The Violence of Maximus

The moment Prince Maximus heard this, he reined back his black courser, spurred it so vehemently that the skin of his courser's stifle-joint burst and blood besprinkled its hoofs. The frantic animal sprang the height of three lances in the air and the length of four lances forward, so that he sped like lightning. Milosh burst into laughter, saying: "God be praised! What was suddenly the matter with that boy!" But his mirth was short-lived, for Prince Maximus now turned his horse straight toward Milosh furiously throwing his lance at his head.4 He struck Milosh so vigorously that both his eyes burst and he fell from his steed. Maximus rushed in and cleft his head asunder; then he took his bride from her leader and sped into the castle.5

When Voïvode Milosh's warriors saw their chief fall, they fiercely attacked the followers of Prince Maximus, and a fight ensued from which but very few returned home.

Maximus becomes a Turk

Prince Maximus, it is said, was so disgusted with what had occurred that he wrote to the doge, inviting him to invade Zablak with a large force and to conquer Montenegro; as for him, he would go to Istamboul and embrace Islamism. This he did.

Now a brother of Milosh, namely, Yovan Obrenbegovitch, suspecting that Maximus's intention was to obtain from the Sultan a great force with which to conquer Montenegro, decided to go to the Sultan for the same purpose. But it was his intention, should he also succeed in obtaining an army from the Sultan, to use it, not against his fatherland, Montenegro, but against Prince Maximus. On their way to Istamboul the two men met and they appeared together before the Sultan, who, knowing well who they were and deeming that they could be usefully employed in his service against the Christians, like many other malcontents from Christian courts, received them most kindly. They adopted the Mohammedan religion and were given Turkish names: Voïvode Yovan was called Mehmed-Bey Obrenbegovitch, and Prince Maximus, Scander-beg Ivanbegovitch. Having served as faithful Turks for nine years, the Sultan, pleased with their conduct, granted them both vizirates: to Mehmed-bey Obrenbegovitch he gave as fief the plain of Ducadyin, and Scander-beg (Prince Ivan's son) he granted Scutari on the River Boyana.

---

[1] Ruler of Zetta and Montenegro, which were separate states at the beginning of the fifteenth century.

[2] This expression occurs in several of the poems and implies the most deeply felt depression of spirits, and disappointment.

[3] In this verse the troubadour expresses the opinion—not at all complimentary to women, but universally prevailing in the Balkans—that "women have long hair and short brains" (*Dooge kosse a pameti kratke*).

[4] Other renderings of this ballad have it that Maximus challenged Milosh to a duel in which the prince was victorious.

[5] Others state that Maximus did not flee but remained and fought till he was nearly exhausted by his numberless wounds, and that then he made a superhuman effort and succeeded in rescuing his bride.

Chapter VIII: The Marriage of Tsar Doushan the Mighty

Doushan sends Theodor to Ledyen

King Michael of Ledyen had a beautiful daughter, Roksanda, and when Tsar Doushan asked her hand in marriage the king immediately consented. The betrothal was arranged by means of couriers, and Doushan had not seen the princess; he therefore summoned Theodor, his counsellor of State: "Listen to me, my trusty Theodor!" said he, "thou shalt go to the white city Ledyen to King Michael, and thou shalt ask him to fix the date for the wedding festivities. Thou shalt also settle with him other customary preliminaries and satisfy thyself that the peerless Roksanda is a fitting tsarina for our Serbian lands." Theodor promised to fulfil his mission faithfully and, having made the necessary preparations, he set out for the Venetian province. When he arrived at the white city Ledyen the king welcomed him courteously and lavished hospitality upon him for a full week.

Then Theodor spoke to the king in this wise: "O my master's friend, thou gallant King Michael! My tsar has not sent me here only that I should drink thy wine; he desires that I should arrange his marriage; tell me, when shall my master come? what time of the year will suit you best to receive him? how many svats shall he bring with him when he comes to take from thee the beautiful maiden Roksanda? My master also instructed me that I should desire of thee to be permitted the happiness of seeing the fair princess."

To this the king answered: "O my friend, Theodor! take my greetings to the tsar and tell him that he is at liberty to bring with him as many svats as he may please; also tell him that he may come for the maiden whenever he may choose; but request him in my name that under no circumstances shall he bring with him his nephews the two Voïnovitchs, Voukashin and Petrashin, for indeed I have heard that they are very quarrelsome when in their cups, and I fear that they may disturb the harmony of our festivities. As to the princess, she shall come to thee at due time and receive at thy hands the ring of thy master, as is the well-established custom."

The Princess Roksanda

At nightfall Theodor was conducted into an unlighted room and while he wondered when the candles would be brought, lo! the princess stood before him, shrouded in the thick gloom. Theodor was grieved at the trick played upon him, but he did not despair. He had with him the magnificent ring of his august master; it was so richly studded with precious stones that as he produced it the whole room was lighted up and the rays shone upon the maiden, who seemed to the ambassador more beautiful than the white veela herself. Theodor presented the betrothal ring and gave the princess also one thousand ducats; her brothers then conducted her back to her apartments.

The rays shone upon the maiden

Next morning Theodor took leave of the king and set out upon his homeward journey; when he arrived at Prisrend the tsar asked eagerly: "O my trusty Theodor!

Didst thou see the maiden Roksanda and didst thou give her my ring? What greetings dost thou bring me from King Michael?"

And Theodor answered: "Yea, my Lord, I saw thy bride and presented her with thy ring; but words fail me to describe the enchanting beauty of the Princess Roksanda! Vain would it be to search for her equal throughout Serbia! And fair and well spoke King Michael: Thou canst go for the maiden whensoever thou choosest, and thou mayest take as many svats as thou pleasest. But the king prays this one thing of thee: that thou shouldest under no circumstances take with thee, the Voinovitchs, thy two nephews, for they are lovers of the wine-cup and are quick to take offence; they may enter into drunken quarrels, and it may be difficult to settle their disputes in a peaceable manner."

When he heard this the tsar struck his knee with his right hand, and exclaimed: "Alas! May God help me! Has the ill fame of my nephews spread as far as that! By my unshakable faith, I shall, immediately after the wedding festivities, have them both hung on the gates of their castle Voutchitrn that they may not any longer bring shame to my name throughout the world."

The Procession Starts

Soon afterward the tsar proceeded to call his svats together and when they had all assembled they presented a brilliant spectacle. The wedding procession rode on its way through the field of Kossovo and as it passed by the walls of the castle Voutchitrn, the two youthful Voinovitchs looked upon the cavalcade and spoke sadly to each other thus: "Our uncle must be angry with us, otherwise he would surely have invited us also to join his wedding party? Some churl must have uttered ill words against us. May a hundred evils befall him who has done so! Our tsar is going to the Venetian land and has not a single hero in his train, neither has he any close relative who might be depended upon in case of dire misfortune. The Venetians are known from ancient times to be very cunning and sly and they may kill our glorious tsar! And yet to accompany him uninvited is more than we dare do."

Thereupon their aged mother spoke thus: "O my children, ye two Voïnovitchs! Ye have a brother in the mountains, Milosh-the-shepherd; though the youngest, he is the greatest hero of ye all and will find some way to uphold the honour of our name. The tsar has never heard about him. I counsel you to send him a message and bid him come to the castle Voutchitrn, mention not the true reason but tell him that his mother, being aged, may die at any moment and that she wishes to give him her blessings. Tell him to make haste if he would find his mother alive!"

This advice seemed good to the two brothers. They wrote a missive and dispatched it with haste to the mountain Shar where Milosh-the-shepherd tarried with his flocks.

The mountain Shar where Milosh-the-shepherd tarried with his flocks

As Milosh read the message his countenance changed and he shed bitter tears. His grief was observed by thirty shepherds who were around him: "O Milosh, our valiant chieftain!" they exclaimed, "Many messages have reached thee, but never yet have we seen thee shed tears when thou didst read them. Whence came this letter and what evil tidings does it bring? Tell us quickly, we beseech thee!"

Milosh sprang to his feet and addressed his shepherds in this wise: "Hearken, O shepherds, my dearest brethren! This message comes from the castle: my mother is on her death-bed and she summons me that she may give me her blessing, that damnation should not fall upon my soul. I must hasten to her side and while I am absent from the mountain I charge ye to watch well the sheep."

When Milosh came near to his white castle, his brothers saw him from a tower and sallied out to meet him; their aged mother also followed. Milosh was astonished to see her and said reproachfully: "Why, O brothers dear, do ye make misfortune when there is no reason, and when all is well with ye! May the Almighty forgive your deception!" And his brothers answered: "Come within, dear brother, there *is* nevertheless great misfortune!"

The young men embraced each other and Milosh kissed his mother's hand. Then his brothers related the story of their uncle's betrothal and how he was proceeding to the Venetian land without having invited his two nephews to ride in the wedding procession, and they besought him in this wise: "O, our dear brother Milosh! Go thou with the tsar, yea, although thou art not invited. Misfortune may befall, and haply thou shalt succour your uncle. Thou canst go and come back again without making thyself known to anyone!"

Milosh was no less eager than his brothers, and he answered gladly: "I will go, O my brothers! Indeed how could I do otherwise? If I were not willing to help our dear uncle, whom else should I be willing to aid?"

Thereupon his brothers began to make all the necessary preparations. Peter went to the stables to saddle his steed Koulash, while Vankashin remained to see that Milosh was fittingly attired. He first put on him a fine shirt which was embroidered with gold from the neck to the waist; downward from the waist it was woven of white silk. Over the shirt he placed three thin, elegant ribbons; then a waistcoat adorned with thirty golden buttons; then a golden cuirasse weighing some fifteen pounds. And in all details he attired him with garments worthy of a prince. Finally he hung upon his broad shoulders a coarse Bulgar shepherd's cloak, which entirely enveloped him, and placed on his head a Bulgarian fur-cap with high point, thus making him look so like a black Bulgar that his own mother would not have recognized him. The brothers now fetched a warrior's lance and mace and the trusty sword of their old father Voïn. Then Peter brought forward Koulash, upon whom he had fastened a bear's skin in order that the tsar might not recognize the well-known steed.

Milosh Joins the Procession

Milosh was now ready to set out, and as he took leave of his brothers they counselled him thus: "When thou comest up with the wedding-guests they will ask thee who thou art and whence thou comest. Thou shalt answer that thou art coming from the Karavallahian land, where thou hast been serving a Turkish lord, Radoul-bey, who would not pay thee thy wages, wherefore thou art looking for a more generous master. Say, moreover, that having received chance tidings of the tsar's wedding, thou has ridden to join thyself to the servants of the party, not for any wages, for thou wilt gladly serve for a piece of bread and a glass of red wine. Thou must, meantime, hold firmly the reins of thy steed, for Koulash is accustomed to go in the line with the tsar's own chargers, and he may betray thee!"

When the brothers had made an end of their counsel Milosh took leave of them and of his mother and turned his steed in the direction of the wedding party, and he came up with them in the mountain Zagoryé. Upon seeing the stranger the svats hailed him: "Whence are thou coming, little young Bulgar?" And Milosh answered from afar as his brothers had counselled. Then the svats welcomed him readily, saying: "Mayest thou be happy with us, little young Bulgar! We are always glad to have one more in our company!"

The princely company, all aglow with the brilliant colours of the resplendent uniforms, their lances and cuirasses gleaming in the sun, rode on until they came to a valley. Now Milosh had a bad habit, acquired in the mountain Shar while watching his sheep, to slumber toward mid-day, and as his Koulash stepped proudly on he fell into a deep sleep and his hand suddenly relaxed on the rein. No sooner did Koulash feel the curb loosen than he arched his neck and flew like an arrow from a bow through the ranks of the cavalcade, overturning horses and riders, till he reached the horses of the tsar, when he ranged himself in line with them and fell into the same slow, measured pace.

By this time the whole procession had fallen into disorder, and a crowd of Lale[1] would have fallen upon the innocent cause of the commotion, had not Doushan intervened to protect him, saying, "Do not strike this youthful Bulgarian, he is a shepherd, and shepherds have a habit of dozing toward noon while watching their sheep; do not be violent, but awaken him gently." Thereupon the svats awakened Milosh, shouting: "Rise, O foolish young Bulgarian! May the Almighty spare thy old mother who could not give thee a better understanding but thou must needs venture to join the company of the tsar!"

The Leap of Koulash

Milosh awoke with a start, and saw the tsar looking upon him with his deep black eyes, and lo! his Koulash was in the royal line! Not a moment did he pause, but, gathering the reins firmly in his hand, he spurred his steed sharply. Koulash for one brief instant quivered from head to heel, then with a frantic bound he sprang into the air the height of three lances; for the length of four lances sideways did he spring, and as for the number of lengths covered by his leap onward, no one could number them! Fire issued from his mouth and tongues of blue flame came out from his nostrils! Twelve thousand svats beheld with awe and admiration the wonderful leap of the Bulgar's steed, and exclaimed as one man: "Father of Mercies, what a mighty wonder!" Then some said to others: "O that so good a horse should be possessed by such a fellow! We have never before seen such a marvel." Others said: "There was, indeed, one charger like this in the stables of our tsar's son-in-law and now is possessed by his nephews the brothers Voïnovitchs."

Among the heroes who admired the steed were Voutché of Dyakovitza, Yanko of Nestopolyé and a youth from Priepolyé; these spake one to another thus: "What a beautiful steed that Bulgar has! There is not its equal to be found in this wedding cavalcade, not even our own tsar has one like it. Let us fall behind and seek an opportunity to deprive him of it."

As they reached Klissoura the three horsemen were far behind the other svats, and Milosh was also riding alone in that place. Then the heroes came near to him and addressed him in seeming courtesy: "Listen to us, thou youthful Bulgar! Wilt thou exchange thy horse for a better one? We shall give thee also one hundred ducats as a bargain-gift, and moreover we shall give thee a plough and a pair of oxen that thou mayest plough thy fields and feed thyself in peace for the rest of thy days!"

But Milosh answered: "Leave me alone, O ye three mighty horsemen! I do not wish for a better horse than the one I have already; for did ye not see that I cannot keep even this one quiet? As to your bargain-gift, what should I do with so many ducats? I do not know how to weigh them, neither am I able to count as high as one hundred. What should I do with your plough and your oxen? My father has never used a plough on his fields and yet his children have never known hunger!"

The Fight for Koulash

At this answer the three horsemen said angrily: "Thou hadst better consider our proposal, O haughty Bulgar, lest we take thy horse by force!" To this menace Milosh answered: "Truly, by force men take lands and cities, and much more easily can three men by force take from me my steed! Therefore I prefer to exchange it, for I am unable to travel on foot." Saying this, Milosh made a pretence to give up his Koulash peaceably, and inserted his right hand under his coarse cloak. They thought he intended to take off his spurs, but they were greatly mistaken, for in a flash out came his six-angled club, and before they had gathered their wits Milosh gave Voutché a gentle tap that tumbled him over and over three times in succession. Milosh then addressed him ironically: "May thy vineyards in thy peaceful estate of Dyakovitza be as fertile as thou art brave!"

Seeing what had befallen his companion, Yanko was in full flight, but it took scarce a moment for Koulash to reach the flying steed, and Milosh let fall upon the shoulders of his rider such a blow that he, too, was hurled to the ground, where he turned over four times ere finding anchorage. "Hold on! O Yanko!" scoffed Milosh, "May the apple-trees in thy peaceful estate bear as abundant fruit as thou art brave to-day!"

There now only remained the young man from Priepolyé who by now had fled to some distance. But his horse's speed could not avail against the swiftness of Koulash, and Milosh soon reached him and with his warrior club gave him a tap that tumbled him over and over no less than seven times. Whether he could hear or not Milosh called aloud: "Hold fast, O young man from Priepolyé! And when thou goest back to thy Priepolyé, I give thee leave to boast before the fair maidens there of how thou hast to-day taken away by force a Bulgar's steed!"

This done, Milosh turned his charger and soon reached the wedding cavalcade. In due course the procession arrived at the white city of Ledyen, and the Serbians put up their white tents beneath its walls. The equerries gave the horses barley, but none did they give to Koulash. When Milosh saw this he took in his left hand a nose-bag and went from horse to horse, taking with his right hand from each a handful until he had filled the bag of his trusty Koulash. Next he went to the principal wine-keeper and prayed that he would give him a glass of wine. But the keeper of the wine refused, saying: "Go away, thou black Bulgar! If thou hadst brought thy rough Bulgarian wooden cup, I might perhaps have poured in it a draught; but these golden cups are not for thee!" Milosh turned on the churlish wine-keeper a dark look and followed it with a tender blow on his cheek that sent three sound teeth into his throat. Then the man, thoroughly cowed, besought Milosh thus: "Stay thy hand, O mighty Bulgar! There is wine in abundance for thee, even if our tsar should thereby go short." But Milosh paid no attention to the fellow, and proceeded to help himself. Then, as his spirits mounted with the generous wine, day dawned and the sun began to shine.

The First Test

As Milosh stood drinking in the fresh beauty of the early morning a page of King Michael called loudly from a tower of the royal castle: "Listen, O Serbian Tsar Doushan! Behold, in the valley beneath the walls of the city is the champion of our king! Thou must fight a duel with him, either thyself or by a substitute. If thou dost not overcome him thou shalt not go from this place safely, neither shalt thou take back with thee so much as one of thy wedding-guests! Still less shalt thou take with thee the princess Roksanda!"

Doushan heard the haughty message and sent a strong-voiced crier among the wedding-guests. Here and there he stood shouting loudly the tsar's message: "Has any mother given birth to a fearless hero who will take up the challenge in our tsar's stead? To him who is brave enough to fight the champion the tsar will grant nobility." But alas! when the crier had gone through the camp no hero had come forward to claim the honour of doing battle for the tsar.

When Doushan heard this, he struck his knee with his right hand, exclaiming: "Woe is me! O mighty Creator! If I had now my darling nephews, the two Voïnovitchs, I should not lack a champion." The tsar had hardly ended his lamentation when Milosh, leading his steed, appeared before the tsar's tent. "O my Lord, thou mighty tsar!" said he, "have I thy leave to fight this duel?"

The tsar answered: "Thou art welcome, O youthful Bulgar! But, alas, there is slender likelihood that thou canst overpower the haughty hector of the king. If, however, thou dost succeed, verily I will ennoble thee!"

Milosh leaped to his saddle, and as he turned his fiery Koulash from the tsar's tent, he carelessly threw his lance on his shoulder with its point turned backward. Seeing this, Doushan called to him: "Do not carry, O my son, thy lance so! Turn the point forward, lest the proud Venetians laugh at thee!" But Milosh answered: "Attend, O my tsar, unto thine own dignity, and be not anxious concerning mine! If need arise I shall easily turn my lance correctly; if not, I may just as well bring it back in this wrong wise!"

As Milosh rode on through the field of Ledyen, the ladies and maidens of Ledyen looked upon him, and, laughing, they exclaimed: "Saints in heaven! a marvel! What a substitute for a Serbian emperor! The young man has even no decent clothes upon him! Be merry, thou hector of the king, for hardly shalt thou need to unsheath thy sword!"

Meantime Milosh reached the tent in which sat the champion of the Venetian king. Before the entrance he had stuck his lance deep into the ground, and to this he had tethered his grey steed. Milosh addressed the hector thus: "Rise up! thou little white Venetian gentleman, we will fight together for the honour of our masters!" But the hector answered angrily: "Away with thee, thou ugly black Bulgar! My sword is not for such as thee! I would not soil my steel on such a ragged fellow!"

This remark made Milosh very angry, and he exclaimed: "Rise up, haughty Venetian! Thou hast indeed richer attire; I shall take it from thee, and then who will have the finer feathers?"

At this the hector sprang to his feet and mounted his grey charger, which he caused to prance and curvet across the field. Milosh stood quietly looking on until suddenly the Venetian fiercely hurled his lance straight to the breast of Milosh. The wary Serbian received it on his golden-headed club and jerked the weapon over his head, breaking it into three pieces as he did so. This sleight-of-hand alarmed the hector and he exclaimed: "Wait a minute, thou ugly black Bulgar! My lance was faulty, wait till I get a better one!" With this he put spurs to his steed, but Milosh shouted after him: "Stop, thou white Venetian! Thou shalt not escape me!" And with this he spurred his Koulash after the cowardly hector and pursued close to the gates of Ledyen. Alas for the fugitive, the gates were closed! For a moment the hector paused irresolute and this moment was his last. Milosh let loose his unerring lance; it whistled though the morning air and the hector was transfixed to the gate. Then Milosh alighted from his steed, struck off the Venetian's head and threw it in Koulash's nose-bag.

Next he caught the grey steed and rode with him to the tsar. "Here, O mighty tsar," said he, "is the head of the king's hector!"

Doushan was overjoyed at his prowess and gave him much gold. "Go, my son," said he, kindly, "drink some good wine, and presently I shall make thee noble!"

The Second Test

Milosh had hardly seated himself at his wine when a page again called loudly from the royal castle: "Behold, O Serbian tsar! In the meadow below thou mayest see three fiery horses saddled, on the back of each there is fastened a flaming sword with point upward. If thou wouldst go in peace from here taking with thee the king's daughter, thou must thyself or by deputy leap over these flaming swords."

Again the tsar sent a crier throughout his camp. "O Serbians," he cried, "has not any mother given birth to a hero who will venture to leap over the three horses and the flaming swords fixed on their backs?"

Again he traversed the entire camp, taking care that his words should come to the ear of every svat, but again no hero came forward to offer himself. Then as the tsar was anxiously meditating on the problem he looked up and, lo! Milosh again stood before him. "O glorious tsar!" said he, "Have I thy permission to essay this feat?" And the tsar readily answered: "Thou mayest surely go, my dear son! But first take off this clumsy Bulgarian cloak! (may God punish the stupid tailor who made it so!)" But

Milosh said: "Sit in peace, O mighty tsar, and drink thy cool wine! Do not be anxious concerning my coarse cloak. If there be a heart in the hero his cloak will not be in his way: if a sheep finds her wool too heavy for her there is no sheep in her nor any wool!"

So saying he rode down to the meadow of Ledyen where stood the three steeds tethered side by side fiercely pawing the ground. The young man dismounted from his Koulash and stationed him several paces from the third steed, by his side, then patting Koulash gently on his proud neck, he said: "Thou shalt stay here quietly until I come again to the saddle!" He passed over to the first steed and went on a little distance, then turned, and dancing first on one foot then on the other, he ran like a swift deer and, leaping high, jumped over the three steeds, over the flaming swords, and alighted safely on the saddle of his own Koulash. This done he gathered the reins of the three chargers and rode with them in triumph to the Serbian tsar.

The Third Test

Very soon the page of the Venetian king came again to the tower of the royal castle and proclaimed: "Hearken, thou tsar of the Serbs! Under the topmost tower of this castle is a slender lance whereon a golden apple is stuck; twelve paces distant is set a ring: thou must shoot an arrow through the ring and transfix the apple—thou or thy deputy!"

This time Milosh would not wait for the crier to do his errand, but straightway went to the tsar and obtained his permission to essay the task. Then, taking his golden bow and arrow, he went to the place indicated, fixed his arrow on the bow string, and the shaft sped straight through the ring to the heart of the apple which he caught in his hand as it fell. Again the tsar bestowed upon him golden ducats beyond number.

The Fourth Test

No sooner was this wonderful exploit completed than the royal page again proclaimed from the castle turret: "Behold, O tsar of the Serbs! The two royal princes have brought out in front of the king's palace three beautiful maidens, all exactly alike and attired in similar robes. The king bids thee guess which of the three is the princess Roksanda. Woe to thee if thou touchest other maiden but Roksanda! Thou shalt not have the princess for thy bride; neither shalt thou go out with thy head upon thy shoulders; still less shall thy guests leave this place!"

When Doushan heard the message he summoned immediately his councillor Theodor and commanded: "Go, Theodor, and tell which is Roksanda!" But Theodor declared that he had seen her but for so brief a time that it would be impossible that he should be able to choose between three maidens all exactly like the one he had seen by the light from his master's ring.

Hearing this the tsar, in despair, struck his knee with his hand, exclaiming: "Alas! alas! After performing many wonderful exploits, must we return without the bride and be the shame of our people?" Just then Milosh, who had become aware of the tsar's difficulty, entered into the imperial presence and spake thus: "Have I thy leave, O tsar, to try to guess which of the maidens is the princess Roksanda?" And the tsar answered joyfully: "Indeed thou hast, O darling son of mine! But slender is the hope that thou shalt guess rightly, since thou hast never seen the princess before!"

Thereupon Milosh answered: "Be not fearful, my glorious Lord! When I was a shepherd in the mountain Shar watching twelve thousand sheep, there have been born in a night three hundred lambs and I have been able to recognize and tell which sheep was dam to each lamb. How much easier will it be to choose Roksanda by her resemblance to her brothers!"

"Go, go then, my darling son! May God help thee to guess rightly! If thou art successful I shall grant thee the whole land of Skender that thou be its lord for thy lifetime!"

Milosh went forth through the wide field until he came to the place where the three maidens stood waiting. With a swift and sudden motion he swept the coarse fur-cap from his head and threw from off his shoulder his heavy cloak, revealing the scarlet velvet and the golden cuirasse which had been hidden underneath. Truly he shone in the verdant field like the setting sun behind a forest! Milosh now spread his cloak on the grass and cast upon it rings, pearls, and precious stones. Then he unsheathed his finely-tempered sword and addressed the three fair maidens thus: "Let her who is the princess Roksanda gather her train and sleeves together and collect these rings, pearls, and precious stones! If any but Roksanda should dare to touch these beautiful things, I swear by my firm faith that I shall instantly cut off her two hands, yea, even as far as her elbows!"

Two of them looked meaningly at their companion

The three beautiful maidens were terrified, and two of them looked meaningly at their companion who stood in the middle. This was the princess, and after a moment's hesitation Roksanda gathered her silky train and sleeves and began to collect the rings, pearls, and precious stones. The two other maidens were about to flee, but Milosh took them gently by their hands and escorted all three to the presence of the tsar, to whom he presented princess Roksanda together with one of her companions who might be her lady-in-waiting; the third maiden, however, he retained for himself. The tsar kissed Milosh between his fiery eyes, still not knowing who he was or whence he came.

The Departure of the Serbians

The masters of the ceremonies now called aloud: "Get ready, all ye svats! It is high time we should hurry homeward!" And the svats made ready for the journey, and soon they set out, taking with them the beautiful princess Roksanda.

As they departed from the gates of the city, Milosh approached the tsar and said: "O my lord, thou Serbian Tsar Doushan, listen to me! There is in the city of Ledyen a terrible hero named Balatchko the Voïvode; I know him and he knows me. Balatchko has three heads: from one of them issues a blue flame, from another rushes a freezing wind. Woe to him against whom these are directed! But if a hero withstands them it is not difficult to slay Balatchko when his wind and flame have left him. The Venetian king has been training him these seven years, for it has been his intention to make use of him to annihilate the royal wedding-party and to rescue princess Roksanda, supposing that thou shouldst succeed in obtaining possession of her. Now it is certain that he will send him to pursue us. Go thou thy way and I will remain behind with three hundred well-chosen heroes, to stop the monster from pursuing thee." Therefore, while the svats went on with the beautiful Princess Roksanda, Milosh, with his three hundred comrades, remained in the verdant forest.

The svats had hardly struck their tents when King Michael summoned Voïvode Balatchko. "O Balatchko, my trusty servant," said he, "canst thou rely upon thy valour and go out against the tsar's svats to bring back my daughter Roksanda?"

And Balatchko replied: "My lord, thou King of Ledyen! First tell me, who was that valorous hero who achieved the great feats to which thou didst challenge the Serbian tsar?" The king of Ledyen answered him: "O Balatchko, our trusty servant! He is no hero; he is only a youthful black Bulgarian." And Balatchko replied: "Nay, thou art mistaken; no black Bulgar is he. I know him well; he is the Prince Milosh Voïnovitch himself, whom not even the Serbian tsar was able to recognize through his shepherd's disguise. Truly he is no ordinary hero, and not to be lightly esteemed by any warrior, however fearless." Nevertheless the king insisted: "Go thou against the svats, O Voïvode Balatchko! If thou dost regain the princess, I will give her to thee for wife!"

The Contest with Balatchko

Hearing this promise, Balatchko saddled his mare Bedevia and went in pursuit of the svats, accompanied by six hundred Venetian cuirassiers. When they reached the forest they saw Koulash standing in the middle of the main road and Milosh on foot behind him. Balatchko addressed the prince, saying: "O Milosh, evidently thou hast waited for me!" With this he loosed his blue flame, which, however, only singed Milosh's furs; whereupon, seeing that he had not greatly harmed the hero, he breathed his freezing wind upon him. Koulash tumbled over and over in the dust three times, but the wind did not affect his master. Exclaiming: "There is something thou didst not expect!" Milosh hurled his six-cornered mace and it gave Balatchko a gentle knock that tumbled him out of his saddle. Then Milosh threw his lance and transfixed the fellow to the ground, after which he cut off all three of his heads and threw them in Koulash's bag. This done, he mounted his steed and led his three hundred Serbians against the Venetian cuirassiers and cleft three hundred heads, the survivors being put to flight. He then hurried on and soon came up with the tsar, at whose feet he cast the three grim heads of Balatchko. The tsar rejoiced to hear of his victory and gave him one thousand ducats; then the procession resumed its march to Prisrend. In the middle of the plain Kossovo, Milosh's way to the fortress of Voutchitrn lay to the right, and he came to the tsar to take leave of him. "May God be with thee, my dear uncle!" said he. Only then did the tsar come to know that the seeming Bulgarian was none else than his nephew Prince Milosh Voïnovitch! Overwhelmed with joy he exclaimed: "Is it thou, my dear Milosh? Is it thou, my dearest nephew?

Happy is the mother who gave thee birth and happy the uncle who has such a valiant nephew! Why didst thou not reveal thyself before? verily I should not have excluded thee from my company."

Woe to him who overlooks his own relatives!

1This is the popular appellation of Serbians living in Batchka and Banat, which provinces are now under Austro-Hungarian rule.

Chapter IX: Tsar Lazarus and the Tsarina Militza

The Tsarina's Forebodings

As they sat at supper together one evening the Tsarina Militza spoke thus unto Tsar Lazarus: "O Lazarus, thou Serbian Golden Crown! Thou art to go to-morrow to the battlefield of Kossovo together with thy dukes and servants, but, alas! thou wilt leave in the palace none who can carry to thee my missives and bring thine from Kossovo to me. Thou takest also with thee my nine brothers Yougovitchs; I pray thee, leave me at least one of my brothers that I may swear[1] by him!"

And the tsar returned answer: "O my lady, thou Tsarina Militza! Which one of thy brothers wouldst thou best like me to leave at home." Thereupon the tsaritza said: "Leave me, I pray, Boshko Yougovitch!"

To this the tsar assented: "O my lady, Tsarina Militza! When the morrow dawns and the sun begins to rise and the gates of the fortress are opened, thou mayest walk out to the main gate whence the whole army will defile with the ensigns—all cavaliers with warrior-lances, headed by Boshko Yougovitch, who will be carrying the flag adorned with a golden cross. Greet him in my name and tell him that I give him leave to remain with thee at our white castle and to yield his flag to whomsoever he may choose!"

Accordingly, when the morrow dawned and the sun shone, the fortress-gates opened and Tsarina Militza appeared at the main gate of the city, and lo! the mighty army was preparing to defile with, in the van, the glorious cavaliers headed by Boshko Yougovitch. Boshko was in the act of mounting his brown horse, a splendid creature, caparisoned with golden trappings; the dropping folds of the flag fell upon his shoulders and over his steed's back. Upon the flag pole was fixed a golden apple and from the great cross hung golden thustles which were knocking gently against Boshko's shoulders.

Tsarina Militza approached her brother and flinging her tender arms around his neck addressed him in her sweet voice thus: "O my darling brother, our tsar has presented thee to me, and desires that thou shalt not go to Kossovo in the war. His charge to thee is: that thou shalt give thy flag to whom thou choosest and remain at Kroushevatz that I may have a brother to swear by!"

But Boshko Yougovitch answered: "Go back, O sister dear, to thy white castle! I would not return, neither would I give up from my hands this flag for the price of Kroushevatz.[2] How could I suffer my comrades to say: 'Look at the coward Boshko Yougovitch! He dares not go to Kossovo, to shed his blood in the cause of the Holy Cross and his orthodox faith!'" Saying this he disengaged himself from his sister's embraces and leapt into his saddle.

Lo! there now comes the aged Youg-Bogdan at the head of a line of his seven other sons! The tsarina endeavoured to stop each one in turn, but in vain. Voïn Yougovitch, the eighth brother, was last in the line; he like the rest of his brothers would not listen, and as he passed on, the poor tsarina fell down at the feet of the horses and swooned. The glorious Lazarus saw his loving consort fall, and understanding the cause of her grief, he shed tears. Glancing quickly right and left he beheld Golouban, his trusty servant, and called to him: "O Golouban, my faithful servant! Dismount from thy charger, and take the tsarina gently in thy heroic arms to her slender tower. God and I will hold thee excused from service in the war, do thou remain at our white castle near the tsarina!"

Hearing this Golouban turned pale, and tears poured down his cheeks as he dismounted from his Laboud.[3] He took the tsarina in his arms and carried her into her slender high tower as the tsar had commanded; but this done he could not resist the desire of his heart to go to Kossovo, so he hurried back to his charger and spurred him swiftly on after his comrades.

News of Battle

Next day, when morning dawned, lo! two ill-omened ravens from the battlefield of Kossovo alighted upon the white tower of the glorious Tsar Lazarus. One spake to the other: "Is this the home of the famed prince, Lazarus? Is there no living soul in the castle?"

One only within the castle heard this. Tsarina Militza walked out upon the balcony of her tower and besought the two black ravens thus: "For the sake of all that ye hold dear, O ye two dark ravens! Whence do ye come? Do ye not fly from the field of Kossovo? Saw ye there two mighty armies? O tell me! Have they met together? Which of them is victorious?"

Thereupon the two ravens answered: "Evil overtake us if we do not speak truth to thee, O fair empress Militza! We fly indeed from the level plain of Kossovo! Yea! There we did see two mighty armies; there did we see two tsars perish!4 Of the Turkish horde but few remain in life; of the Serbs, those who live are covered with wounds and blood!"

The Trusty Miloutin

The ravens had hardly spoken when the tsarina perceived a horseman approaching whom she recognized. His left arm hung helpless; he was covered with seventeen wounds; blood ran over his steed. The tsarina called to him in accents of terror: "Alas, alas! Is it thou, my trusty Miloutin? Hast thou then betrayed thy tsar on Kossovo the level field?"

But Miloutin answered slowly and with pain: "Help me, O my lady, to alight from my brave steed! Bathe my face with cooling water and refresh me with rosy wine, for heavy wounds have overwhelmed me!"

And the tsarina went to him and helped him to dismount from his bloody steed, bathed his face with some cooling water and brought wine unto his dried lips. When she had thus restored him somewhat, she spake again: "What dreadful thing has happened, O thou trusty servant, in Kossovo that level field? Where perished the glorious Prince Lazarus? Where perished the aged Youg Bogdan? Where perished the nine Yougovitchs? Where perished Voïvode Milosh? Where perished Vouk Brankovitch? Where perished Ban Strahinya?"

Thereat the warrior groaned heavily: "All remain on Kossovo, O my lady! Where the glorious Prince Lazarus perished, there were broken many, many lances, both Turkish and Serbian, but more Serbian than Turkish: defending, O my lady, their beloved lord, their lord the glorious Prince Lazarus. And thy father, O lady, perished in the first onset. Thy nine brothers perished too—faithful did they abide to one another. Till all perished, there mightest thou have seen the valiant Boshko, his flag fluttering in the breeze as he rushed hither and thither, scattering the Turks like a falcon amongst timid doves. There, by the streamlet Sitnitza, where blood was running above a hero's knees, perished Ban Strahinya.

"But our heroes did not die alone! Twelve thousand Turks lie prone upon the plain. Sultan Mourat$_5$ was slain by Voïvode Milosh. May God forgive all his sins! The hero has bequeathed to the Serbian race a memory of noble deeds that shall be recounted by the bards as long as men live and Kossovo stays. As for the traitor Vouk, accursed be she who gave him birth! He betrayed our tsar on Kossovo, leading astray, O my lady! twelve thousand fierce cuirassiers of our people! Accursed for ever be his progeny!"

Historical Note

The bards invariably throw all responsibility for the great calamity to the Serbian arms, inflicted upon them in that celebrated battle on Kossovo, upon Vouk Brankovitch, who was one of the sons-in-law of Tsar Lazarus. Some of our historians are convinced that there is a great deal of truth in this *licencia poetica*, and they point to the fact that the mediæval history of Serbia contains many instances of such malcontents as Vouk Brankovitch who, seduced by fair promises from cunning Turkish statesmen, went to Stamboul to become useful tools in the hands of Ottoman generals, who were thereby aided in their conquests of the Slavs of the Balkans. But the truth is that our calamity was due mainly to the disobedience of the Serbian Lords who ruled almost independently over Bosnia and Herzegovina. These lords failed to comply with Tsar Lazarus' mobilisation proclamation, and it was due to this that the Serbian army was considerably smaller than the Turkish.

Be this as it may, the defeat which the Serbians sustained in that memorable battle left a very deep impression upon the nation, and Serbians have believed ever since that it was solely due to this disaster that the Serbian empire was crushed by the Turk. This feeling persisted in the hearts of the oppressed Serbians through four centuries and was manifested in repeated insurrections against their oppressors in the beginning of the last century under the leadership of two Serbian princes, George Petrovitch, grandfather of the present King Peter I Karageorgevitch, in the year 1804, and Milosh Obrenovitch in 1815. But another century had to pass ere the opportunity came for a decisive battle by which satisfaction could be obtained for the battle on Kossovo. This opportunity offered on the famous field of Koumanovo in 1913, where perished more Turks than did Serbians five centuries ago. Only then was Serbia happy! The present writer went through the Balkan Campaigns of 1912–1913, and was a witness of glorious deeds and feats of arms by his countrymen which, relatively speaking, by no means yield to those of their mediæval ancestors led by Milosh Obilitch, Marko Kralyevitch, Ban Strahinya, and others. It was an imposing sight when the victorious Serbian army returned to Belgrade at the conclusion of the war. The soldiers entered through numberless triumphal gates, over some of which were huge inscriptions: "For Kossovo: Koumanovo" and "For Slivnitza: Bregalnitza."

The untiring Serbian bards have now turned their attention to the exploits of modern heroes at Monastir, Koumanovo, Perlep (Prilip), Scutari (Skadar), &c., and they will thus immortalize for the delight of future generations the final triumph of the Serb over the oppressor of his race, from whom he has wrested the empire of his valiant ancestors—if not in its entirety as under the rule of Tsar Doushan the Powerful, yet as it was in extent in the time of Tsar Lazarus.

What Tsar Lazarus lost, therefore, has now been virtually regained by his brave countrymen under the wise leadership of our present King Peter I.

---

[1] The love of a sister for her brother in Serbia is proverbial. Entire ballads are devoted to beautiful examples of such love. There is no greater and more solemn oath for a sister in Serbia than that sworn by the name of her brother.

[2] Kroushevatz was the capital of the vast Serbian empire during the reign of Tsar Lazarus Hrebélianovitch at the time of the famous battle of Kossovo (A.D. 1389).

[3] Laboud means *white swan* in Serbian.

[4] The Turkish sultan, Amourath I, perished by the hand of Voïvode Milosh. That great Serbian hero stabbed him with his secret poniard when conducted as an alleged traitor to the sultan's presence.

[5] Corrupted form of Amourad or Amourath.

Chapter X: The Captivity and Marriage of Stephan Yakshitch[1]

The Veela's Warning

Dawn had not appeared, neither had Danitza[2] yet shown her face when from the heights of the mountain Avala by Belgrade a veela called aloud upon Demitrius and Stephan, the two brothers Yakshitchs: "O ye brothers Yakshitchs! Ill fate hath this morn brought to ye! See ye not that the mighty Turk has made ready to assail the glorious town Belgrade from three sides? Hearken! I will tell ye the pashas by name. The Vizier of Tyoopria is come with forty thousand troops; the Pasha of Vidin leads an army of thirty thousand; and the Pasha of Novi Bazar has brought with him twenty thousand fierce Yanissaries! If ye will not believe, climb ye to the top of your towers and look over upon the broad field of Belgrade!"

Hearing this adjuration Demitrius looked out, and saw, indeed, all that the veela had said. If rain had fallen from the skies, no drop would have fallen on the ground, so thick was the multitude of Turks and their horses! He was seized with terror at the sight, and, without pausing a moment, he ran to his stable, saddled his steed, and, unlocking the main gates of the fortress, rushed out, leaving the keys in the gate. He did not slacken rein until he reached a great forest, and by this time the sun was already high in the heavens. Dismounting from the saddle he seated himself on the banks of the cooling river Yahorika, and soliloquized thus: "Alas, Demitrius, mayst thou perish! To whose care hast thou left thy only brother Stephan?"

Overcome with remorse for his cowardice he would have returned to Belgrade, but it was too late. The Turks had already entered the city through the open gates. There was none to oppose them, and after indulging in outrage and pillage they had carried away many captives, among whom was Stephan Yakshitch. Him they did not behead because of his unusual beauty, and because they were well acquainted with his heroism, the fame of which was known far and near. They brought Stephan to the presence of the Vizier of Tyoopria, who was so pleased to see him that he ordered his hands to be freed, and gave him back his horse and arms. He also held a great feast and accompanied it with the firing of innumerable cannon. After this the Vizier of Tyoopria returned with the whole army in triumph to Stamboul, where he brought his distinguished prisoner into the sultan's presence.

Stephan and the Sultan

The mighty Padishah was seated on his sidjadé,[3] and after presenting Stephan the vizier took a seat near by. Stephan made a profound obeisance and kissed the slipper and the knee of the sultan. The sultan then invited him to a seat near to him and spake thus: "O heroic Stephan Yakshitch! If thou wilt become a Turk! (may Allah favour thee!) I will make thee my Grand Vizier of Bosnia in the City of Travnik! Thou shalt have seven other viziers to obey thy orders; I will give thee in marriage my only daughter, and will care for thee as for my own son!"

To this Stephan answered firmly: "O Great Padishah! Thou mighty ruler of the world! I shall never turn Turk and renounce the Holy Cross. Yea, even if thou offered me thy own throne! I am ready to give my life for the holy Christian faith!"

At these bold words the sultan was very angry, and gave orders that Stephan should be executed. But Stephan had a good friend in the Vizier of Tyoopria, who at this juncture prayed the sultan not to give way to his wrath. "Do not, in the name of Allah, O my Padishah," said he, "have so valorous a young man beheaded! I have given him my word of honour that thou, O Sultan, will not take his life! Deliver him to me for ransom! I will give thee as many golden ducats as he weighs on thy balance, and will keep him safely in my castle at Tyoopria where, I give thee my firm faith, I will make him love the creed of Mohammed."

The sultan graciously acceded to his vizier's request and Stephan departed with the Turk to his province.

Stephan at Tyoopria

When the vizier came to Tyoopria he invited Stephan to participate in all the luxury of his castle, and during one whole year he endeavoured by courtesy and kindness to convert the Serbian prince to the Mussulman faith. Then, as all his efforts had failed, he called together his hodjas[4] and kadis,[5] as well as all the noblemen of his district, and these men spoke to Stephan thus: "O Stephan, the vizier has ordered us to convert thee unto the true faith; if thou wilt submit to us in this thing he will give thee in marriage his only daughter—she is more beautiful than the white veela herself—and he will have thee to be appointed the Grand Vizier of Novi Bazar. But if thou refused to become a Turk, his djelat[6] will cleave thy head asunder."

Thereupon Stephan answered: "I thank ye, venerable hodgas and kadis! But I would rather lose my life for the sake of our holy faith and the law of our Lord Jhesu, than live to become a Turk!"

The vizier turned sadly away and ordered his djelat to behead Prince Stephan. But again Stephan's good fortune befriended him. The Grand Vizier of Novi Bazar came to the Vizier of Tyoopria and implored him not to behead the young man. "Dost thou not remember," said he, "that thou didst promise that his life should not be taken from him? 'Twere better to deliver him to me on ransom: I will give twice his weight in golden ducats, and I declare solemnly that when I have him in my province of Novi Bazar, I shall not fail to induce him to embrace Islam!"

The Vizier of Tyoopria agreed to his friend's offer and Stephan was thus a second time delivered from death.

Stephan at Novi Bazar

Arriving at Novi Bazar the vizier summoned his servant Hoossein. "Listen, Hoossein, my trusty servant!" said he.

"Take thou this dearly bought prisoner, and conduct him through the donjons, until thou comest to the twelfth; there leave him and shut the twelve doors behind thee carefully, so that he shall see neither the sun nor the moon. Methinks he will soon be willing to adopt our Mussulman faith!"

Hoossein did as he was commanded, and Stephan remained a prisoner for half a year, when the vizier took pity on him. Summoning his only daughter Haykoona, he said to her: "My darling daughter, my pure gold! Hearken to thy father's words! Go back to thy tower, open thy golden cupboards, and adorn thyself with thy richest apparel. Put on thy prettiest dress of rosy silk adorned with velvet ribbons and golden threads, and cover all with thy gold-woven cloak. In thy right hand take a golden apple and under thy arm take this bottle; in it is a beverage prepared from forest plants and flowerets. It is called 'water of oblivion'; I have been told that he who washes his face with it and drinks of it must hate his relatives and his religion. Take ye these to the lowest seraïs and open the twelve doors, closing carefully each of them in turn after thee. When thou comest to Prince Stephan give him this wonderful bottle. He will surely bathe his face with its contents and drink: then he will forget his faith, embrace Islam and marry thee!"

The Turkish maiden could have wished for no greater good fortune, for ever since she first saw the handsome Serbian prince she had felt strange pains. In her dreams she saw nobody but him, and in the daytime she was consumed with fevers.

Stephan and the Vizier's Daughter

Therefore she complied with her father's wish with alacrity, and when she reached Stephan she greeted him tenderly: "Hail, O Serbian Hero! May God be with thee!" And the chivalrous prince returned the greeting: "May God help thee, O peerless Haykoona!"

The beautiful maiden then said: "O Prince Stephan, I value thee more than my black eyes! I sorrow to see thy face thus darkened and thy life so miserable in the prison-donjons of my father. Take this bottle of cooling water; bathe thy heroic visage with the liquid and drink a little of it!"

The hero took the bottle from those beauteous hands; but he was wise! Without hesitation he shattered it against the stony wall, taking great care that not a drop of the liquid should besprinkle him. The Turkish maiden flushed with anger, but a moment later she composed herself, and casting upon the prince a tender glance, she said to him sweetly: "Do, I pray thee, become a Turk and marry me! I love thee more than my black eyes."

But Stephan answered: "I beseech thee, in thy Allah's name, speak not so, O Princess Haykoona. I shall never turn Turk and forget my Christian faith! Yea, I am ready always to give my life for it!"

The beauteous lady turned aside impatiently, but her anger soon passed, and again looking tenderly at the young prince, she exclaimed with sudden passion, "Kiss me, O my beloved!"

But Stephan was proof against temptation, and he answered sternly: "O Turkish lady, may misfortune attend thee! Thou knowest that my faith forbids that a Christian should kiss a Turk! The skies above would burst asunder and stones would fall upon our heads!"

The vizier's daughter really loved the prince, and although it was not easy for her haughty spirit to brook such a refusal of her advances, she presently spake again in this wise: "O Prince Stephan, truly I love thee more than my own eyes! I would not for the entire wealth of this world be baptized, but if thou wilt promise me thy love and wilt marry me I will even embrace the Christian faith! Let us take much gold from my father's treasury and flee together to thy glorious Belgrade."

Hearing this, the young prince sprang joyfully to his feet and opened his arms to the beauteous maiden. He was by no means insensible to her charms, and he exclaimed with fervour: "Thou hast my princely promise that I shall love thee and be faithful to thee—as it is the duty of a true knight so to be. May the Lord Jhesu in Heaven be my witness!"

Then the vizier's daughter opened the twelve doors one after the other and the young couple soon stood in the glorious fresh air under the sky, which was bespangled with silver stars, and radiant with the light of the moon.

From the vizier's treasury they took three tovars of gold, and from his stables his two best horses. And the maiden gave Stephan a sabre studded with large diamonds—it was worth half of Novi Bazar—saying: "Take this sword, my darling lord: that thou mayest not be compelled to give way to inferior heroes, if we should be molested on our way!"

Then they mounted the horses and urged them swiftly away: in one night they put a distance between them and the vizier's castle which a caravan could not cover in less than three days and three nights. At dawn of the next day they reached Belgrade, and Prince Stephan immediately summoned twelve monks, who baptized the fair Turkish maiden, after which the young couple were happily united.

The Ending of the Ballad

The bard finishes his ballad with the following stereotyped ending very usual with Montenegrins:

"This happened once upon a time; let us, O brethren, pray of God to grant our holy Vladika[7] good health! Amen, O God, to whom we always pray!"

Serbian bards did not as a rule end in this manner, but contented themselves with wishing good health to their audiences.

Historical Note

During the long course of the imposition of Ottoman dominion upon the suffering Christian races of the Balkans there were always at the courts of the Christian princes malcontents whom the cunning Turkish statesmen easily seduced from their allegiance to their rightful lords, and to whom they extended hospitality in Constantinople, often overwhelming them with riches and honours. In return they have rendered most important services to the sultans in their many campaigns, being, of course, well acquainted with the strategic dispositions of their countrymen, and often with important state secrets. Sometimes such traitorous men have served the Turk in their own country by sowing the seed of dissatisfaction with their rulers among the peasantry, assuring them that they would be better off under Ottoman rule. The influence of such renegades prevailed upon the peasantry in Bosnia and Herzegovina, at the time of the Battle of Kossovo (1389), to rise against their rulers, and they did not participate in that memorable battle.

Very few instances of such treachery, however, occurred in Montenegro, which has been from the earliest times the home of the noblest of Serbian aristocrats and heroes, and where the adoption of the faith of Islam, no matter for what reason, or from what motive, was considered as the greatest cowardice of which a Christian could be guilty.

---

[1] A ballad of Montenegro, county Byelopavlitch.

[2] Danitza is the Morning Star. The Serbian bards often begin their poems with a reference to the dawn and "Danitza." Several well-known ballads begin thus: "The Moon scolds the star Danitza: Where hast thou been? Wherefore hast thou wasted much time?" And Danitza in order to exonerate herself, invariably relates to the Moon something she has seen in the night during her absence; usually some wrongful deed by a Turk or dishonourable conduct on the part of a young man to his brother or other relatives, such as an unjust division of patrimony, &c.

[3] *Sidjadé*, a divan.

[4] *Hodja*, a Mussulman priest.

5*Kadi*, an Ottoman judge.

6*Djelat*, an executioner.

7*Vladika* means in Serbian 'Bishop.' In Montenegro members of the Petrovitch-Niegosh family were bishops as well as political rulers. It was Vladika Danilo Petrovitch, uncle of the present king of Montenegro, who first assumed the title of prince as an hereditary one.

Chapter XI: The Marriage of King Voukashin

The Message to Vidossava

King Voukashin[1] of Skadar on Boyana[2] wrote a book[3] and dispatched it to Herzegovina, to the white city of Pirlitor[4] opposite the mountain Dourmitor. He wrote it secretly, and secretly he dispatched it to the hands of beauteous Vidossava, the lonely consort of Voïvode Momtchilo. These were the words in the book:

"Hail Vidossava, Momtchilo's consort! Why dost thou dwell in the midst of ice and snow? When thou lookest up from thy castle walls thou seest Mount Dourmitor adorned with ice and snow, yea, even in summer as in mid-winter; when thou lookest down, lo! thither rushes thy turbulent River Tarra carrying on its waves wood and stones. There are no fords, neither are there bridges to span it; around it are only pine-trees and fragments of rock. Why shouldst thou not give poison to thy husband or betray him unto me? Then mightest thou fly to me on this level sea-coast in my white city on Boyana. I will gladly espouse thee and thou shalt become my queen. Thou shalt spin silk upon a golden spindle, sit upon silk cushions and wear velvet embroidered with gold. And how glorious is this city of Skadar on Boyana! When thou lookest upon the fertile slopes above the walls thou wilt see innumerable fig-trees and olive-trees, and vineyards full of grapes; when thou lookest beneath, behold! the plain will be white with nodding wheat, and green with the verdure of the meadows. Through the meadows green-limpid Boyana is flowing; in its stream are all kinds of fish which thou wilt have served fresh at table when thou dost so desire."

Vidossava's Treachery

When Vidossava had read the book she wrote a reply in fine characters: "My Lord, thou King Voukashin! It is not an easy task to betray Voïvode Momtchilo, still less is it easy to poison him. Momtchilo has a sister, by name Yevrossima, who prepares his dishes and partakes of each before him. He has nine brothers and twelve first cousins who pour wine into his golden cup; they always drink before him of each draught. Also, O king! Voïvode Momtchilo possesses a steed named Yaboutchilo; it has wings and can fly any distance its master wishes. Nor is this all! My spouse has a sword adorned with diamonds as big as a maiden's eyes; with this, he fears no one but God. But attend to me, O King Voukashin! Gather a numberless army together; bring thy heroes to the lake, and hide there in the woods. It is Momtchilo's custom to hunt each Sunday morning; he rides out with his nine brothers and his twelve cousins, and attended by forty guards from his castle. On the eve of next Sunday I will burn off Yaboutchilo's wings; the jewelled sword I will dip in salted blood that Momtchilo may not be able to unsheath it: thus thou shalt be able to vanquish him."

When this book reached King Voukashin's hands, his heart rejoiced and he assembled a large force and marched to Herzegovina. He marched to the lake by Momtchilo's castle, where he hid in the neighbouring woods.

On the eve of Sunday, Momtchilo retired to his bedchamber to rest upon the silken cushions, when lo! his consort came to him. She did not lay on the cushions, but stood by her spouse and her tears fell upon his head. Feeling the warm tears upon his knightly cheeks, the Voïvode looked up and said: "O Vidossava, my faithful consort! What great trouble afflicts thee, that thou shouldst shed tears upon my head?"

And Vidossava answered: "My Lord, thou Voïvode Momtchilo! I have no trouble but for thee! I have heard tell of a marvel which I have not seen with my own eyes. It is said that thou hast a wondrous winged steed but I cannot believe the story. It is some evil portent, and I fear thou wilt perish!"

The Winged Horse

Momtchilo was usually cautious, but this time he fell into the trap. "Vidossava, my dear consort," said he, tenderly, "if that be all thy trouble I will easily console thee. Thou shalt see the wings of my steed Tchile:5 when the first cocks crow go down to the new stables, Tchile will then unfold his wings, as thou wilt see."

Saying this, he composed himself once more to slumber. But not so Vidossava. She watched to hear the first rooster's crow, and at the sound she sprang to her feet, lit a lantern and a candle, took some fat of mutton and some tar, and hurried to the stables. And behold! she saw Yaboutchilo unfold a pair of wings which reached down to his hoofs. Vidossava anointed the pinions with the fat and tar and set fire to them with the flame of her candle. What did not burn she bound tightly under the belt of the steed. This done, she, the youthful one, went to the armoury and dipped Momtchilo's favourite sword into salted blood. Then she returned to her consort's chamber.

Momtchilo's Dream

At daybreak Momtchilo awoke and spake thus to Vidossava: "Vidossava, my beloved spouse! I have had this night a strange dream: there appeared suddenly a cloud of fog from the accursed land of Vassoye and wrapped itself round Dourmitor. I rode through the cloud with my nine darling brothers and twelve first-cousins, together with my forty guards. In that fog, O my darling Vidossava! we lost sight of each other, never to meet again! God alone knows what this dream means, but I have a presentiment that some evil will befall us soon!"

Vidossava endeavoured to reassure her lord. "Do not fear, my darling lord!" she said; "dreams are false, God is true!"

The Ambuscade

Momtchilo attired himself for hunting and walked out from his white tower to the courtyard, where his nine brothers, twelve cousins, and forty guards awaited him. His spouse led to him his Yaboutchilo; he sprang to the saddle, and without more ado rode with his followers to the hunt. All unsuspecting, they reached the lake, when suddenly a great force surrounded them. Momtchilo grasped his sword, but, alas! he was unable to unsheathe it. Then he exclaimed bitterly: "Hark, my beloved brethren! My consort Vidossava has betrayed me; give me a sword!"

Speedily his brothers obeyed; they gave him the best sword they had. Then Momtchilo said again: "Listen, my beloved brothers: ye shall attack the wings of the army and I will storm it in the centre."

God adored, what a mighty wonder! 'Would that some from among ye, brethren,[6] could have been there to see: how Voïvode Momtchilo wielded his sword and cleared his way through the press of his foes!' Howbeit, more were crushed by Yaboutchilo than by the hero's sword! But, alas! a sad misfortune had befallen him: when he had gained clear of the foe his brothers' nine black steeds followed after him; but their saddles were empty!

When Momtchilo saw this his heroic heart burst from great sorrow for the loss of his nine beloved brothers: his sword-arm dropped limp at his side, and knowing that he could fight no more, he spurred Yaboutchilo, intending that he should unfold his wings and fly to his castle.

But, alas! for the first time his charger did not respond to the spur. Then Momtchilo spake reproachfully thus: "O Yaboutchilo, may wolves devour thee! Many times hast thou flown from here merely in pastime, and now when I am in sore straits thou wilt not fly!"

And the steed answered, neighing: "My Lord, mighty Voïvode Momtchilo! Do not curse me, nor try to force me further. To-day I cannot fly! May God punish thy Vidossava! Last night she burnt the pinions of my two wings. What did not burn she tied tightly under my belt. O my beloved master! thou hadst better escape as thou mayest. I cannot help thee!"

When Momtchilo heard this, tears fell down his heroic visage. He alighted heavily from his well-loved Yaboutchilo; after a last caress he gathered himself together, and in three leaps he found himself before the portals of his castle. And lo! the massive gates were closed and locked.

Brother and Sister

Seeing this, Momtchilo called aloud upon his sister: "O Yevrossima, my darling sister! Stretch down to me a roll of linen that I may climb the castle wall and escape ere my pursuers come up with me!"

Yevrossima heard the appeal and answered through copious tears: "Alas, my darling brother, thou Voïvode Momtchilo! How can I drop down to thee a length of white linen, seeing that my sister-in-law, thine own faithless Vidossava, hath bound my hair to a beam?"

But sisters have soft hearts for their brothers,[7] and Yevrossima, for the sake of her only brother, jerked her head with such force that she left her hair on the beam; then she seized a length of linen, made one end fast, and threw the other end over the wall from the rampart. Momtchilo seized the linen and quickly climbed almost to the top of the rampart. He was on the point of springing into the fortress when his faithless spouse ran thither swiftly and, with a sharp sword, cut the linen above Momtchilo's hands.

By this time the forces of Voukashin had come up, and Momtchilo was precipitated upon their swords and lances. Seeing the hero fall, the king hastened to the spot, and with a fierce thrust ran him through the heart. So fiercely did he lunge that the end of the sword penetrated the wall.

The Death of Momtchilo

Voïvode Momtchilo was a rare hero, and he was able to speak these last words to King Voukashin: "My last request to thee, O King Voukashin, is that thou shouldst not marry my faithless Vidossava, for she will betray thee also. To-day she hath betrayed me to thee; to-morrow she will deal with thee in like manner! Far better would it be to marry my dear sister Yevrossima, the loveliest of maidens. She will always be faithful to thee and will bear thee a hero like unto myself."

This spake Voïvode Momtchilo, struggling with pale death: this he said and his soul flew heavenward.

The gates of the castle were now opened, and the faithless Vidossava came out to welcome King Voukashin. After she had greeted him she led the way to her white tower and gave him a seat at her golden table. She offered him fine wines and many lordly dishes. Then she went to the armoury and brought Momtchilo's armour and weapons. But, marvellous to relate!

Momtchilo's helmet, which fitted him closely, fell down to King Voukashin's shoulders. One of Momtchilo's top-boots was big enough for King Voukashin's two feet. Momtchilo's golden rings were too large for three of King Voukashin's fingers together. Momtchilo's sabre was one whole yard too long when King Voukashin tried it on his belt!

The Punishment of Vidossava

Seeing all this, King Voukashin exclaimed: "Alas! Woe is me! May God forgive me! What a faithless monster this youthful Vidossava must be to betray such a hero, whose equal would be vainly sought throughout the whole world! How could I, the wretched one, expect such a woman to be faithful to me?"

So saying, he called loudly to his servants, who took Vidossava and bound her fair limbs to the tails of four horses and drove them from the castle Pirlitor. Thus, dreadful fate! she was torn to pieces alive.

Then the king pillaged Voïvode Momtchilo's castle and led away Yevrossima to his palace at Skadar on Boyana. Later, he deserved her love and married her, and she bore unto him Marko and Andrias. Truly Marko inherited the heroism of Voïvode Momtchilo, and thus his uncle's prediction was fulfilled.

Historical Note

Primitive as may be the customs illustrated in this ballad of the fourteenth century, it is undoubtedly worthy of a place in my collection. It was taken down by Vouk St. Karadgitch from the lips of the Serbian bard, and I cannot sufficiently express my regret for my inability to convey in English the beautiful and audacious similes and the eloquent figures of speech which adorn the original.

The French mediæval troubadour rarely chose as his theme the faithlessness of women; probably because incidents like the one described in our ballad were either unknown or too common to be considered interesting. But if the Serbian bards did not, excepting in this rare instance, sing of the fickleness and treachery of the weaker sex, it was that Serbian public opinion could not suffer the contemplation of faithlessness on the part of either husband or wife. No doubt the bard, wandering from one monastery to another, found in some chronicle a few facts concerning the marriage of King Voukashin which he elaborated much as did the French troubadour who dealt similarly with the slender historic fact relative to the battle at Ronceval. The public opinion of the epoch is reflected in the barbarous punishment which the bard, moved by his austerity, inflicts upon Vidossava. It is interesting to note that in my researches I have not found one ballad in which faithlessness on the part of a husband occurs.

In the ballads concerning the royal Prince Marko we see that he was always chivalrous toward women, especially toward widows and oppressed maidens, irrespective of their social position or their religion. He is willing to succour Turkish maidens, for whom he is ready to jeopardize his life. In the ballad entitled "The Captivity and Marriage of Stephan Yakshitch" the bard tells of advances made to Stephan by a passionate Turkish maiden, which he repels with indignation at the mere idea of an alliance between a Christian and a Mussulman woman. King Voukashin might have corresponded with Voïvode Momtchilo's wife previous to her marriage, but if so it must have been rather a political attachment than an affair of the heart.

---

[1] King Voukashin, the father of Prince Marko, was a vassal king to the Emperor Doushan the Powerful.

[2] Boyana is the river upon the banks of which Scutari is built.

[3] The Serbian bards of the fourteenth century invariably use the word "book" when speaking of a letter.

[4] Or, according to some bards, *Piritor*. It is said that the walls of the castle still exist in Herzegovina.

[5] *Tchile*, diminutive of *Yaboutchilo*, the full name of the steed.

[6] It must be remembered that these ballads are recited by bards before great gatherings of people of all ages and both sexes, hence such direct addresses.

[7] This is one more instance of the intensity of sisterly love to which we have previously referred.

Chapter XII: The Saints Divide the Treasures[1]

The Bard begins!

Merciful Creator! Does it thunder, or is the earth quaking? Or can it be the tempestuous ocean hurling its waves against the shore?[2]

Nay! It is not thunder, neither is the earth quaking, nor is the stormy ocean beating upon the shore!

Lo! the saints are dividing among themselves the treasures of Heaven, of Earth and of Sea: Saint Peter and St. Nicholas, St. John and St. Elias; with them, too, is St. Panthelias.

Suddenly there comes Beata Maria, tears streaming down her white face.

"Dear sister ours," spake St. Elias, "thou Beata Maria! What great misfortune hath befallen thee that thou shouldst shed tears down thy cheeks?"

Thereupon, amid her sobs, Beata Maria said: "O my dear brother, thou Thunderer Elias! How could I refrain from shedding tears, since I am just come from India—from India, that accursed country? In that degraded land there is utter lawlessness: the common people do not respect their superiors; children do not obey their parents; parents crush their own children under their feet (may their cheeks blush at the divan[3] before the very God of truth!) A koom prosecutes a brother koom before the judge and bears false witness against him—thus losing his own soul, and damaging one who has acted as a witness at his wedding or baptism; brother challenges brother to duels; a bride is not to be entrusted with safety to the care of a dever, and, alas! even more dreadful things have I seen!"

The Thunderer Elias returned answer: "O sister dear, thou Beata Maria! Wipe those tears from thy tender face! When we have divided these treasures we will go to the divan unto our Almighty creator. Him we will pray, the Truthful One, that He may, in His Infinite Grace, grant us the Keys of the Seven Heavens, with which we may lock them. I will seal the clouds that no drop of rain may fall therefrom, neither abundant rain nor soft dew. Also, the silvery moonbeams shall not shine at night. Thus for three full years there shall be a heavy drought, and neither wheat nor wine shall grow, yea, not as much as is needful for the Holy Mass."

Beata Maria was comforted, and wiped away the tears from her milk-white face. And the saints turned again to the division of the treasures: Peter chose wine and wheat and the Keys of the Heavenly Empire; Elias chose the lightning and thunder; Panthelias, great heats; John chose brotherhood and koomhood as well as the Holy Cross; Nicholas chose the seas with the galleys upon them.

The Wrath of God

Then one and all went to divan with the Almighty, to Whom for three white days and three obscure nights they prayed incessantly. They prayed and, indeed, their prayers were heard: God gave them the Keys of the Heavens.

They locked the Seven Heavens; they affixed seals upon the clouds and lo, for full three years, there fell no drop of rain, neither rain nor silent dew! Neither shone the silvery moonlight, nor did wine grow or wheat spring up from the parched ground,—not even as much as is requisite for the needs of Holy Church.

Behold! The black earth cracked; the living dropped in it. God sent an awful plague which smote both old and young, severing those who were dear to each other. The small remnant who remained alive bitterly repented and turned to the Lord God in whom they truly believed, and who now blessed them.

And God's benediction which He gave to those people yet remains: there should be winter and summer once in each year!

As it was long ago, so it is nowadays.
"God Adored, may our thanks reach Thee!
What has been, may it never happen again!"

---

[1] This ballad is in all probability a remnant of the mythologic traces of a great prehistoric catastrophe, and it illustrates more than any other ancient memorial of the poetic Serbian people, the striking similarity in the beliefs of nations.

[2] This opening might perplex many readers if it were not explained that the commotion is not caused by the saints, but is due to the device, familiar to a Serbian audience, whereby the bard gives his ballad an effective start, and obtains the close attention of his peasant hearers.

[3] *Divan* means in Serbian any state gathering. In this passage it means the Supreme Judgment.

Chapter XIII: Three Serbian Ballads

I. The Building of Skadar (Scutari)[1]

The following poems are reprinted here from Sir John Bowring's *Servian Popular Poetry*, London, 1827. These translations will serve to give to English readers some idea of the form of the national decasyllabic verse from which the matter of the greater part of this book is taken.
Brothers three combined to build a fortress,
Brothers three, the brothers Mrnyavtchevitch,
Kraly Vukashin[2] was the eldest brother;
And the second was Uglesha-Voivode;
And the third, the youngest brother Goïko.
Full three years they labour'd at the fortress,
Skadra's fortress on Boyana's river;
Full three years three hundred workmen labour'd.
Vain th' attempt to fix the wall's foundation.
Vainer still to elevate the fortress:
Whatsoe'er at eve had raised the workmen
Did the veela raze ere dawn of morning.
When the fourth year had begun its labours,
Lo! the veela from the forest-mountain
Call'd—"Thou King Vukashin! vain thine efforts!
Vain thine efforts—all thy treasures wasting!
Never, never, wilt thou build the fortress,
If thou find not two same-titled beings,
If thou find not Stoyan and Stoyana:
And these two—these two young twins so loving,
They must be immured in the foundation.
Thus alone will the foundations serve thee:
Thus alone can ye erect your fortress."
When Vukashin heard the veela's language,
Soon he call'd to Dessimir, his servant:

"Listen, Dessimir, my trusty servant!
Thou hast been my trusty servant ever;
Thou shalt be my son from this day onward.
Fasten thou my coursers to my chariot:
Load it with six lasts of golden treasures:
Travel through the whole wide world, and bring me,
Bring me back those two same-titled beings:
Bring me back that pair of twins so loving:
Bring me hither Stoyan and Stoyana:
Steal them, if with gold thou canst not buy them.
Bring them here to Skadar on Boyana[3]
We'll inter them in the wall's foundation:
So the wall's foundations will be strengthened:
So we shall build up our Skadra's fortress."
Dessimir obey'd his master's mandate;
Fasten'd, straight, the horses to the chariot;
Fill'd it with six lasts of golden treasures;
Through the whole wide world the trusty servant
Wander'd—asking for these same-named beings—
For the twins—for Stoyan and Stoyana;
Full three years he sought them,—sought them vainly:
Nowhere could he find these same-named beings:
Nowhere found he Stoyan and Stoyana.
Then he hasten'd homeward to his master;
Gave the king his horses and his chariot;
Gave him his six lasts of golden treasures:
"Here, my sov'reign, are thy steeds and chariot:
Here thou hast thy lasts of golden treasures:
Nowhere could I find those same-named beings:
Nowhere found I Stoyan and Stoyana."
When Vukashin had dismiss'd his servant,
Straight he call'd his builder master Rado.
Rado call'd on his three hundred workmen;
And they built up Skadar on Boyana;
But, at even did the veela raze it:

Vainly did they raise the wall's foundation;
Vainly seek to build up Skadra's fortress.
And the veela, from the mountain-forest,
Cried, "Vukashin, listen! listen to me!
Thou dost spill thy wealth, and waste thy labour:
Vainly seek'st to fix the wall's foundations;
Vainly seek'st to elevate the fortress.
Listen now to me! Ye are three brothers:
Each a faithful wife at home possesses:—
Her who comes to-morrow to Boyana,
Her who brings the rations to the workmen—
Her immure deep, down, in the wall's foundations:—
So shall the foundations fix them firmly:
So shall thou erect Boyana's fortress."
When the king Vukashin heard the veela,
Both his brothers speedily he summon'd:
"Hear my words, now hear my words, my brothers!
From the forest-hill the veela told me,
That we should no longer waste our treasures
In the vain attempt to raise the fortress
On a shifting, insecure foundation.
Said the veela of the forest-mountain,
Each of you a faithful wife possesses;
Each a faithful bride that keeps your dwellings:
Her who to the fortress comes to-morrow,
Her who brings their rations to the workmen—
Her immure within the wall's foundations;
So will the foundations bear the fortress:
So Boyana's fortress be erected.
Now then, brothers! in God's holy presence
Let each swear to keep the awful secret;
Leave to chance whose fate 'twill be to-morrow
First to wend her way to Skadar's river."
And each brother swore, in God's high presence,
From his wife to keep the awful secret.

When the night had on the earth descended,
Each one hastened to his own white dwelling;
Each one shared the sweet repast of evening;
Each one sought his bed of quiet slumber.
Lo! there happen'd then a wond'rous marvel!
First, Vukashin on his oath he trampled,
Whisp'ring to his wife the awful secret:
"Shelter thee! my faithful wife! be shelter'd!
Go not thou to-morrow to Boyana!
Bring not to the workmen food to-morrow!
Else, my fair! thy early life 'twill cost thee:
And beneath the walls they will immure thee!"
On his oath, too, did Uglesha trample!
And he gave his wife this early warning:
"Be not thou betray'd, sweet love! to danger!
Go not thou to-morrow to Boyana!
Carry not their rations to the workmen!
Else in earliest youth thy friend might lose thee!
Thou might be immured in the foundation!"
Faithful to his oath, young Goïko whisper'd
Not a breath to warn his lovely consort.
When the morning dawn'd upon the morrow,
All the brothers roused them at the day-break,
And each sped, as wont, to the Boyana.
Now, behold! two young and noble women;
They—half-sisters—they, the eldest sisters—
One is bringing up her snow-bleach'd linen,
Yet once more in summer sun to bleach it.
See! she comes on to the bleaching meadows;
There she stops—she comes not one step further.
Lo! the second, with a red-clay pitcher;
Lo! she comes—she fills it at the streamlet;
There she talks with other women—lingers—
Yes! she lingers—comes not one step farther.
Goïko's youthful wife at home is tarrying,

For she has an infant in the cradle
Not a full moon old; the little nursling:
But the moment of repast approaches;
And her aged mother then bestirs her;
Fain would call the serving-maid, and bid her
Take the noon-tide meal to the Boyana.
"Nay, not so!" said the young wife of Goïko;
"Stay, sit down in peace, I pray thee, mother!
Rock the little infant in his cradle:
I myself will bear the food to Skadra.
In the sight of God it were a scandal,
An affront and shame among all people,
If, of three, no one were found to bear it."
So she staid at home, the aged mother,
And she rock'd the nursling in the cradle.
Then arose the youthful wife of Goïko;
Gave them the repast, and bade them forward.
Call'd around her all the serving maidens;
When they reach'd Boyana's flowing river,
They were seen by Mrnyavtchevitch Goïko,
On his youthful wife, heart-rent, he threw him;
Flung his strong right arm around her body;
Kiss'd a thousand times her snowy forehead:
Burning tears stream'd swiftly from his eyelids,
And he spoke in melancholy language:
"O my wife, my own! my full heart's-sorrow!
Didst thou never dream that thou must perish?
Why hast thou our little one abandoned?
Who will bathe our little one, thou absent?
Who will bare the breast to feed the nursling?"
More, and more, and more, he fain would utter;
But the king allow'd it not. Vukashin,
By her white hand seizes her, and summons
Master Rado,—he the master-builder;
And he summons his three hundred workmen.

But the young espoused one smiles, and dreams it
All a laughing jest,—no fear o'ercame her.
Gathering round her, the three hundred workmen
Pile the stones and pile the beams about her.
They have now immured her to the girdle.
Higher rose the walls and beams, and higher;
Then the wretch first saw the fate prepared her,
And she shriek'd aloud in her despair;
In her woe implored her husband's brothers:
"Can ye think of God?—have ye no pity?
Can ye thus immure me, young and healthful?"
But in vain, in vain were her entreaties;
And her brothers left her thus imploring.
Shame and fear succeeded then to censure,
And she piteously invoked her husband:
"Can it, can it be, my lord and husband,
That so young, thou, reckless, would'st immure me?
Let us go and seek my aged mother:
Let us go—my mother she is wealthy:
She will buy a slave,—a man or woman,
To be buried in the wall's foundations."
When the mother-wife—the wife and mother,
Found her earnest plaints and prayers neglected,
She address'd herself to Neimar Rado:[4]
"In God's name, my brother, Neimar Rado,
Leave a window for this snowy bosom,
Let this snowy bosom heave it freely;
When my voiceless Yovo shall come near me,
When he comes, O let him drain my bosom!"
Rado bade the workmen all obey her,
Leave a window for that snowy bosom,
Let that snowy bosom heave it freely
When her voiceless Yovo shall come near her,
When he comes, he'll drink from out her bosom.

Once again she cried to Neimar Rado,
"Neimar Rado! In God's name, my brother!
Leave for these mine eyes a little window,
That these eyes may see our own white dwelling,
When my Yovo shall be brought toward me,
When my Yovo shall be carried homeward."
Rado bade the workmen all obey her,
Leave for those bright eyes a little window,
That her eyes may see her own white dwelling,
When they bring her infant Yovo to her,
When they take the infant Yovo homeward.
So they built the heavy wall about her,
And then brought the infant in his cradle,
Which a long, long while his mother suckled.
Then her voice grew feeble—then was silent:
Still the stream flow'd forth and nursed the infant:
Full a year he hung upon her bosom;
Still the stream flow'd forth—and still it floweth.[5]
Women, when the life-stream dries within them,
Thither come—the place retains its virtue—
Thither come, to still their crying infants!

The veela razing the walls of Skadar

II. The Stepsisters
Near each other grew two verdant larches,
And, between, a high and slender fir-tree:
Not two larches were they—not two larches,
Not a high and slender fir between them—
They were brothers, children of one mother.
One was Paul; the other brother, Radool,
And, between them, Yelitza, their sister.
Cordial was the love her brothers bore her;
Many a token of affection gave her,
Many a splendid gift and many a trifle,
And at last a knife, in silver hafted,
And adorn'd with gold, they gave their sister.
When the youthful wife of Paul had heard it,
Jealousy swell'd up within her bosom:
And she call'd, enraged, to Radool's lady:
"Sister mine! thou in the Lord my sister,
Dost thou know some plant of demon-virtue,
Which may bring our sister to perdition?"
Radool's wife her sister swiftly answered:
"In the name of God, what mean'st thou, sister?
Of such cursed weeds I know not.—Did I,
Never would I tell thee of them, never;
For my brothers love me; yes! they love me—
To their love full many a gift bears witness."
When Paul's youthful wife had heard her sister,
To the steed she hastened in the meadow,
Gave the steed a mortal wound, and hurried
To her husband, whom she thus accosted:—
"Evil is the love thou bear'st thy sister,
And thy gifts are worse than wasted to her;
She has stabb'd thy courser in the meadow."
Paul inquired of Yelitza, his sister,
"Why this deed, as God shall recompense thee?"

High and loudly, then the maid protested:
"By my life, it was not I, my brother;
By my life and by thy life, I swear it!"
And the brother doubted not his sister.
Which when Paul's young wife perceived, at even
To the garden secretly she hasten'd,
Wrung the neck of Paul's grey noble falcon,—
To her husband sped she then and told him:
"Evil is the love thou bear'st thy sister,
And thy gifts to her are worse than wasted;
Lo! she has destroy'd thy favourite falcon."
Paul inquired of Yelitza, his sister,
"Tell me why, and so may God reward thee!"
But his sister swore both high and loudly:
"'Twas not I, upon my life, my brother;
On my life and thine, I did not do it!"
And the brother still believed his sister.
When the youthful bride of Paul discover'd
This, she slunk at evening,—evening's meal-time,
Stole the golden knife, and with it murder'd,
Murder'd her poor infant in the cradle!
And when morning's dawning brought the morning,
She aroused her husband by her screaming
Shrieking woe; she tore her cheeks, exclaiming:
"Evil is the love thou bear'st thy sister,
And thy gifts to her are worst than wasted;
She has stabb'd our infant in the cradle!
Will thine incredulity now doubt me?
Lo! the knife is in thy sister's girdle."
Up sprang Paul, like one possess'd by madness:
To the upper floor he hastened wildly;
There his sister on her mats was sleeping,
And the golden knife beneath her pillow
Swift he seized the golden knife,—and drew it—
Drew it, panting, from its silver scabbard;—

It was damp with blood—'twas red and gory!
When the noble Paul saw this, he seized her,—
Seized her by her own bright hand and cursed her:
"Let the curse of God be on thee, sister!
Thou didst murder, too, my favourite courser;
Thou didst murder, too, my noble falcon;
But thou should'st have spared the helpless baby."
Higher yet his sister swore, and louder—
"'Twas not I, upon my life, my brother;
On my life and on thy life, I swear it!
But if thou wilt disregard my swearing,
Take me to the open fields—the desert;
Bind thy sister to the tails of horses;
Let four horses tear my limbs asunder."
But the brother trusted not his sister:
Furiously he seized her white hand—bore her
To the distant fields—the open desert:
To the tails of four fierce steeds he bound her,
And he drove them forth across the desert;—
But, where'er a drop of blood fell from her,
There a flower sprang up,—a fragrant flow'ret;
Where her body fell when dead and mangled,
There a church arose from out the desert.

Little time was spent, ere fatal sickness
Fell upon Paul's youthful wife;—the sickness
Nine long years lay on her,—heavy sickness!
'Midst her bones the matted dog-grass sprouted,
And amidst it nestled angry serpents,
Which, though hidden, drank her eyelight's brightness.
Then she mourn'd her misery—mourn'd despairing;
Thus she spoke unto her lord and husband:
"O convey me, Paul, my lord and husband!
To thy sister's church convey me swiftly;
For that church, perchance, may heal and save me."

So, when Paul had heard his wife's petition,
To his sister's church he swiftly bore her.
Hardly had they reach'd the church's portal,
When a most mysterious voice address'd them:
"Come not here, young woman! come not hither!
For this church can neither heal nor save thee."
Bitter was her anguish when she heard it;
And her lord the woman thus entreated:
"In the name of God! my lord! my husband!
Never, never bear me to our dwelling.
Bind me to the wild steeds' tails, and drive them;
Drive them in the immeasurable desert;
Let them tear my wretched limbs asunder."
Paul then listened to his wife's entreaties:
To the tails of four wild steeds he bound her;
Drove them forth across the mighty desert.
Wheresoe'er a drop of blood fell from her,
There sprang up the rankest thorns and nettles.
Where her body fell, when dead, the waters
Rush'd and formed a lake both still and stagnant.
O'er the lake there swam a small black courser:
By his side a golden cradle floated:
On the cradle sat a young grey falcon:
In the cradle, slumbering, lay an infant:
On its throat the white hand of its mother:
And that hand a golden knife was holding.

She wrung the neck of Paul's grey falcon

III. The Abduction of the Beautiful Iconia

Golden wine drinks Theodore of Stalatch6
In his Castle Stalatch, on Morava;
Pours him out the wine his aged mother.
While the wine-fumes to his head were rising,
Thus his mother spoke unto the hero:
"Son of mine! thou Theodore of Stalatch!
Tell me, wherefore hast thou not espoused thee?
Thou art in thy youthful days of beauty:
In thy dwelling now thine aged mother
Fain would see thy children play around her."
And he answer'd—Theodore of Stalatch—
"God is witness, O my aged mother!
I have roamed through many a land and city,
But I never found the sought-for maiden;
Or, when found the maiden, found I never
Friendly feelings in thy mind towards her;
And where thou hast shown thy friendly feeling,
There I found the maiden false and faithless.
But, as yesterday, at hour of sunset,
I was wandering near Ressava's river,
Lo! I glanced on thirty lovely maidens
On its banks their yarn and linen bleaching:
'Midst them was the beauteous Iconia,
Fairest daughter of the Prince Miloutin,
He the princely sovereign of Resseva.
She, indeed, would be a bride to cherish;
She, indeed, were worthy of thy friendship:
But that maiden is betrothed already;
She is promised unto George Irene—
To Irene, for Sredoi, his kinsman.
But I'll win that maiden—I will win her,
Or will perish in the deed, my mother!"
But his mother counsell'd him and warn'd him—

"Say not so, my son! the maid is promised;
'Tis no jest! she is of monarchs' kindred."
But the hero cared not for his mother:
Loud he called to Dobrivoy, his servant—
"Dobrivoy! come hither, trusty servant!
Bring my brown steed forth, and make him ready—
Make him ready with the silver saddle;
Rein him with the gold-embroider'd bridle."
When the steed was ready, forth he hasten'd,
Flung him on his back, and spurr'd him onward
To the gentle river of Morava,
Flowing through Ressava's quiet levels.
And he reach'd Ressava's gentle river:
There again he saw the thirty maidens—
There he saw the beauteous Iconia.
Then the hero feign'd a sudden sickness;
Ask'd for help; and sped her courteous greeting—
"God above be with thee, lovely maiden!"
And the loveliest to his words made answer,
"And with thee be bliss, thou stranger-warrior!"
"Lovely maiden! for the love of heaven,
Wilt thou give me one cup of cooling water?
For a fiery fever glows within me;
From my steed I dare not rise, fair maiden!
For my steed, he hath a trick of evil—
Twice he will not let his rider mount him."
Warm and earnest was the maiden's pity,
And, with gentle voice, she thus addressed him:
"Nay! not so—not so, thou unknown warrior!
Harsh and heavy is Ressava's water;
Harsh and heavy e'en for healthful warriors;
How much worse for fever-sickening tired ones!
Wait, and I a cup of wine will bring thee."
Swiftly tripp'd the maiden to her dwelling;
With a golden cup of wine return'd she,

Which she reach'd to Theodore of Stalatch.
Out he stretch'd his hand; but not the wine cup,
But the maiden's hand, he seized, and flung her,
Flung her on his chestnut steed behind him:
Thrice he girt her with his leathern girdle,
And the fourth time with his sword-belt bound her;
And he bore her to his own white dwelling.

1*Skadar* or Skadra, derived from the Italian appellation *Scodra*, otherwise Scutari, the present capital of Albania. Scutari has belonged from time immemorial to the Serbians.

2Kraly means King.

3Boyana is the name of the river washing the wall of Skadar.

4*Neimar* means 'architect.'

5Sir John Bowring, writing in 1827, states that a small stream of liquid carbonate of lime is shown on the walls of Scutari as evidence of the truth of this story. Vouk St. Karadjitch, says that the Serbian people even to-day believe that no great building can be successfully erected without the immuring of some human being. Therefore they avoid the neighbourhood of such buildings while they are being erected, for it is said that even the spirit of such an unfortunate being can be immured, whereby a speedy death would ensue. *Srpske Narodne Pyesme*, Vienna, 1875, vol. ii. p. 124, footnote 20.

6A ruined fortress on the banks of the River Morava. The same name is borne by a city in Central Serbia, situated not far from the castle of Theodore.

Chapter XIV: Folk Lore

I. The Ram with the Golden Fleece

Once upon a time when a certain hunter went to the mountains to hunt, there came toward him a ram with golden fleece. The hunter took his rifle to shoot it, but the ram rushed at him and, before he could fire, pierced him with its horns and he fell dead. A few days later some of his friends found his body; they knew not who had killed him and they took the body home and interred it. The hunter's wife hung up the rifle on the wall in her cottage, and when her son grew up he begged his mother to let him take it and go hunting. She, however, would not consent, saying: "You must never ask me again to give you that rifle! It did not save your father's life, and do you wish that it should be the cause of your death?"

One day, however, the youth took the rifle secretly and went out into the forest to hunt. Very soon the same ram rushed out of a thicket and said: "I killed your father; now it is your turn!" This frightened the youth, and ejaculating: "God help me!" he pressed the trigger of his rifle and, lo! the ram fell dead.

The youth was exceedingly glad to have killed the golden-fleeced ram, for there was not another like it throughout the land. He took off its skin and carried the fleece home, feeling very proud of his prowess. By and by the news spread over the country till it reached the Court, and the king ordered the young hunter to bring him the ram's skin, so that he might see what kind of beasts were to be found in his forests. When the youth brought the skin to the king, the latter said to him: "Ask whatever you like for this skin, and I will give you what you ask!" But the youth answered: "I would not sell it for anything."

It happened that the prime minister was an uncle of the young hunter, but he was not his friend; on the contrary, he was his greatest enemy. So he said to the king: "As he does not wish to sell you the skin, set him something to do which is surely impossible!" The king called the youth back and ordered him to plant a vineyard and to bring him, in seven days' time, some new wine from it. The youth began to weep and implored that he might be excused from such an impossible task; but the king insisted, saying: "If you do not obey me within seven days, your head shall be cut off!"

The Youth finds a Friend

Still weeping, the youth went home and told his mother all about his audience with the king, and she answered: "Did I not tell you, my son, that that rifle would cost you your life?" In deep sorrow and bewilderment the youth went out of the village and walked a long way into the wood. Suddenly a girl appeared before him and asked: "Why do you weep, my brother?" And he answered, somewhat angrily: "Go your way! You cannot help me!" He then went on, but the maiden followed him, and again begged him to tell her the reason of his tears, "for perhaps," she added, "I may, after all, be able to help you." Then he stopped and said: "I will tell you, but I know that God alone can help me." And then he told her all that had happened to him, and about the task he had been set to do. When she heard the story, she said: "Do not fear, my brother, but go and ask the king to say exactly where he would like the vineyard planted, and then have it dug in perfectly straight lines. Next you must go and take a bag with a sprig of basil in it, and lie down to sleep in the place where the vineyard is to be, and in seven days you will see that there are ripe grapes."

"Why do you weep, my brother?"

He returned home and told his mother how he had met a maiden who had told him to do a ridiculous thing. His mother, however, said earnestly: "Go, go, my son, do as the maiden bade; you cannot be in a worse case anyhow." So he went to the king as the girl had directed him, and the king gratified his wish. However, he was still very sad when he went to lie down in the indicated place with his sprig of basil.

When he awoke next morning he saw that the vines were already planted; on the second morning they were clothed with leaves; and, by the seventh day, they bore ripe grapes. Notwithstanding the girl's promise the youth was surprised to find ripe grapes at a time of year when they were nowhere to be found; but he gathered them, made wine, and taking a basketful of the ripe fruit with him, went to the king.

The Second Task

When he reached the palace, the king and the whole court were amazed. The prime minister said: "We must order him to do something absolutely impossible!" and advised the king to command the youth to build a castle of elephants' tusks.

Upon hearing this cruel order the youth went home weeping and told his mother what had transpired, adding: "This, my mother, is utterly impossible!" But the mother again advised him, and said: "Go, my son, beyond the village; may be you will again meet that maiden!"

The youth obeyed, and, indeed, as soon as he came to the place where he had found the girl before, she appeared before him and said: "You are again sad and tearful, my brother!" And he began to complain of the second impossible task which the king had set him to perform. Hearing this, the girl said: "This will also be easy; but first go to the king and ask him to give you a ship with three hundred barrels of wine and as many kegs of brandy, and also twenty carpenters. Then, when you arrive at such and such a place, which you will find between two mountains, dam the water there, and pour into it all the wine and brandy. Elephants will come down to that spot to drink water, and will get drunk and fall on the ground. Then your carpenters must at once cut off their tusks, and carry them to the place where the king wishes his castle to be built. There you may all lie down to sleep, and within seven days the castle will be ready."

When the youth heard this, he hurried home, and told his mother all about the plan of the maiden. The mother was quite confident, and counselled her son to do everything as directed by the maiden. So he went to the king and asked him for the ship, the three hundred barrels of wine and brandy, as well as the twenty carpenters; and the king gave him all he wanted. Next he went where the girl had told him, and did everything she had advised. Indeed, the elephants came as was expected, drank, and then duly fell down intoxicated. The carpenters cut off the innumerable tusks, took them to the chosen place, and began building, and in seven days the castle was ready. When the king saw this, he was again amazed, and said to his prime minister: "Now what shall I do with him? He is not an ordinary youth! God alone knows who he is!" Thereupon the officer answered: "Give him one more order, and if he executes it successfully, he will prove that he is a supernatural being."

The elephants came as was expected

The Third Task

Thus he again advised the king, who called the youth and said to him: "I command you to go and bring me the princess of a certain kingdom, who is living in such and such a castle. If you do not bring her to me, you will surely lose your life!" When the youth heard this, he went straight to his mother and told her of this new task; whereupon the mother advised him to seek his girl friend once more. He hurried to where beyond the village he had met the girl before, and as he came to the spot she reappeared. She listened intently to the youth's account of his last visit to the court, and then said: "Go and ask the king to give you a galley; in the galley there must be made twenty shops with different merchandise in each; in each shop there must, also, be a handsome youth to sell the wares. On your voyage you will meet a man who carries an eagle; you must buy his eagle and pay for it whatever price he may ask. Then you will meet a second man, in a boat carrying in his net a carp with golden scales; you must buy the carp at any cost. The third man whom you will meet, will be carrying a dove, which you must also buy. Then you must take a feather from the eagle's tail, a scale from the carp, and a feather from the left wing of the dove, and give the creatures their freedom. When you reach that distant kingdom and are near the castle in which the princess resides, you must open all shops and order each youth to stand at his door. And the girls who come down to the shore to fetch water are sure to say that no one ever saw a ship loaded with such wonderful and beautiful things in their town before; and then they will go and spread the news all over the place. The news will reach the ears of the princess, who will at once ask her father's permission to go and visit the galley. When she comes on board with her ladies-in-waiting, you must lead the party from one shop to another, and bring out and exhibit before her all the finest merchandise you have; thus divert her and keep her on board your galley until evening, then you must suddenly set sail; for by that time it will be so dark that your departure will be unnoticed. The princess will have a favourite bird on her shoulder, and, when she perceives that the galley is sailing off, she will turn the bird loose and it will fly to the palace with a message to her father of what has befallen her. When you see that the bird has flown you must burn the eagle's feather; the eagle will appear, and, when you command it to catch the bird, it will instantly do so. Next, the princess will throw a pebble into the sea, and the galley will immediately be still. Upon this you must burn the scale of the carp at once; the carp will come to you and you must instruct it to find the pebble and swallow it. As soon as this is done, the galley will sail on again. Then you will proceed in peace for a while; but, when you reach a certain spot between two mountains, your galley will be suddenly petrified and you will be greatly alarmed. The princess will then order you to bring her some water of life, whereupon you must burn the feather of the dove, and when the bird appears you must give it a small flask in which it will bring you the elixir, after which your galley will sail on again and you will arrive home with the princess without further adventure."

The youth returned to his mother and she advised him to do as the girl counselled him. So he went to the king and asked for all that was necessary for his undertaking, and the king again gave him all he asked for.

On his voyage everything was accomplished as the girl had foretold, and he succeeded in bringing home the princess in triumph. The king and his prime minister from the balcony of the palace saw the galley returning, and the prime minister said: "Now you really must have him killed as soon as he lands; otherwise you will never be able to get rid of him!"

When the galley reached the port, the princess first came ashore with her ladies-in-waiting; then the handsome young men who had sold the wares, and finally the youth himself. The king had ordered an executioner to be in readiness, and as soon as the youth stepped on shore he was seized by the king's servants and his head was chopped off.

It was the king's intention to espouse the beautiful princess, and, as soon as he saw her, he approached her with compliments and flattery. But the princess would not listen to his honeyed words; she turned away and asked: "Where is my captor, who did so much for me?" And, when she saw that his head had been cut off, she immediately took the small flask and poured some of its contents over the body and, lo! the youth arose in perfect health. When the king and his minister saw this marvellous thing, the latter said: "This young man must now be wiser than ever, for was he not dead, and has he not returned to life?" Whereupon the king, desirous of knowing if it were true that one who has been dead knows all things when he returns to life, ordered the executioner to chop off his head, that the princess might bring him to life again by the power of her wonderful water of life.

But, when the king's head was off, the princess would not hear of restoring him to life, but immediately wrote to her father, telling him of her love for the youth and declaring her wish to marry him, and described to her father all that had happened. Her father replied, saying that he approved of his daughter's choice, and he issued a proclamation which stated that, unless the people would elect the youth to be their ruler, he would declare war against them. The men of that country immediately recognized that this would be only just, and so the youth became king, wedded the fair princess, and gave large estates and titles to all the handsome youths who had helped him on his expedition.

II. A Pavilion neither in the Sky nor on the Earth[1]

Once upon a time there lived a tsar, who had three sons and one daughter. The latter was kept in a cage by her father, for he loved her as he loved his own eyes. When the girl grew up she begged her father's permission to go out one evening with her brothers, and the tsar granted her wish. No sooner had she left the palace than a dragon flew down, seized the princess and, despite her brothers, disappeared with her into the clouds. The princes hastened to tell their father what had happened, and they implored him to let them go in search of their sister.

Thereupon their unhappy father gave each of them a horse and other necessary equipment for a long journey, and they started out upon their quest. After journeying a long way, they sighted in the distance a pavilion, which was neither in the sky nor on the earth, but was hanging midway between. When they came underneath this, it occurred to them that their sister might be hidden in it, and they began to consider how best they might reach it. Finally they decided that one of them must kill his horse, cut its hide into strips, make a thong, and, fastening one end to an arrow, shoot it from the bow so strongly that it should strike deeply into the framework of the pavilion, thus making a way up which they could climb.

The two younger brothers proposed to the eldest that he should kill his horse, but he refused. Neither would the second brother consent to do so; then the youngest brother, seeing that it could not be helped, killed his horse, made its hide into a lengthy thong, fixed one end to his arrow, and shot straight up to the pavilion, where the arrow stuck firmly.

Next they had to discuss who should climb up the thong; again the two elder brothers refused, so it fell to the youngest to perform this exploit. Being very agile, he soon reached the pavilion; wandering from one room to another, he finally came to an apartment where, to his great joy, he saw his sister sitting with the sleeping dragon's head on her knee. When the princess beheld her brother, she feared exceedingly for his life, and implored him to escape before the dragon awoke.

Sitting with the sleeping dragon's head on her knee

The Prince slays the Dragon

The courageous youth, however, would not obey his sister, but seized his mace and struck the dragon on the head. The monster pointed with one of his claws to the place where he had been struck and said to the maiden: "Something bit me here!" Again the prince raised his mace and delivered a blow upon the monster's head; but the dragon apparently did not mind, for he pointed again indifferently to the place, saying: "Again something has bitten me!"

The young prince was on the point of striking the third time, when his sister pointed to a spot where only the dragon might receive a mortal wound, and directing his blow upon the place indicated, the dragon instantly succumbed. The princess at once freed herself of the dragon's head, ran swiftly to kiss her brother, and then was eager to show him the different rooms.

First, she took him into a room in which stood a black steed fastened to a stall and decked with a saddle and harness adorned with pure silver. Next she led him into a second room, where they found a white horse, also ready to be mounted, but its harness was of pure gold. Then she took him into a third room, where was a beautiful Arab steed whose saddle, stirrups and bridle were studded with precious stones.

The princess next conducted her brother to a chamber in which a maiden was sitting at a golden tambourette engaged in embroidering with golden threads. From thence she led him into a second apartment where a girl was spinning gold threads. At last they entered a third room in which a maiden sat threading pearls, and before her, upon a golden plate, was a golden hen with its chickens, sorting the pearls.

Having satisfied his curiosity, the prince returned to the room where he had left the dead dragon, and threw the carcass down to earth; and at the mere sight of the dragon's body the two brothers were terrified out of their wits. Next the prince slowly let down his sister, and, after her, the three maidens, together with their work. While he was thus engaged he shouted to his brothers and made gestures indicating to whom each of the girls should belong. He reserved for himself the one who had been threading pearls, not forgetting the golden hen and the chickens.

The Perfidy of the Brothers

His brothers, envying the heroism of the young prince and jealous of his successful exploits, were now guilty of a dastardly trick; they cut the thong in order that he might not be able to reach the earth, and taking their sister with all the booty they hurriedly decamped.

On the way home the princes met a shepherd watching his sheep, and they prevailed upon him to disguise himself and to impersonate their youngest brother, ordering their sister and the three maidens to keep strictly their secret.

Some time elapsed, and one day the youngest prince had tidings that his brothers and the disguised shepherd were on the point of marrying the three maidens. This information seems to have been singularly complete, for on the day of his eldest brother's wedding, mounted on the black steed, he flew down and alighted in front of the church. There he awaited the moment for the procession to come out, and, as his brother was preparing to mount his horse, he approached him swiftly, raised his club and struck him a heavy blow so that he fell instantly. The young prince then remounted the black horse and was instantly transported to the mysterious pavilion.

On the wedding-day of his second brother the feat, this time on the white horse, was repeated, none guessing who the strange aggressor was.

Next came the turn of the shepherd. On the day of his wedding with the third maiden, the young prince, mounted on the Arab, alighted in the churchyard just at the moment when the wedding procession started to return. This time he struck the bridegroom on the head so heavily that he fell dead. The guests hurriedly alighted from their horses and surrounded the prince, who made no attempt to escape, but revealed himself as the third son of their tsar. He told them that the pretended prince, whom he had just sent to the other world, was but a common shepherd, and that his brothers, out of envy, had caused him to remain in the magic pavilion where he had discovered his sister and killed the dragon. All that he said was immediately confirmed by his sister and the three maidens. When the tsar heard this he was very angry with his two elder sons, and drove them for ever from his palace. But as for his valiant youngest son, he united him to the third maiden and left him the crown and all he possessed when he died.

III. Pepelyouga

On a high pasture land, near by an immense precipice, some maidens were occupied in spinning and attending to their grazing cattle, when an old strange-looking man with a white beard reaching down to his girdle approached, and said: "O fair maidens, beware of the abyss, for if one of you should drop her spindle down the cliff, her mother would be turned into a cow that very moment!"

So saying the aged man disappeared, and the girls, bewildered by his words, and discussing the strange incident, approached near to the ravine which had suddenly become interesting to them. They peered curiously over the edge, as though expecting to see some unaccustomed sight, when suddenly the most beautiful of the maidens let her spindle drop from her hand, and ere she could recover it, it was bounding from rock to rock into the depths beneath. When she returned home that evening she found her worst fears realized, for her mother stood before the door transformed into a cow.

A short time later her father married again. His new wife was a widow, and brought a daughter of her own into her new home. This girl was not particularly well-favoured, and her mother immediately began to hate her stepdaughter because of the latter's good looks. She forebade her henceforth to wash her face, to comb her hair or to change her clothes, and in every way she could think of she sought to make her miserable.

One morning she gave her a bag filled with hemp, saying: "If you do not spin this and make a fine top of it by tonight, you need not return home, for I intend to kill you."

The poor girl, deeply dejected, walked behind the cattle, industriously spinning as she went, but by noon when the cattle lay down in the shade to rest, she observed that she had made but little progress and she began to weep bitterly.

Now, her mother was driven daily to pasture with the other cows, and seeing her daughter's tears she drew near and asked why she wept, whereupon the maiden told her all. Then the cow comforted her daughter, saying: "My darling child, be consoled! Let me take the hemp into my mouth and chew it; through my ear a thread will come out. You must take the end of this and wind it into a top." So this was done; the hemp was soon spun, and when the girl gave it to her stepmother that evening, she was greatly surprised.

Next morning the woman roughly ordered the maiden to spin a still larger bag of hemp, and as the girl, thanks to her mother, spun and wound it all her stepmother, on the following day, gave her twice the quantity to spin. Nevertheless, the girl brought home at night even that unusually large quantity well spun, and her stepmother concluded that the poor girl was not spinning alone, but that other maidens, her friends, were giving her help. Therefore she, next morning, sent her own daughter to spy upon the poor girl and to report what she saw. The girl soon noticed that the cow helped the poor orphan by chewing the hemp, while she drew the thread and wound it on a top, and she ran back home and informed her mother of what she had seen. Upon this, the stepmother insisted that her husband should order that particular cow to be slaughtered. Her husband at first hesitated, but as his wife urged him more and more, he finally decided to do as she wished.

The Promise

On learning what had been decided, the stepdaughter wept more than ever, and when her mother asked what was the matter, she told her tearfully all that had been arranged. Thereupon the cow said to her daughter: "Wipe away your tears, and do not cry any more. When they slaughter me, you must take great care not to eat any of the meat, but after the repast, carefully collect my bones and inter them behind the house under a certain stone; then, should you ever be in need of help, come to my grave and there you will find it."

The cow was killed, and when the meat was served the poor girl declined to eat of it, pretending that she had no appetite; after the meal she gathered with great care all the bones and buried them on the spot indicated by her mother.

Now, the name of the maiden was 'Marra,' but, as she had to do the roughest work of the house, such as carrying water, washing and sweeping, she was called by her stepmother and stepsister 'Pepelyouga' (Cinderella). One Sunday, when the stepmother and her daughter had dressed themselves for church, the woman spread about the house the contents of a basketful of millet, and said: "Listen, Pepelyouga; if you do not gather up all this millet and have dinner ready by the time we return from church, I will kill you!"

When they had gone, the poor girl began to weep, reflecting, "As to the dinner I can easily prepare it, but how can I possibly gather up all this millet?" But that very moment she recalled the words of the cow, that, if she ever should be struck by misfortune, she need but walk to the grave behind the house, when she would find instant help there. Immediately she ran out, and, when she approached the grave, lo! a chest was lying on the grave wide open, and inside were beautiful dresses and everything necessary for a lady's toilet. Two doves were sitting on the lid of the chest, and as the girl drew near, they said to her: "Marra, take from the chest the dress you like the best, clothe yourself and go to church; as to the millet and other work, we ourselves will attend to that and see that everything is in good order!"

Marra goes to Church

Marra needed no second invitation; she took the first silk dress she touched, made her toilet and went to church, where her entrance created quite a sensation. Everybody, men and women, greatly admired her beauty and her costly attire, but they were puzzled as to who she was, and whence she came. A prince happened to be in the church on that day, and he, too, admired the beautiful maiden.

Just before the service ended, the girl stole from the church, went hurriedly home, took off her beautiful clothes and placed them back in the chest, which instantly shut and became invisible. She then rushed to the kitchen, where she discovered that the dinner was quite ready, and that the millet was gathered into the basket. Soon the stepmother came back with her daughter and they were astounded to find the millet gathered up, dinner prepared, and everything else in order. A desire to learn the secret now began to torment the stepmother mightily.

Next Sunday everything happened as before, except that the girl found in the chest a silver dress, and that the prince felt a greater admiration for her, so much so that he was unable, even for a moment, to take his eyes from her.

On the third Sunday, the mother and daughter again prepared to go to church, and, having scattered the millet as before, she repeated her previous threats. As soon as they disappeared, the girl ran straight to her mother's grave, where she found, as on the previous occasions, the open chest and the same two doves. This time she found a dress made of gold lace, and she hastily clad herself in it and went to church, where she was admired by all, even more than before. As for the tsar's son, he had come with the intention not to let her this time out of his sight, but to follow and see whither she went. Accordingly, as the service drew near to its close, and the maiden withdrew quietly as before, the enamoured prince followed after her. Marra hurried along, for she had none too much time, and, as she went, one of her golden slippers came off, and she was too agitated to stop and pick it up. The prince, however, who had lost sight of the maiden, saw the slipper and put it in his pocket. Reaching home, Marra took off her golden dress, laid it in the chest, and rushed back to the house.

Marra took off her golden dress

The Prince's Quest

The prince now resolved to go from house to house throughout his father's realm in search of the owner of the slipper, inviting all fair maidens to try on the golden slipper. But, alas! his efforts seemed to be doomed to failure; for some girls the slipper was too long, for others too short, for others, again, too narrow. There was no one whom it would fit.

Wandering from door to door, the sad prince at length came to the house of Marra's father. The stepmother was expecting him, and she had hidden her stepdaughter under a large trough in the courtyard. When the prince asked whether she had any daughters, the stepmother answered that she had but one, and she presented the girl to him. The prince requested the girl to try on the slipper, but, squeeze as she would, there was not room in it even for her toes! Thereupon the prince asked whether it was true that there were no other girls in the house, and the stepmother replied that indeed it was quite true.

That very moment a cock flew on to the trough and crowed out lustily: "*Kook-oo-ryeh-koooo!* Here she is under this very trough!"

The stepmother, enraged, exclaimed: "Sh——! Go away! May an eagle seize you and fly off with you!" The curiosity of the prince was aroused; he approached the trough, lifted it up, and, to his great surprise, there was the maiden whom he had seen thrice in church, clad in the very same golden dress she had last worn, and having only one golden slipper.

When the prince recognized the maiden he was overcome with joy. Quickly he tried the slipper on her dainty foot; it not only fitted her admirably, but it exactly matched the one she already wore on her left foot. He lifted her up tenderly and escorted her to his palace. Later he won her love, and they were happily married.

IV. Animals' Language

The universality of folk-lore is curiously illustrated in the following tale which is strikingly like a story native to the negroes of Western Africa. In this the hero is granted, as a boon by the King of the Animals, the gift of understanding animal language; he is warned that if he divulges to any that he possesses this gift he will die on the instant; he is made rich by the possession of it; he laughs at a conversation between animals which he overhears; his wife demands to know the cause of his laughter. To this point the two stories are identical, but in the West African tale the man divulges the secret and pays the penalty with his life, whereas the Serbian conclusion is very much less tame, as will be seen.

A wealthy peasant had a shepherd, who served him for a great number of years most honestly and faithfully. One day, as he drove his sheep through a forest to the pasture, he heard a hissing sound, and wondered what it could be. Listening carefully he went nearer and nearer to the spot whence the sound came, and he saw that the forest was on fire and that the hissing proceeded from a snake that was surrounded by flames. The shepherd watched to see what the poor creature would do in its trouble: and when the snake saw the shepherd, it exclaimed from the midst of the flames: "O shepherd, I pray of you, save me from this fire!" Then the shepherd reached out his crook and the snake entwined itself swiftly round the stick, round his arm, on to his shoulders and round his neck.

The snake entwined itself swiftly round his arm

When the shepherd realized what was happening he was seized with horror, and cried out: "What are you about to do, ungrateful creature! Did I save your life only to lose my own?" And the snake answered him: "Have no fear, my saviour! But take me to my father's house! My father is the king of the snake-world."

The shepherd endeavoured to move the snake to pity and prayed it to excuse him, for he could not leave his sheep. Thereupon the snake said to him: "Be comforted, my friend! Do not trouble about your sheep; nothing amiss will happen to them, but now do hasten to my father's house!" So the shepherd went with the snake round his neck through the forest, till he came at length to a doorway constructed entirely of serpents. When they came near the gate, the shepherd's guide hissed to its servants, whereupon all the snakes instantly untwined themselves, leaving a way open for the shepherd, who passed through unmolested. Then the snake said to its preserver: "When we come before my father he will surely give you, as reward for your kindness to me, whatever you may wish: gold, silver and precious stones; but you should not accept anything of that kind. I would advise you to ask for the language of animals. He will undoubtedly be opposed to your wish, but finally he will yield."

They now entered the apartments of the king, who, with evident relief, inquired: "My son, where have you been all this time?" The reptile then told all about the fire in the forest and of the kindness of the shepherd, who had saved his life. At this the snake-king turned with emotion to the shepherd: "What reward can I give you for having saved the life of my son?" he said. The shepherd answered: "I desire nothing but the power of understanding and speaking the language of animals." But the monarch said: "That is not for you, for if I give you that power, and you should impart the secret to another, you will instantly die. Therefore choose some other gift." But the shepherd insisted: "If you wish to reward me, give me the language of animals: if you do not care to gratify my wish, no more need be said; I bid you farewell!" And indeed he turned to go, but the king, seeing his determination, stopped him, exclaiming: "Come here, my friend! Since you so strongly desire the language of animals, the gift shall not be withheld; open your mouth!" The shepherd obeyed, and the snake-king blew into his mouth, and said: "Now, blow into my mouth!" The shepherd did as he was told, and the snake-king blew a second time in the shepherd's mouth, and then said: "Now you have the language of animals. Go in peace; but be sure not to impart your secret to another, else you will die that very moment!"

The shepherd took leave of his friends and as he returned through the woods he heard and understood everything the birds, plants and other living creatures were saying to each other. When he reached his flock and found all his sheep safe as had been promised, he lay on the grass to rest.

The Buried Treasure

Hardly had he settled himself, than two ravens alighted on a tree near by and began to converse: "If this shepherd knew what is under the spot where that black lamb is lying, he would surely dig in the earth; he would discover a cave full of silver and gold."

The shepherd at once went to his master and told him of the buried treasure. The latter drove a cart to the place indicated, dug deeply in the earth and lo! he found a cave full of silver and gold, the contents of which he placed in his cart and carried home. This master was an honest and generous man, and he gave the entire treasure to his shepherd, saying: "Take this, my son; it was to you that God gave it! I would advise you to build a house, to marry and start some good business with this gold."

The shepherd did as his kindly master advised him, and, little by little he multiplied his wealth and became the richest man, not only in his village, but in the whole district. He now hired his own shepherds, cattle-drivers and swineherds to keep his great property in good order. One day, just before Christmas, he said to his wife: "Prepare wine and food, for to-morrow we will go to our farms and feast our servants." His wife did as he bade, and the next morning they went to their farms, and the master said to his men: "Now come one and all, eat and drink together; as for the sheep I will myself watch them to-night."

So the kind man went to guard his sheep. About midnight, wolves began to howl and his dogs barked a defiance. Said the wolves in their own language to the dogs: "Can we come and kill the sheep? There will be enough for you also." Thereupon the dogs answered in their own tongue: "O come by all means, we also would like to have a feast!" But amongst the dogs there was a very old one who had only two teeth left. That faithful animal barked furiously at the wolves: "To the devil with you all! So long as I have these two teeth, you shall not touch my master's sheep!" And the master heard and understood every word they uttered. Next morning he ordered his servants to kill all his dogs, except the old one. The servants began to implore their master, saying:

"Dear master, it is a pity to kill them!" But the master would not suffer any remonstrance, and sternly ordered: "Do as I bid you!" Then he and his wife mounted their horses and started for home, he on a horse and she on a mare. As they journeyed, the horse left the mare a little behind and he neighed, saying: "Hurry up, why do you dawdle behind?" And the mare answered: "Eh, it is not hard for you—you are carrying only your master, and I am carrying a despotic woman whose rules are a burden to the whole household."

The Importunate Wife

Hearing this, the master turned his head and burst into laughter. His wife noticing his sudden mirth, spurred on her mare, and when she reached her husband she asked him why he had laughed. He answered: "There is no reason, I just laughed." But the woman was not satisfied with this reply and would not give her husband any peace. He endeavoured in vain to excuse himself, saying: "Don't keep on asking me; if I tell you the true reason why I laughed, I shall instantly die!" But she did not believe her husband, and the more he refused to tell her, the more she insisted that he should do so, until at last the poor man was worn out by her persistence.

Directly they arrived home, therefore, the man ordered a coffin to be made, and, when it was ready and he had it placed in front of the house-door, he said to his wife: "I shall lie down in this coffin, for the moment I tell you why I laughed, I shall die." So he laid himself in the coffin, and as he took a last look around, he saw his faithful old dog, coming from the fields. The poor animal approached his master's coffin and sat near his head howling with grief. When the master saw this, he requested his wife to give it food. The woman brought bread and gave it to the dog, who would not even look at it, still less eat it. The piece of bread attracted a cock, which came forward and began to peck at it; the dog reproached him saying: "You insatiable creature! You think of nothing but food, and you fail to see that our dear master is about to die!"

To this reprimand the cock retorted: "Let him die, since he is such a foolish man! I have a hundred wives, and I gather them all round a grain of corn, which I happen to find; and then, when they have all assembled, I swallow it myself! If any of them should protest, I just peck at them; but he, the fool, is not able to rule a single wife."

At this the man jumped out of the coffin, took a stick and called to his wife: "Come in the house, wife, and I shall tell you why I laughed!"

Seeing the obvious intention of her husband, the woman begged him to desist, and promised that nevermore would she be curious, or try to pry into his affairs.

V. The Stepmother and her Stepdaughter

Once upon a time there was a girl who lived with her stepmother. The woman hated her stepdaughter exceedingly, because she was more beautiful than her own daughter, whom she had brought with her to the house. She did her utmost to turn the poor girl's own father against her, and with such success that he soon began to scold and even to hate his own child.

One day the woman said to her husband: "We must send your daughter away. She must go into the world to seek her fortune!" And he answered: "How can we send the poor girl away? Where could she go alone?" But the wicked stepmother replied: "To-morrow you must take her far into the woods, leave her there and hurry home, or I will no longer live with you."

The unfortunate father at length gave way, and said: "At least prepare the girl something for her journey, that she may not die of hunger." The stepmother therefore made a cake, and gave it to the girl next morning as she was leaving the house. The man and his daughter trudged on until they were right in the depth of the woods, and then the father stole away and returned home.

The girl, alone in the woods, wandered all the rest of that day in search of a path, but could not find one. Meanwhile it grew darker and darker, and at length she climbed a tree, fearing lest some wild beast should devour her if she remained through the night on the ground. And indeed, all night long the wolves howled under the tree so ravenously that the poor girl, in her nervous terror, could hardly keep from falling.

Next morning she descended the tree and wandered on again in search of some way out, but the more she walked the denser grew the forest, and there seemed to be no end to it. When it grew dark again, she looked about for another suitable tree in the branches of which she might safely pass the night, but suddenly she noticed something shining through the darkness. She thought it might, perhaps, be a dwelling, and she went toward it. And indeed, she came soon to a large fine house, the doors of which were open. She entered, and saw many elegant rooms, in one of which was a large table with lights burning on it. She thought this must be the dwelling of brigands, but she had no fear at all, for she reasoned with herself: "Only rich people need fear robbers; I, a poor simple girl, have nothing to be afraid of; I shall tell them that I am ready to work for them gladly if they will give me something to eat."

A Strange Dwelling

Then she took the cake from her bag, made the sign of the cross[2] and began her meal. No sooner had she begun to eat than a cock appeared and flew near her as if begging for a share. The good girl crumbled a piece of her cake and fed him. Shortly afterward a little dog came and began in his own way to express friendly feeling toward her. The girl broke another piece of her cake, gently took the little dog in her lap, and began feeding and caressing it. After that a cat came in too, and she did the same with her.

Suddenly she heard a loud growling, and she was terrified to see a lion coming toward her. The great beast waved his tail in such a friendly manner, and looked so very kind, however, that her courage revived, and she gave him a piece of her cake, which the lion ate; and then he began to lick her hand. This proof of gratitude reassured the girl completely, and she stroked the lion gently, and gave him more of the cake.

All at once the girl heard a great clashing of weapons, and nearly swooned as a creature in a bear-skin entered the room. The cock, the dog, the cat and the lion all ran to meet it, and frisked about it affectionately, showing many signs of pleasure and rejoicing. She, poor creature, did not think this strange being could be anything but cruel, and expected it would spring upon her and devour her. But the seeming monster threw the bear-skin from its head and shoulders, and at once the whole room gleamed with the magnificence of its golden garments. The girl almost lost her senses when she saw before her a handsome man of noble appearance. He approached her and said: "Do not fear! I am not a lawless man, I am the tsar's son; and when I wish to hunt, I usually come here, disguised in this bear-skin, lest the people should recognize me. Save you, no one knows that I am a man; people think I am an apparition, and flee from me. No one dares to pass near this house, still less to enter it, for it is known that I dwell in it. You are the first who has ventured to come in; probably you knew that I was not a ghost?"

Thereupon the girl told the prince all about her wicked stepmother, and declared that she knew nothing of this dwelling or who lived in it. When the young prince heard her story, moved with indignation and pity, he said: "Your stepmother hated you, but God loved you. I love you very much, too, and if you feel you could return my love, I would like to marry you—will you be my wife?" "Yes," replied the maiden.

Next morning the prince took the girl to his father's palace and they were married. After some time the prince's bride begged to be allowed to go and pay a visit to her father. The prince gladly allowed her to do as she wished, and donning a fine robe embroidered with gold she went to her old home. Her father happened to be absent, and her stepmother, seeing her coming, feared that she had come to revenge herself; therefore she hurried out to meet her, saying: "You see now that I sent you on the road of happiness?" The stepdaughter embraced the woman and kissed her; she also embraced her stepsister. Then she sat down to await her father's return, but at length, as he did not come, she was compelled reluctantly to leave without seeing him. On going away she gave much money to her stepmother, nevertheless when she had got some distance from the house, the ungrateful woman steathily shook her fist at her, muttering: "Wait a little, you accursed creature, you shall certainly not be the only one so elegantly dressed; to-morrow I shall send my own daughter the same way!"

The Envy of the Stepmother

The husband did not return until late in the evening, when his wife met him, saying: "Listen, husband! I propose that my own daughter should be sent out into the world that she may also seek her fortune; for your girl came back to visit us to-day and lo! she was glittering in gold." The man sighed and agreed.

Next morning the woman prepared for her daughter several cakes and some roast meat and sent her with the father into the forest. The unfortunate man guided her as he had led his own daughter, into the heart of the forest, and then stole off leaving her alone. When the girl saw that her father had disappeared she walked on slowly through the woods, till she came to the gates of the same house in which her stepsister had found happiness. She entered, closed the door and resolved not to open it for anybody. Then she took a cake out of her bag and began her meal. Meanwhile the cock, the dog and the cat came in, and began to frisk about her playfully expecting that she would give them something to eat, but she exclaimed angrily: "Get away, you ugly creatures! I have hardly enough for myself; I will not give you any!" Then she began to beat them; whereat the dog howled, and the lion, hearing his friend's lamentation, rushed in furiously and killed the unkind girl.

Next morning the prince rode out with his wife to hunt. They came to the house, and saw what had happened, and when the princess recognized her stepsister's dress, she gathered up the torn garment and carried it to her father's house. This time she found her father at home, and he was indeed very happy to learn that his dear daughter was married to a handsome prince. When, however, he heard what had befallen his wife's daughter he was sad indeed, and exclaimed: "Her mother has deserved this punishment from the hand of God, because she hated you without reason. She is at the well, I will go and tell her the sad news."

When his wife heard what had happened, she said: "O husband! I cannot bear the sight of your daughter; let us kill both her and the tsar's son! Do this thing or I will jump at once into the well." The man indignantly answered: "Well then, jump! I shall not murder my own child!"

And the wicked woman said: "If you cannot kill her, I cannot bear to look at her!" Thereupon she jumped into the well and was killed.

VI. Justice and Injustice

There was a king who had two sons, one of whom was cunning and unjust, and the other good and just. In due time the king died, and the unjust son said to his brother: "As you are younger than I, you cannot expect me to share the throne with you, so you had better go away from the palace. Take these three hundred *tzechins*[3] and a horse to ride: this is to be your share of the inheritance." The younger brother took the gold and his horse, and reflecting he said: "God be praised! How much of the entire kingdom has fallen to me!"

Some time later the two brothers met by chance on a road, and the younger saluted the elder thus: "God help you, brother!" And the elder answered: "May God send you a misfortune! Why do you for ever mention the name of God to me? Injustice is better than justice." Thereupon the good brother said: "I wager that injustice is not better than justice!"

So they laid as a wager one hundred *tzechins* and agreed to accept the decision of the first passer-by whom they should happen to meet. Riding on a little farther they met Satan, who had disguised himself as a monk, and they requested him to decide their contest. Satan immediately answered that injustice is better than justice; so the just brother lost one hundred *tzechins*. Then they made another wager in the same sum, and again a third; and each time the Devil—differently disguised on each occasion—pronounced for injustice. Finally the good brother lost even his horse; but he was quite unconvinced and he reflected: "Ah, well! I have lost all my *tzechins*, it is true, but I have still my eyes, and I shall wager my eyes this time." So they made the bet once more, but the unjust brother did not even wait anybody's arbitration, he took out his poniard and pierced his brother's eyes, saying: "Now, let justice help you, when you have no eyes!"

The poor youth said to his cruel brother: "I have lost my eyes for the sake of God's justice, but I pray you, my brother, give me a little water in a vessel that I may wash my wounds and take me under the pine-tree, near the spring!" The unjust brother did as he was asked and then departed.

The Healing Water

The unfortunate youth sat without moving until late in the night, when some veele came to the spring to bathe, and he heard one of them say to her sisters: "Do you know, O sisters, that the royal princess suffers from leprosy, and the king, her father, has consulted all the famous physicians, but no one can cure her? But if the king knew the healing qualities of this water, he would surely take a little and bathe his daughter with it, and she would recover perfect health." When the cocks began to crow, the veele disappeared and the prince crept to the spring to test its wonderful properties. He bathed his eyes, and lo! his sight was instantly restored; then he filled his vessel with the water, and hurried to the king, whose daughter was suffering from leprosy. Arriving at the palace he told the officers on guard that he could cure the princess in a day and a night. The officers informed the king, who at once allowed him to try his method and the suffering princess was restored. This pleased the king so much that he gave the young prince half of his kingdom, as well as his daughter for his wife. So the just brother became the king's son-in-law, and a Councillor of State.

The veele came to the spring to bathe

The tidings of this great event spread all over the kingdom, and finally came to the ears of the unjust prince. He thought that his brother must have found his good fortune under the pine-tree, so he went there himself to try his luck. Arrived there, he pierced his own eyes. Late in the night, the veele came to bathe, and the prince heard them discuss with astonishment the recovery of the royal princess. "Some one must have spied upon us," said one of them, "when we discussed about the qualities which this water possesses; perhaps somebody is watching us even now. Let us look around us!" When they came under the pine-tree, they found there the young man who had come seeking good fortune, and they immediately tore him into four.

And thus was the wicked prince recompensed for his injustice.

VII. He Who Asks Little Receives Much

Once upon a time there lived three brothers, who instead of much property had only a pear-tree. Each would watch that tree in turn, whilst the other two went away from home to work for hire. One night God sent His angel to see how the brothers lived, and, should they be in misery, to improve their position. The angel came disguised as a beggar, and when he found one of the brothers watching the tree, he went forward and asked him for a pear. The youth plucked some of the fruit from his own part of the tree, handed them to the beggar, and said: "Accept these pears from my share of the tree, but I cannot give you those belonging to my brothers." The angel took the fruit, thanked the youth, and disappeared.

The next day it was the turn of the second brother to watch the fruit, and the angel, again in the semblance of a beggar, came and asked for a pear. This brother likewise gave from his own part of the tree, saying: "Take these, they are my own; but of those belonging to my brothers I dare not offer you." The angel took the fruit gratefully and departed.

The third brother had a similar experience.

When the fourth day came, the angel disguised himself as a monk, and came very early so that he could find all three brothers at home, and he said to the youths: "Come with me, I shall improve your state of life," whereupon they obeyed without question.

Soon they arrived at a river where the water was flowing in torrents, and the angel asked the eldest brother: "What would you like to have?" He answered: "I should like all this water to be changed into wine and to belong to me." The angel made the sign of the cross with his stick, and lo! wine was flowing instead of water, and that very moment there appeared on the banks of the streamlet many barrels, and men filling them with wine; in one word, there was a whole village. Then the angel turned again to the young man and said: "Here is what you wished; farewell!" and he continued his journey with the others.

The three went on till they came to a field where they saw numbers of doves, and the angel asked the second brother: "Now, what is it that you would like?" And he answered: "I should like all these doves to be changed into sheep, and to be mine!" The angel again made the sign of the cross in the air, and lo! sheep instead of doves covered the field. Suddenly there appeared many dairies; maidens were busy milking the sheep, others pouring out the milk, others again making cream. There was also a slaughter-house, and men busy, some cutting the meat into joints, others weighing it, others again selling the meat and receiving the money for it. Then the angel said: "Here is all you wished for; farewell!"

The angel now proceeded with the youngest brother, and having crossed the field he asked him what he would like to have. The young man answered: "I should consider myself the happiest of men if God were graciously pleased to grant me a wife of pure Christian blood!" Thereupon the angel replied: "Oh, that is rather difficult to find; in the whole world there are but three such women, two of whom are married. The youngest is a maid, it is true, but she is already sought in marriage by two wooers."

Journeying on, they came to a city where a mighty tsar dwelt with his daughter. She, indeed, was of pure Christian blood. The travellers entered the palace and found two princes already there with their wedding apples[4] laid upon a table. Then the young man also placed his apple on the table. When the tsar saw the newcomers he said to those around him: "What shall we do now? Those are imperial princes, and these men look like beggars!" Thereupon the angel said: "Let the contest be decided thus: the princess shall plant three vines in the garden, dedicating one to each of the three wooers; and he on whose vine grapes are found next morning, is to be the one whom the princess shall marry!" This plan was agreed to by all, and the princess accordingly planted three vines.

When the next morning dawned, lo! grapes hung in clusters on the vine dedicated to the poor man. So the tsar could not refuse his daughter to the youngest brother. After the marriage, the angel led the young couple to the forest, where he left them for a full year.

The Angel Returns

Then God sent again His angel, saying: "Go down to earth and see how those poor ones are living now: if they are in misery, it may be you will be able to improve their condition!" The angel obeyed immediately, and disguising himself again as a beggar, he went first to the eldest brother and asked him for a glass of wine. But the rich man refused, saying: "If I were to give every one a glass of wine, there would be none left for myself!" Upon this the angel made the sign of the cross with his stick, and the stream began instantly to flow with water as before. Then he turned to the man and said: "This was not for you; go back under the pear-tree and continue to guard it!"

Then the angel went on to the second brother, whose fields were covered with sheep, and asked him for a slice of cheese; but the rich man refused, saying: "If I were to give everybody a slice of cheese, there would be none left for myself!" Again the angel made the sign of the cross with his stick, and lo! all the sheep turned instantly into doves, who flew away. Then he said to the second brother: "Of a surety that was not for you, go under the pear-tree and watch it!"

Finally the angel went to the youngest brother in order to see how he was living, and found him with his wife in the forest, dwelling as a poor man in a hut. He begged to be admitted into their hut, and to pass the night there. They welcomed him very cordially, but they explained that they could not entertain him as well as they would like to do. "We are," they added, "very poor people." To which the angel answered: "Do not speak so, I shall be quite content with what you have!" They wondered then what to do, for there was no corn in their hut to make real bread; they usually ground the bark of certain trees and made bread from it. Such bread the wife now made for their guest, and placed it in the oven to bake. When she came later to inspect her baking, she was pleasantly surprised to find a fine loaf of real bread.

When the couple saw this wonder they lifted their hands toward heaven and gave thanks: "We thank thee, O God! that we are now able to entertain our guest!" After they had placed the bread before their guest, they brought a vessel of water, and lo! when they came to drink, they found it was wine.

Then the angel once more made the sign of the cross with his stick over the hut, and on that spot instantly rose a beautiful palace, containing an abundance of everything. Then the angel blessed the couple and disappeared. The modest and pious man and woman lived there happily ever after.

On that spot instantly rose a beautiful palace

VIII. Bash Tchelik or Real Steel

There lived once a tsar who had three sons and three daughters. When old age overtook him and the hour came for him to die he called his children to him, and desired his sons to give their sisters to the first wooers who might ask them in marriage. "Do as I tell you," added the dying tsar, "or dread my curse!"

Shortly after the tsar had passed away there came one night a fearful knocking at the palace gate, so that the whole building shook, and a great roaring, screaming, and blowing was heard; it seemed as if the palace was assailed by some awful tempest. All the courtiers were seized with unspeakable fear, and suddenly a voice from outside was heard: "O princes, open the door!" Thereupon the eldest brother exclaimed: "Do not open!" The second brother added: "Do not open for anything!" But the youngest brother said: "I must open the door!" and he sprang to the door and flung it open. As he did so something came in, but the brothers could see only a bright light, out of which proceeded these urgent words: "I have come to ask your eldest sister in marriage, and to take her away this moment; for I have no time to lose, neither shall I come a second time to demand her! Answer quickly, will you give her or not? That is what I must know."

The eldest brother answered: "I will not give her. I cannot see you, and do not know who you are or even whence you came. To-night is the first time I have heard your voice, and you insist upon taking my sister away at once. Should I not know where I could visit my sister sometimes?"

The second brother also said: "I will not consent that my sister should be taken away to-night!"

But the youngest brother protested, saying: "If you will not give her, I will. Do you not remember our father's words?" Thereupon he took his sister by the hand,[5] and presented her to the invisible wooer, saying: "May she be a loyal and dutiful wife!"

The moment the princess passed over the threshold every one in the palace fell to the ground in terror, so fearsome was the lightning and so loud the peals of thunder. The whole building shook as if about to fall. The storm, however, passed and daybreak came. That morning close search was made to see if any trace could be found of the strange visitant or the way it had gone; but, alas! all their efforts were vain.

The second night, about the same time, a similar noise was heard again round the palace, and a voice at the door exclaimed: "O princes, open the door!"

Seized with fear they dared not disobey. Then the pitiless voice spake again: "Give me your second sister; I have come to ask her in marriage!"

The eldest brother protested: "I will not consent!" The second brother said: "I will not give away our sister!" But the youngest brother was willing. "I will give her!" said he; "have you already forgotten what our father commanded at the hour of his death?"

Thereupon the youngest prince took his sister by the hand and presented her to the unseen visitor, saying: "Take her, may she be loyal and dutiful to you!" So the visitant departed with the princess, and next morning no trace of him could be found.

The third night at the same hour the earth quaked and the palace rocked on its foundations, so mighty was the tumult around it. And again a mysterious voice was heard from without. The princes opened the door, and the unseen presence entered and said: "I come to ask your youngest sister in marriage!" The two elder brothers exclaimed simultaneously: "We will not give our sister by night; we must know to whom we are giving her, so that we may visit her when we wish to do so!" But once more the youngest brother exclaimed: "I will give her, if you will not! Have you, then, forgotten what our father told us? It is not so very long ago!" So saying, he took the maiden and presented her to the invisible power, saying: "Take her with you! And may she bring you joy and happiness!"

The Princes set Out

Next morning the brothers debated the fate of their sisters, and sorrow filled their hearts. "Great Heaven!" they said, "what a mighty wonder! We know not what has befallen our sisters; neither do we know where they have gone nor whom they have married!" At length they decided to go in search of their beloved sisters, and making the necessary preparations for their journey they set out on the quest.

They journeyed for some time and then lost their way in a dense forest, in which they wandered for a whole day. When darkness fell, they agreed that they must pass the night at some place where they could find water, so when they came to a lake, they decided to pass the night there, and sat down to eat. When they were ready to compose themselves to sleep, the eldest proposed to his brothers that they should sleep while he kept guard. So the two younger brothers went to sleep, and the eldest watched.

About midnight the lake became agitated, and the watcher was seized with horror when he saw in the middle of it something moving straight toward him. As it came nearer, he saw clearly that it was a monstrous alligator with two huge ears. The monster attacked the prince with all its strength, but the gallant young man received it on the point of his sword and swiftly cleft its head asunder. Then he cut off the ears, placed them in his bag, but threw the carcass back into the lake. Soon after this, morning broke; but the two younger brothers slept quietly on, unconscious of their brother's exploit.

In due time the prince awakened the young men and, without mentioning what had happened, he recommended that they should continue their journey. They travelled the whole day long and, having again lost their way in another dense forest, they decided to pass the coming night by a small lake, and they quickly made a fire. After they had eaten, the second brother said: "To-night you two sleep, and I shall watch." And so the eldest and the youngest brothers slept, while the second kept guard.

Suddenly the water of the lake began to stir, and lo! an alligator with two heads appeared and rushed furiously upon the three brothers. But the second brother was no coward; he gave the monster a fearful blow with his gleaming sabre and the alligator fell dead. Then the prince cut off its four ears, placed them in his bag, and threw the horrible carcass into the lake. The two sleeping brothers knew nothing of all this and slept till sun-rise. Then the gallant prince exclaimed: "Get up, my brothers, it is high time!" And they instantly arose, and prepared to continue their journey, without knowing whither they should go.

A great fear seized their hearts when they found themselves in a horrible desert; they wandered in this for three long days, and, as their food was consumed, they feared now lest they should die of hunger in this strange land, which seemed to have no end. Then they addressed their fervent prayers to the Almighty that He might be pleased to afford them some guidance, and lo! they saw at length a large sheet of water. Great was now their joy, and they took counsel with each other and agreed to pass the night on the shores of that lake.

Having quenched their thirst, they made a bright fire, and when the hour for sleep approached, the youngest brother proposed: "To-night it is my turn; you two go to sleep and I shall watch!" So the two elder brothers went to sleep, and the youngest brother kept awake, looking sharply about him, often casting his eyes over the lake. Toward midnight he noticed a disturbance in the water, and as he looked in wonder the lake grew so agitated that a wave overflowed the shore and nearly extinguished the fire. The next moment a horrible alligator with three heads appeared and rushed furiously on the brothers, obviously intending to devour them. But the youngest prince was no less brave than his two brothers; he unsheathed his sword, and as the monster came on with jaws wide agape, he gave it three fearful blows in rapid succession, slashing off its three heads. Then he cut off the six ears and placed them in his bag, and threw the body and the heads back into the lake.

The Nine Giants

Meantime the fire had smouldered out, and having no materials with which to make a fresh fire, and not wishing to awake his brothers, the prince went a short distance into the desert in the hope of finding some fuel, but without success. He climbed upon a rock, and looking around he saw at length the glare of a fire. As it seemed that the fire was not very far off, he decided to go and get brands with which to relight his own fire. So he descended from the rock and hastening for some time through the desert, he came at last to a cave in which he saw nine giants sitting round a big fire and roasting on spits two men, one on each side. Upon the fire there stood a caldron full of the limbs of men.

When the prince saw all this, he was seized with horror, and would readily have gone back, but it was too late. So he saluted the giants thus: "Good evening, my comrades, I have been in search of you for a long time!" They welcomed him in a friendly manner and returned the greeting, saying: "May God favour you, since you are one of us!" The wily prince added: "Why, I shall remain one of your faithful friends for ever, and would give my life for your sake!" "Eh!" exclaimed the giants, "since you intend to join us, no doubt you are ready to eat man's flesh, and to join our company when we go in search of prey?" Thereupon the tsar's son answered: "Most decidedly! I shall do willingly everything that you, yourselves, do." Hearing this the giants retorted: "That is well for you then! Come and sit here with us!" Then the whole company, sitting round the fire, and taking the meat out of the caldron, began to eat. The tsar's son pretended to eat, but he deceived them cleverly, for instead of eating he threw the meat behind him.

After supper the giants exclaimed: "Now let us go to hunt, for we must have something to eat to-morrow!" So they started out, all nine of them, the prince being the tenth of the party. "Come with us," said the giants to the prince, "we will go to a neighbouring city in which lives a tsar: for from that city we have been supplying ourselves with food for many years!" When they arrived at that place, the giants uprooted two fir-trees, and, reaching the walls of the city, they placed one tree against it and ordered the prince: "Go up to the top of the wall, and we will hand you the second tree, which you will fix on the other side of the wall, so that we can climb down the stem of it into the city." The prince obeyed, and, when he was on the top of the wall, he said: "I do not know how to do it, I am not familiar with this place, and I cannot manage to throw the tree over the wall; please come up, one of you, and show me how to do it!" Thereupon one of the giants climbed up, took the top of the tree and threw the stem over the wall, holding fast the highest branch in his hands. The prince utilised this opportunity to draw his sword, and, unseen by those below, with one stroke he cut off the giant's head, and pushed his body over the wall. Then he said to the others: "Now come up one by one, so that I can let you down into the city as I did our first comrade." The giants, suspecting nothing, climbed up one after the other; and the prince cut off their heads till he had killed the whole nine. Then he slowly descended the pine-tree and reached the ground within the city walls.

Walking through the streets he was surprised to see no living soul there, and the whole city seemed to be deserted! So he reasoned to himself: "Those ugly giants must have annihilated all the inhabitants of this city!"

The Sleeping Princess

He continued wandering about till he saw at length a very tall tower, through one of the vent-holes of which shone a light. He opened the door and went straight to the room from which he judged the light to have come. It was magnificently decorated with gold and velvet, and lying on a resplendent couch, was a maiden sleeping. The girl was exceedingly beautiful, and as the prince devoured her with his eyes he was horrified to see a snake on the wall; it poised its hideous head with the obvious intention of striking the girl on her forehead between the eyes, but the prince rushed swiftly forward with drawn poniard and pierced the serpent's head so that it was nailed to the wall, exclaiming as he did so: "May God grant that my poniard cannot be drawn out of the wall by any hand but mine!" He then hurried away, climbing the city wall by the same way as he had come. When he arrived at the giants' cave, he took a brand from the fire, and hastened to the place where he had left his brothers, and found them still sleeping. He made a fresh fire, and, as meantime the sun had risen, he now awoke his brothers and they immediately continued their journey. That same day they came to a road which led to the city of which we have heard. It was the custom of the tsar who lived in that city to walk abroad every morning and to lament the great destruction of his people by the giants. His greatest anxiety was lest his only daughter would one day be their prey. On this particular morning he walked unusually early through the streets, which were all empty. After a time he came to a part of the city wall against which the tall pine-tree of the giants leaned. He approached closely and found the bodies of the nine giants, the terrible enemies of his people, lying upon the ground with their heads cut off. When the tsar saw this wonder he rejoiced exceedingly, and the people soon gathered around him and prayed that God might grant happiness and long life to the hero who had killed the giants. At that very moment servants came hurriedly from the palace and informed the tsar that a snake had very nearly caused the death of his daughter. Hearing this the tsar ran to his daughter, and entering her room he was amazed to see a large, hideous serpent nailed to the wall. He tried at once to pluck out the poniard, but was not able to do so.

He was horrified to see a snake on the wall

Then the tsar issued a proclamation throughout his vast empire to the effect that if the hero who had killed the nine giants and pierced the snake would come to court

323

he should receive great gifts and the hand of the tsar's daughter in marriage. This proclamation spread quickly all over the land, and by the tsar's orders, in every inn on the principal roads an official was stationed whose duty it was to ask every traveller if he had heard of the hero who had killed the nine giants. If any man should know anything about the matter, he was at once to come before the tsar and tell what he knew, and was to be rewarded. And the tsar's commands were strictly carried out.

After some time the three princes in search of their sisters came to pass the night at one of the inns of that country, and, after supper, they began an animated conversation with the inn-keeper, in the course of which the witty host boasted of his exploits, and at length asked the princes: "Tell me now, what heroic deeds have you young men performed?"

Thereupon the eldest brother started thus: "When my brothers and I set out on our expedition in search of our sisters, we decided to pass the first night on the shores of a lake in the midst of a deserted forest. There I proposed that my brothers should go to sleep while I remained to keep watch. As soon as they fell asleep, a terrible alligator rose from the lake to devour my brothers, but I received it on the point of my sword and cleft its hideous head asunder: if you do not believe, here are the ears of the monster!" Saying this, the eldest brother took out of his bag the ears of the alligator and placed them on the table.

When the second brother heard this, he said: "And I was on guard, my brothers, while you were sleeping the second night; and from the lake appeared an alligator with two heads. I rushed at it with my sword and cut off both its heads: if you do not believe me, see! here are the four ears of the monster!" Saying this, he produced the ears from his bag and placed them on the table to the great astonishment of the listeners.

The Hero Found

But the youngest brother kept silent. And the inn-keeper asked him: "By my faith, young man, your brothers are veritable heroes, let us hear whether you have performed any heroic exploit?" Then the youngest brother began to relate: "I have also done a little. When we arrived at the shores of a lake on the third night in that desert to pass the night, you, my brothers, went to rest, and I remained awake to keep watch. About midnight, the lake was greatly agitated and an alligator with three heads rushed out with the intention of swallowing you, but I received it on the point of my sword and successfully cleft its three heads asunder: if you do not believe me, see! here are the six ears of the monster!" This astounded even his brothers, and the young man continued: "Meantime our fire was extinguished, and I went in search of fuel. Wandering over the desert, I came across nine giants ..." and so he proceeded to relate to them all his surprising deeds. When the story came to an end the inn-keeper hurried off and told everything to the tsar, who gave him money and ordered that the brothers should be brought to him. When they appeared the tsar asked the youngest prince: "Is it really you who have done all those wonders in my city, and saved the life of my only daughter?" "Yes, your Majesty!" answered the prince. Thereupon the tsar moved with great joy and gratitude, gave his daughter in marriage to the gallant prince and appointed him his prime minister. As to his brothers, the tsar said: "If you wish to remain with your brother, I shall find you wives and shall order castles to be built for you!" But the two princes thanked his Majesty and declared that they were already married and that they wished to continue their search for their lost sisters.

The tsar approved of this resolution, and having been supplied with two mules loaded with gold the two brothers said their farewells and departed. The youngest brother soon began to think of his three sisters; he would have been sorry to leave his wife to go in search of them, and in any case the tsar, his father-in-law, would not permit him to leave the court. Nevertheless the prince wasted away slowly in grief for his sisters.

One day the tsar went forth to hunt, and said to the prince: "Remain in the palace, and take these nine keys and keep them in your pocket. You can open three or four rooms with those keys, there you will find unbounded gold, silver and precious stones. In fact, if you wish to do so, you can open even the eight rooms, but do not dare to open the ninth. Ill indeed will be your fate if you do!"

Bash Tchelik

As soon as the tsar had left the palace, the young prince began to open the doors, one after the other, of all the eight rooms, and truly he saw much gold, silver and other precious things. At length he came to the ninth room, and reasoned to himself: "I have survived many extraordinary adventures, nothing ever surprised me; why should I now be afraid to venture into this room?"

Saying this, he opened the door, and what do you think he saw there? In the middle of the room stood a strange man, whose legs were bound in iron up to the knees and his arms up to the elbows; in the four corners of the room there were chains fastened to thick beams, and all the chains met in a ring round the man's neck, so that he could not make the slightest movement. In front of him was a fountain from which the water streamed through a golden pipe into a golden basin. Near him stood a golden mug, incrusted with precious stones. Despite his longing to drink the water, the man could not move to reach the mug. When the prince saw all this, he was indeed astounded, and drew back, but the man groaned: "For heaven's sake, come to me!" The prince approached him and the man said: "Do a good deed! Give me now a cup of water, and know for certain, that I will reward you with another life!"

The prince thought within himself: "Is there anything better than to possess two lives?" So he took the mug, filled it with water, and handed it to the man, who drank eagerly. Then the prince asked him: "Tell me now, what is your name?" The man answered: "My name is Bash Tchelik (Real Steel)." The prince made a movement toward the door, but the man again implored him: "Give me another mug of water, and I shall give you a second life!" The prince thought: "Now, if he gives me a second life, I shall have, together with my own, three lives! This will be quite wonderful!" So he again filled the mug and handed it to the strange prisoner, who emptied it greedily. The prince turned toward the door, but the man exclaimed: "O hero, do not go! Come back a moment! Since you have done two good deeds, do yet a third, and I will give you a third life as reward. Take this mug, fill it with water, and pour it over my head!"

The prince had no desire to refuse; he filled the cup with water, and poured it over the man's head. No sooner had he done this than Bash Tchelik broke the iron chains around his neck, jumped up with the speed of lightning, and, lo! he had wings. He rushed through the door before the surprised prince could make a movement, and, having snatched up the daughter of the tsar, the wife of his deliverer, he flew into the air and disappeared.

When the tsar returned from the hunt, his son-in-law told him all that had happened, and the tsar was indeed greatly saddened, and exclaimed: "Why did you do this? Did I not tell you not to open the ninth room?" The prince humbly answered: "Do not be angry, I shall go in search of Bash Tchelik, for I must fetch my wife." But the tsar tried to dissuade him, saying: "Do not go, for anything in the world! You do not yet know this man; it cost me many an army before I succeeded in taking him prisoner. Remain in peace where you are, and I will find for you a still better wife than my daughter was, and rest assured that I shall continue to love you as my own son!" However, the young prince would not listen to his father-in-law's advice, but took money for his travelling expenses, saddled a horse and went in search of Bash Tchelik.

The Prince finds his Sister

Some time later the young man came to a city. From the window of a castle a girl cried out: "O prince, alight from your charger and come into our courtyard!" The prince did as he was invited; the girl met him in the courtyard, and he was greatly astonished to recognize in her his eldest sister. They embraced and kissed each other, and his sister said: "Come within, my brother." When they were inside, the prince asked his sister who her husband was, and she answered: "I have married the king of dragons, and he has sworn that he will kill my brothers the first time he comes across them. Therefore, I will hide you, and shall ask him first what he would do to you if you appeared. Should he declare that he would do you no harm, I would tell him of your presence." So she hid both her brother and his horse. Toward evening the dragon flew home, and the whole castle shone. As soon as he entered, he called his wife: "My dear, there is a smell of human bones! Tell me at once who is here!" She answered: "There is nobody!" But the dragon added: "That cannot be!" Then his wife asked him: "Please answer truly, would you harm my brothers if one of them should come here to see me?" And the king of dragons said: "Your eldest and your second brother I would slaughter and roast, but your youngest brother I would not harm." Then she said: "My youngest brother, and your brother-in-law, is here." Thereupon the king said: "Let him come in." And when the prince appeared, the king of dragons stretched forth his arms, embraced his brother-in-law, and said: "Welcome, O brother!" And the prince answered: "I hope you are well?" Then they related to each other all their adventures from beginning to end, and sat down to supper.

At length the prince told his brother-in-law that he was searching for Bash Tchelik, and the dragon advised him, saying, "Do not go any further! I will tell you all about him; the very day when he escaped from his prison, I met him with five thousand of my dragons, and, after a severe battle, he escaped victorious. So you see, there is slender hope for you, alone, to overpower him. Therefore I advise you, as a friend, to abandon your plan, and return home in peace; and if you are in need of money I will give you any amount of it." But the prince answered: "I thank you very much for all your good wishes and advice, but I cannot do otherwise than go in search of Bash Tchelik!" And he thought: "Why should I not do so, since I have three superfluous lives?"

When the king of dragons saw that he could not dissuade the prince, he handed a feather he was wearing to him, and said: "Take this, and if you are ever in need of my help, you have only to burn it, and I will come at once to your aid with all my forces." The prince thankfully took the feather and started once more in pursuit of Bash Tchelik.

The Second Sister

Wandering for some time he came at length to another city, and, as he was riding under the tower of a magnificent castle, a window opened and he heard a voice calling him: "Alight from your steed, O prince, and come into our courtyard!" The prince complied immediately, and when he entered the courtyard, he was greatly surprised to see his second sister, who threw herself into his arms, weeping for joy. Then she showed her brother into her private apartment, and he asked: "To whom are you married, sister dear?" And she answered: "My husband is the king of the eagles." When the king returned home his loving wife welcomed him, but he exclaimed at once: "Who is the daring man now in my castle? Tell me directly!" She lied and said: "No one!" Then they began their supper, and the princess asked her husband: "Tell me truly, would you do any harm to my brothers if one of them should dare to come here to see me?" And the eagle-king answered: "As to your eldest and your second brother, I declare that I would kill them; but your third brother I would welcome and help as much as I could." Then she took heart and told him: "Here is my youngest brother, and your brother-in-law, who has come to see us!" Then the king ordered his servants to bring the prince before him, and when the servants obeyed and the prince appeared, he stood up and embraced and kissed his brother-in-law, saying: "Welcome, my dear brother-in-law!" And the prince, touched by his kindness, answered most courteously: "Thank you, my brother! I hope you are well!" The king at once bade him be seated at table, and after supper the prince related his wonderful adventures, and finished by telling them about his search for Bash Tchelik. Hearing this, the eagle-king counselled his brother-in-law most urgently to give up his hazardous plan, adding: "Leave that fiend alone, O dear brother-in-law! I would advise you to remain here; you will find everything you desire in my castle." But the adventurous prince would not listen to this advice for a moment, and on the morrow he prepared to resume his search for Bash Tchelik. Then the eagle-king, seeing that the prince's resolution was unshakable, plucked out of his garment a beautiful feather, handed it to his brother-in-law, and said: "Take this feather, O brother, and if you ever should need my help you will have but to burn it, and I will at once come to your aid with the whole of my army." The prince accepted the feather most gratefully, took his leave, and went away in pursuit of his enemy.

The Third Sister

After some time he came to a third city, in which he found in the same manner his youngest sister. She was married to the king of the falcons, who also welcomed him in a friendly manner, and gave him a feather to burn in case of need.

The Prince finds his Wife

After wandering from one place to another, he finally found his wife in a cave. When his wife saw him she exclaimed: "How in the world did you come here, my dear husband?" And he told her all about his adventures and said: "Let us flee together, my wife!" But she replied: "How could we flee, when Bash Tchelik will surely overtake us: he would kill you, and he would take me back and punish me." Nevertheless, the prince, knowing well that he had three additional lives, persuaded his wife to go with him.

No sooner had they left the cavern than Bash Tchelik heard of their departure and hurried after them. In a short time he reached them, took back the princess, and reproached the prince; "O prince, you have stolen your wife! This time I forgive you, because I recollect having granted you three lives. So you can go, but if you dare come again for your wife I shall kill you!" Thereupon Bash Tchelik disappeared with the princess, and her husband remained to wonder what he should do next. At length he decided to try his luck again, and when he was near the cave he chose a moment when Bash Tchelik was absent, and again took away his wife. But Bash Tchelik again learnt of their departure quickly, and in a short time reached them again. Now he drew his bow at the prince, saying: "Do you prefer to be shot by this arrow, or to be beheaded by my sabre?" The prince asked to be pardoned again, and Bash Tchelik forgave him, saying: "I pardon you this time also, but know surely that should you dare come again to take away your wife I shall kill you without mercy."

The prince tried his luck yet a third time, and, being again caught by Bash Tchelik, once more implored to be pardoned. Because he had given him of his own free will three lives, Bash Tchelik listened to his plea, but said: "Be warned; do not risk losing the one life God gave you!"

The prince, seeing that against such a power he could do nothing, started homeward, pondering in his mind, however, how he could free his wife from Bash Tchelik. Suddenly an idea came to him: he recalled what his brothers-in-law had said when giving him a feather from their garments. So he thought: "I must go once more and try to rescue my wife; if I come to any harm I will burn the feathers and my brothers-in-law will come to my aid."

Thereupon the prince returned to the cave of Bash Tchelik, and his wife was greatly surprised to see him and exclaimed: "So, you are tired of life, since you have come back a fourth time for me!" But the prince showed his wife the feathers and explained their uses, and prevailed upon her to try once more to escape. No sooner had they left the cavern, however, than Bash Tchelik rushed after them shouting: "Stop, prince! You cannot escape me!" The prince, seeing that they were in imminent peril, hastily burnt all three feathers, and when Bash Tchelik came up with drawn sabre ready to kill him, oh! what a mighty wonder! At the same moment came flying to the rescue the dragon-king with his host of dragons, the eagle-king with all his fierce eagles, and the falcon-king with all his falcons. One and all fell furiously upon Bash Tchelik, but despite the shedding of much blood Bash Tchelik seemed to be invincible, and at length he seized the princess and fled.

After the battle the three brothers-in-law found the prince dead, and immediately decided to recall him to life. They asked three dragons which of them could bring, in the shortest possible time, some water from the Jordan. The first said: "I could bring it in half an hour!" The second declared: "I will bring it in ten minutes!" The third asserted: "I can bring it in nine seconds!" Thereupon the king dispatched the third dragon, and, indeed, he used all his fiery might and returned in nine seconds. The king took the healing water, poured it upon the gaping wounds of their brother-in-law, and, as they did so, the wounds were healed up and the prince sprang to his feet alive.

Then the kings counselled him: "Since you have been saved from death go home in peace." But the prince declared that he would once more try to regain his beloved wife. The kings endeavoured to dissuade him, saying: "Do not go, for you will be lost if you do! You know well that you have now only the one life which God gave you." But the prince would not listen. Thereupon the kings said: "Since it cannot be otherwise, then go! But do not vainly think to flee with your wife! Request your wife to ask Bash Tchelik where his strength lies, and then come and tell us, in order that we may help you to conquer him."

The Secret of Strength

This time the prince went stealthily to the cavern and, as counselled by the kings, told his wife to inquire from Bash Tchelik wherein lay his strength. When Bash

Tchelik returned home that evening, the princess asked: "I pray you, tell me where lies your strength?" Bash Tchelik, hearing this laughed and said: "My strength is in my sabre!" The princess knelt before the sabre and began to pray. Thereupon Bash Tchelik burst into louder laughter, exclaiming: "O foolish woman! My strength is not in my sabre, but in my bow and my arrows!" Then the princess knelt before the bow and the arrows, and Bash Tchelik, shouting with laughter, said: "O foolish woman! My strength is neither in my bow nor in my arrows! But tell me who instructed you to ask me where my force lies? If your husband were alive I could guess it was he who demanded it!" But the princess protested that no one urged her, and he believed what she said.

After some time the prince came, and when his wife told him that she could not learn anything from Bash Tchelik, he said: "Try again!" and went away.

When Bash Tchelik returned home the princess began again to ask him to tell the secret of his strength. Then he answered: "Since you esteem my heroism so much, I will tell you the truth about it." And he began: "Far away from here is a high mountain, in that mountain there lives a fox, in the fox is a heart, in that heart there lives a bird: in that bird lies my whole strength. But it is very hard to catch that fox, for it can turn itself into anything!"

Next morning, when Bash Tchelik left the cave, the prince came and learned the secret from his wife. Then he went straight to his brothers-in-law who, upon hearing his tale, went at once with him to find the mountain. This they were not long in doing, and they loosed eagles to chase the fox, whereat the fox quickly ran into a lake and there it transformed itself into a six-winged duck. Then the falcons flew to the duck and it mounted into the clouds. Seeing this, the dragons pursued it; the duck changed again into a fox; the other eagles surrounded it, and at length it was caught.

Then the three kings ordered the fox to be cut open and its heart taken out. This done, they made a great fire and from the fox's heart took a bird which they threw into the fire, and it was burnt to death. So perished Bash Tchelik, and thus did the prince finally regain his beloved and loyal wife.

IX. The Golden Apple-tree and the Nine Peahens

Once there was a king who had three sons. In the garden of the palace grew a golden apple-tree, which, in one and the same night would blossom and bear ripe fruit. But during the night a thief would come and pluck the golden apples, and none could detect him. One day the king deliberating with his sons, said: "I would give much to know what happens to the fruit of our apple-tree!" Thereupon the eldest son answered: "I will mount guard to-night under the apple-tree, and we will see who gathers the fruit."

When evening came, the prince laid himself under the apple-tree to watch; but as the apples ripened, he fell asleep and did not wake until next morning, when the apples had vanished. He told his father what had happened, and his brother, the second son, then offered to keep guard that night. But he had no more success than his elder brother.

It was now the turn of the youngest son to try his luck, and, when night came on, he placed a bed under the tree, and lay down and went to sleep. About midnight he awoke and glanced at the apple-tree. And lo! the apples were just ripening and the whole castle was lit up with their shining. At that moment nine peahens flew to the tree and settled on its branches, where eight remained to pluck the fruit. The ninth, however, flew to the ground and was instantly transformed into a maiden so beautiful that one might in vain search for her equal throughout the kingdom.

The pea-hen instantly turned into a maiden

The prince immediately fell madly in love with his visitor and the fair maiden was not at all unwilling to stay and converse with the young man. An hour or two soon passed but at last the maiden said that she might stay no longer. She thanked the prince for the apples which her sisters had plucked, but he asked that they would give him at least one to carry home.

The maiden smiled sweetly and handed the young man two apples, one for himself, the other for his father, the king. She then turned again into a peahen, joined her sisters and all flew away.

Next morning the prince carried the two apples to his father. The king, very pleased, praised his son, and on the following night, the happy prince placed himself under the tree, as before, next morning again bringing two apples to his father. After this had happened for several nights, his two brothers grew envious, because they had not been able to do what he had done. Then a wicked old woman offered her services to the malcontent princes, promising that she would reveal the secret to them. So on the next evening the old woman stole softly under the bed of the young prince and hid herself there. Soon afterward the prince came and at once went to sleep just as before. When midnight came, lo! the peahens flew down as usual; eight of them settling on the branches of the apple-tree, but the ninth, descending on the bed of the prince, instantly turned into a maiden. The old woman, seeing this strange metamorphosis, crept softly near and cut off a lock of the maiden's hair, whereupon the girl immediately arose, changed again into a peahen, and disappeared together with her sisters. Then the young prince jumped up and wondering what had been the reason for the sudden departure of his beloved began to look around. He then saw the old woman, dragged her from under his bed, and ordered his servants to fasten her to the tails of four horses and so to destroy her.

But the peahens never came again, to the great sorrow of the prince, and for all that he mourned and wept.

Weeping will not move any mountain, and at length the prince resolved to go through the wide world in search of his sweetheart and not return home until he had found her. As a good son, he asked leave of his father who tried hard to make him give up such a hazardous scheme and promised him a much more beautiful bride in his own vast kingdom—for he was very sure that any maiden would be glad to marry such a valiant prince.

The Prince's Quest

But all his fatherly advice was vain, so the king finally allowed his son to do what his heart bade, and the sorrowful prince departed with only one servant to seek his love. Journeying on for a long time, he came at length to the shore of a large lake, near which was a magnificent castle in which there lived a very old woman, a queen, with her only daughter. The prince implored the aged queen, "I pray thee, grandmother, tell me what you can about the nine golden peahens?" The queen answered: "O, my son, I know those peahens well, for they come every day at noon to this lake and bathe. But had you not better forget the peahens, and rather consider this beautiful girl, she is my daughter and will inherit my wealth and treasures, and you can share all with her." But the prince, impatient to find the peahens, did not even listen to what the queen was saying. Seeing his indifference, the old lady bribed his servant and gave him a pair of bellows, saying: "Do you see this? When you go to-morrow to the lake, blow secretly behind your master's neck, and he will fall asleep and will not be able to speak to the peahens."

The faithless servant agreed to do exactly as the queen bade, and when they went to the lake, he used the first favourable occasion and blew with the bellows behind his poor master's neck, whereupon the prince fell so soundly asleep that he resembled a dead man. Soon after, the eight peahens flew to the lake, and the ninth alighted on the prince's horse and began to embrace him, saying: "Arise, sweetheart! Arise, beloved one! Ah, do!" Alas! the poor prince remained as if dead. Then after the peahens had bathed, all disappeared.

Shortly after their departure the prince woke up and asked his servant: "What has happened? Have they been here?" The servant answered that they had indeed been there; that eight of them bathed in the lake, while the ninth caressed and kissed him, trying to arouse him from slumber. Hearing this, the poor prince was so angry that he was almost ready to kill himself.

Next morning the same thing happened. But on this occasion the peahen bade the servant tell the prince that she would come again the following day for the last time. When the third day dawned the prince went again to the lake, and fearing to fall asleep he decided to gallop along the marge instead of pacing slowly as before. His deceitful servant, however, pursuing him closely, again found an opportunity for using the bellows, and yet again the prince fell asleep.

Shortly afterward the peahens came; eight of them went as usual to bathe, and the ninth alighted on the prince's horse and tried to awaken him. She embraced him and spoke thus: "Awake, my darling! Sweetheart, arise! Ah, my soul!" But her efforts were futile; the prince was sleeping as if he were dead. Then she said to the servant: "When thy master awakes tell him to cut off the head of the nail; then only he may be able to find me again."

Saying this the peahen disappeared with her sisters, and they had hardly disappeared when the prince awoke and asked his servant: "Have they been here?" And the malicious fellow answered: "Yes; the one who alighted on your horse ordered me to tell you that, if you wish to find her again, you must first cut off the head of the nail." Hearing this the prince unsheathed his sword and struck off his faithless servant's head.

The Quest Resumed

The prince now resumed his pilgrimage alone, and after long journeying he came to a mountain where he met a hermit, who offered hospitality to him. In the course of conversation the prince asked his host whether he knew anything about the nine peahens; the hermit replied: "O my son, you are really fortunate! God himself has shown you the right way. From here to their dwelling is but half a day's walk; to-morrow I will point you the way."

The prince rose very early the next morning, prepared himself for the journey, thanked the hermit for giving him shelter, and went on as he was directed. He came to a large gate, and, passing through it, he turned to the right; toward noon he observed some white walls, the sight of which rejoiced him very much. Arriving at this castle he asked the way to the palace of the nine peahens, and proceeding he soon came to it. He was, of course, challenged by the guards, who asked his name and whence he came. When the queen heard that he had arrived, she was overwhelmed with joy, and turning into a maiden she ran swiftly to the gate and led the prince into the palace.

There was great feasting and rejoicing when, later, their nuptials were solemnized, and after the wedding the prince remained within the palace and lived in peace.

Now one day the queen went for a walk in the palace grounds accompanied by an attendant, the prince remaining in the palace. Before starting the queen gave her spouse the keys of twelve cellars, saying: "You may go into the cellars, all but one; do not on any account go into the twelfth; you must not even open the door!"

The prince soon began to speculate upon what there could possibly be in the twelfth cellar; and having opened one cellar after the other, he stood hesitatingly at the door of the twelfth. He who hesitates is lost, and so the prince finally inserted the key in the lock and the next moment had passed into the forbidden place. In the middle of the floor was a huge cask bound tightly round with three strong iron hoops. The bung-hole was open and from within the cask came a muffled voice which said: "I pray thee, brother, give me a drink of water, else I shall die of thirst!" The prince took a glass of water and poured it through the bung-hole; immediately one hoop burst. Then the voice spake again: "O brother give me more water lest I should die of thirst!" The good-hearted prince emptied a second glass into the cask, and a second hoop instantly came asunder. Again the voice implored: "O brother, give me yet a third glass! I am still consumed by thirst!" The prince made haste to gratify the unseen speaker, and as he poured in the water the third hoop burst, the cask fell in pieces, and a great dragon struggled out from the wreck, rushed through the door and flew into the open. Very soon he fell in with the queen, who was on her way back to the palace, and carried her off. Her attendant, affrighted, rushed to the prince with the intelligence, and the news came as a thunderbolt.

For a time the prince was as one distraught, but then he became more calm and he resolved to set out again in search of his beloved queen. In his wanderings he came to a river, and, walking along its bank, he noticed in a little hole a small fish leaping and struggling. When the fish saw the prince it began to beseech him piteously: "Be my brother-in-God! Throw me back into the stream; some day I may, perhaps, be useful to you! But be sure to take a scale from me, and when you are in need of help rub it gently." The prince picked up the fish, took a scale from it, and threw the poor creature into the water; then he carefully wrapped the scale in his handkerchief.

Continuing his wanderings, he came to a place where he saw a fox caught in an iron trap, and the animal addressed him, saying: "Be my brother-in-God! Release me, I pray, from this cruel trap; and some day, perhaps, I may be helpful to you. Only take a hair from my brush, and, if you are in need, rub it gently!" The prince took a hair from the fox's tail and set him free. Journeying on, he came upon a wolf caught in a trap. And the wolf besought him in these words: "Be my brother-in-God, and release me! One day you may need my help, therefore, take just one hair from my coat, and if you should ever need my assistance, you will have but to rub it a little!" This likewise the prince did.

Some days elapsed and then, as the prince went wearily on his way, he met a man in the mountains, to whom he said: "O my brother-in-God! Can you direct me to the castle of the king of the dragons?" Luckily the man knew of this castle and was able to tell the way to it; he also informed the prince exactly how long the journey would take.

The Prince finds his Wife

The prince thanked the stranger and continued his journey with fresh vigour until he came to where the king of the dragons lived. He entered the castle boldly and found his wife there; after their first joy of meeting, they began to consider how they could escape. Finally, they took swift horses from the stables, but they had hardly set out before the dragon came back. When he found that the queen had escaped, he took counsel with his courser: "What do you advise? Shall we first eat and drink, or shall we pursue at once!" The horse answered: "Let us first refresh ourselves, for we shall surely catch them." After the meal, the dragon mounted his horse and in a very few minutes they reached the fugitives. Then he seized the queen and said to the prince: "Go in peace! I pardon you this time, because you released me from that cellar: but do not venture to cross my path again, for you will not be forgiven a second time."

The poor prince started sadly on his way, but he soon found that he could not abandon his wife. Whatever the cost he must make another attempt to rescue her, and so he retraced his steps, and on the following day entered the castle again and found his wife in tears. It was evident that they must use guile if they were to elude the magical powers of the dragon-king, and after they had thought upon the matter, the prince said: "When the dragon comes home to-night, ask where he got his horse; perchance I may be able to procure a steed that is equally swift: only then could we hopefully make another attempt to escape." Saying this he left his wife for a time. When the dragon-king returned, the queen began to caress him and to pleasantly converse; at length she said: "How I admire your fine horse! Certainly he is of no ordinary breed! Where did you find such a swift courser?" And the dragon-king replied: "Ah! his like is not to be got by every one! In a certain mountain lives an old woman, who has in her stables twelve wondrous horses; none could easily tell which is the finest! But in a corner stands one that is apparently leprous; he is, in fact, the best of the stable, and whoever becomes his master, may ride even higher than the clouds. My steed is a brother of those horses, and if anyone would get a horse from that old woman he must serve her for three days. She has a mare and a foal, and he who is her servant must tend them for three days and three nights; if he succeeds in guarding them and returns them to the old woman, he is entitled to choose a horse from her stable. But, if the servant does not watch well over the mare and its foal, he will indeed lose his life."

The old Woman and her Horses

Next morning, when the dragon had left the castle, the prince came and the queen told him what she had heard.

Hastily bidding his wife farewell, he went with all speed to the mountain, and finding the old woman, he said to her: "God help you, grandmother!" And she returned the greeting: "May God help you also, my son! What good wind brought you here, and what do you wish?" He answered: "I should like to serve you." Thereupon the old woman said: "Very well, my son! If you successfully watch my mare and its foal for three days, I shall reward you with a horse which you yourself are at liberty to choose from my stable; but if you do not keep them safe, you must die."

Then she led the prince into her courtyard, where he saw stakes all around placed close together, and on each save one was stuck a human head. The one stake kept shouting out to the old woman: "Give me a head, O grandmother! Give me a head!" The old woman said: "All these are heads of those who once served me; they did not succeed in keeping my mare and its foal safe, so they had to pay with their heads!" But the prince was not to be frightened at what he saw, and he readily accepted the old woman's conditions.

When evening came, he mounted the mare and rode it to pasture, the foal following. He remained seated on the mare, but, toward midnight, he dozed a little and finally fell fast asleep. When he awoke he saw, to his great consternation, that he was sitting upon the trunk of a tree holding the mare's bridle in his hand. He sprang down and went immediately in search of the tricky animal. Soon he came to a river, the sight of which reminded him of the little fish, and taking the scale from his handkerchief, he rubbed it gently between his fingers, when lo! the fish instantly appeared and asked: "What is the matter, my brother-in-God?" The prince answered: "My mare has fled, and I do not know where to look for her!" And the fish answered: "Here she is with us, turned into a fish, and her foal into a small one! Strike once upon the water with the bridle and shout: 'Doora! Mare of the old woman!'"

The prince did as the fish told him; at once the mare and her foal came out of the water; he bridled the mare, mounted and rode home; the young foal trotting after. The old woman brought the prince some food without a word; then she took the mare into the stable, beat her with a poker, and said: "Did I not tell you to go down among the fish?" The mare answered: "I have been down to the fish, but the fish are his friends and they betrayed me to him." Thereupon the old woman said: "To-night you go among the foxes!"

When evening came, the prince mounted the mare again and rode to the field, the foal following its mother. He determined again to remain in the saddle and to keep watch, but, toward midnight, he was again overcome by drowsiness and became unconscious. When he awoke next morning, lo! he was seated on a tree-trunk holding fast the bridle. This alarmed him greatly, and he looked here and he looked there. But search as he would, he could find no trace of the mare and her foal. Then he remembered his friend the fox, and taking the hair from the fox's tail out of his handkerchief, he rubbed it gently between his fingers, and the fox instantly stood before him. "What is the matter, my brother-in-God?" said he. The prince complained of his misfortune, saying that he had hopelessly lost his mare. The fox soon reassured him: "The mare is with us, changed to a fox, and her foal into a cub; just strike once with the bridle on the earth, and shout out 'Doora, the old woman's mare!'" He did so, and sure enough the mare at once appeared before him with the foal. So he bridled her and mounted, and when he reached home the old woman gave him food, and took the mare to the stable and beat her with a poker, saying: "Why did you not turn into a fox, you disobedient creature?" And the mare protested: "I did turn into a fox; but the foxes are his friends, so they betrayed me!" At this the old woman commanded: "Next time you go to the wolves!"

When evening came the prince set out on the mare and the same things befell as before. He found himself, the next morning, sitting on a tree-trunk, and this time he called the wolf, who said: "The mare of the old woman is with us in the likeness of a she-wolf, and the foal of a wolf's cub; strike the ground once with the bridle and exclaim: 'Doora! the mare of the old woman!'" The prince did as the wolf counselled, and the mare reappeared with her foal standing behind her.

He mounted once again and proceeded to the old woman's house, where, on his arrival, he found her preparing a meal. Having set food before him, she took the mare to the stable and beat her with a poker. "Did I not tell you to go to the wolves, you wretched creature?" she scolded. But the mare protested again, saying: "I did go to the wolves, but they are also his friends and they betrayed me!" Then the old woman went back to the house and the prince said to her: "Well, grandmother, I think I have served you honestly; now I hope you will give me what you promised me!" The old woman replied: "O my son, verily a promise must be fulfilled! Come to the stable; there are twelve horses; you are at liberty to choose whichever you like best!"

The Prince's Choice

Thereupon the prince said firmly: "Well, why should I be particular? Give me the leprous horse, standing in that corner." The old woman tried by all means in her power to deter him from taking that ugly horse, saying: "Why be so foolish as to take that leprous jade when you can have a fine horse?" But the prince kept to his choice, and said: "Give me rather the one I selected, as it was agreed between us!"

The old woman, seeing that he would not yield, gave way, and the prince took leave of her and led away his choice. When they came to a forest he curried and groomed the horse, and it shone as if its skin were of pure gold. Then he mounted, and, the horse flying like a bird, they reached the dragon-king's castle in a few seconds.

The prince immediately entered and greeted the queen with: "Hasten, all is ready for our flight!" The queen was ready, and in a few seconds they were speeding away, swift as the wind, on the back of the wonderful horse.

Shortly after they had gone, the dragon-king came home, and finding that the queen had again disappeared, he addressed the following words to his horse: "What shall we do now? Shall we refresh ourselves, or shall we go after the fugitives at once?" And his horse replied: "We may do as you will, but we shall never reach them!"

Upon hearing this the dragon-king at once flung himself upon his horse and they were gone in a flash. After a time the prince looked behind him and saw the dragon-king in the distance. He urged his horse, but it said: "Be not afraid! There is no need to run quicker." But the dragon-king drew nearer, so close that his horse was able to speak thus to its brother: "O brother dear, tarry, I beseech you! else I shall perish in running at this speed!" But the prince's horse answered: "Nay, why be so foolish as to carry that monster? Fling up your hoofs and throw him against a rock, then come with me!" At these words the dragon-king's horse shook its head, curved its back, and kicked up its hoofs so furiously that its rider was flung on to a rock and killed. Seeing this, the prince's horse stood still, its brother trotted up, and the queen mounted on it. So they arrived happily in her own land, where they lived and ruled in great prosperity ever after.

X. The Bird Maiden

There was once a king who had an only son, whom, when he had grown up, he sent abroad to seek a suitable wife. The prince set out on his journey, but, although he travelled over the whole world, he did not succeed in finding a bride. Finally, after having exhausted his patience and his purse, he decided to die, and, that there should not remain any trace of him, he climbed a high mountain, intending to throw himself from the summit. He was on the point of jumping from the pinnacle, when a voice uttered these mysterious words: "Stop! Stop! O man! Do not kill yourself, for the sake of three hundred and sixty-five which are in the year!"

The prince endeavoured in vain to discover whence the voice came, and, seeing no one, he asked: "Who are you that speak to me? Show yourself! If you knew of my troubles, you would surely not hinder me!" Thereupon an old man appeared, with hair as white as snow, and said to the unfortunate prince: "I am well aware of all you suffer; but listen to me. Do you see yonder high hill?" The king's son answered: "Yes, indeed." "Very well," continued the old man, "seated day and night in the same spot on the summit of that hill there is an old woman with golden hair, and she holds a bird in her lap. He who succeeds in securing that bird will be the happiest man in the world. But if you wish to try your luck you must be cautious; you must approach the old woman quietly, and, before she sees you, you must take her by the hair. Should she see you before you seize her, you will be turned to stone then and there, just as it has happened to many young men whom you will see there in the form of blocks of marble."

The Old Witch

When the prince heard these words, he reflected: "It is all one to me; I shall go, and, if I succeed in seizing her, so much the better for me; but if she should see me before I catch her, I can but die, as I had already resolved to do." So he thanked the old man, and went cheerfully to try his luck. He soon climbed the other hill and saw the old woman, whom he approached very warily from behind. Fortunately the old woman was absorbed in playing with the bird, and so the prince was able to get quite near without being perceived. Then he sprang suddenly forward and seized the old woman by her golden hair; whereupon she screamed so loudly that the whole hill shook as with an earthquake. But the courageous prince held her fast. Then the old woman exclaimed: "Release me, and ask whatever you wish!" And the prince answered: "I will do so if you let me have that bird, and if you at once recall to life all these young men whom you have bewitched." The old woman was forced to consent, and she gave up the bird. Then from her lips she breathed a blue wind toward the petrified figures, so that instantly they became living men once more. The noble prince expressed the joy in his heart by kissing the bird in his hands, whereupon it was transformed into a most beautiful girl, whom, it appeared, the enchantress had bewitched in order to lure young men to a horrid fate. The king's son was so pleased with his companion that he promptly fell in love with her. On their way from that place the maiden gave him a stick, and told him that it would do everything he might wish. Presently the prince wished that he had the wherewithal to travel as befitted a prince and his bride; he struck a rock with the stick, and out poured a torrent of golden coins, from which they took all they needed for their journey. When they came to a river, the prince touched the water with his stick, and a dry path appeared, upon which they crossed dryshod. A little farther on they were attacked by a pack of wolves, but the prince protected his bride with his stick, and one by one the wolves were turned into ants.

And many other adventures they had, but in the end they arrived safely at the prince's home. Then they married and they lived happily ever after.

The old woman was absorbed in playing with the bird

XI. Lying for a Wager

One day a father sent his boy to the mill with corn to be ground, and, at the moment of his departure, he warned him not to grind it in any mill where he should happen to find a beardless man.[6]

When the boy came to a mill, he was therefore disappointed to find that the miller was beardless.

"God bless you, Beardless!" saluted the boy.

"May God help you!" returned the miller.

"May I grind my corn here?" asked the boy.

"Yes, why not?" responded the beardless one, "my corn will be soon ground; you can then grind yours as long as you please."

But the boy, remembering his father's warning, left this mill and went to another up the brook. But Beardless took some grain and, hurrying by a shorter way, reached the second mill first and put some of his corn there to be ground. When the boy arrived and saw that the miller was again a beardless man, he hastened to a third mill; but again Beardless hurried by a short cut, and reached it before the boy. He did the same at a fourth mill, so that the boy concluded that all millers are beardless men. He therefore put down his sack, and when the corn of Beardless was ground he took his turn at the mill. When all of his grain had been ground Beardless proposed: "Listen, my boy! Let us make a loaf of your flour."

The boy had not forgotten his father's injunction to have nothing to do with beardless millers, but as he saw no way out of it, he accepted the proposal. So Beardless now took all the flour, mixed it with water, which the boy brought him, and thus made a very large loaf. Then they fired the oven and baked the loaf, which, when finished, they placed against the wall.

Then the miller proposed: "Listen, my boy! If we were now to divide this loaf between us, there would be little enough for either of us, let us therefore tell each other stories, and whoever tells the greatest lie shall have the whole loaf for himself."

The boy reflected a little and, seeing no way of helping himself, said: "Very well, but you must begin."

Then Beardless told various stories till he got quite tired. Then the boy said: "Eh, my dear Beardless, it is a pity if you do not know any more, for what you have said is really nothing; only listen, and I shall tell you now the real truth."

The Boy's Story

"In my young days, when I was an old man, we possessed many beehives, and I used to count the bees every morning; I counted them easily enough, but I could never contrive to count the beehives. Well, one morning, as I was counting the bees, I was greatly surprised to find that the best bee was missing, so I saddled a cock, mounted it, and started in search of my bee. I traced it to the sea-shore, and saw that it had gone over the sea, so I decided to follow it. When I had crossed the water, I discovered that a peasant had caught my bee; he was ploughing his fields with it and was about to sow millet. So I exclaimed: 'That is my bee! How did you get it?' And the ploughman answered: 'Brother, if this is really your bee, come here and take it!' So I went to him and he gave me back my bee, and a sack full of millet on account of the services my bee had rendered him. Then I put the sack on my back, and moved the saddle from the cock to the bee. Then I mounted, and led the cock behind me that it might rest a little. As I was crossing the sea, one of the strings of my sack burst, and all the millet poured into the water. When I had got across, it was already night, so I alighted and let the bee loose to graze; as to the cock, I fastened him near me, and gave him some hay. After that I laid myself down to sleep. When I rose next morning, great was my surprise to see that during the night, the wolves had slaughtered and devoured my bee; and the honey was spread about the valley, knee-deep and ankle-deep on the hills. Then I was puzzled to know in what vessel I could gather up all the honey. Meantime I remembered I had a little axe with me, so I went into the woods to catch a beast, in order to make a bag of its skin. When I reached the forest, I saw two deer dancing on one leg; so I threw my axe, broke their only leg and caught them both. From those two deer I drew three skins and made a bag of each, and in them gathered up all the honey. Then I loaded the cock with the bags and hurried homeward. When I arrived home I found that my father had just been born, and I was told to go to heaven to fetch some holy water. I did not know how to get there, but as I pondered the matter I remembered the millet which had fallen into the sea. I went back to that place and found that the grain had grown up quite to heaven, for the place where it had fallen was rather damp, so I climbed up by one of the stems. Upon reaching heaven I found that the millet had ripened, and an angel had harvested the grain and had made a loaf of it, and was eating it with some warm milk. I greeted him, saying: 'God bless you!' The angel responded: 'May God help you!' and gave me some holy water. On my way back I found that there had been a great rain, so that the sea had risen so high that my millet was carried away! I was frightened as to how I should descend again to earth, but at length I remembered that I had long hair—it is so long that when I am standing upright it reaches down to the ground, and when I sit it reaches to my ears. Well, I took out my knife and cut off one hair after another, tying them end to end as I descended on them. Meantime darkness overtook me before I got to the bottom, and so I decided to make a large knot and to pass the night on it. But what was I to do without a fire! The tinder-box I had with me, but I had no wood. Suddenly I remembered that I had in my vest a sewing needle, so I found it, split it and made a big fire, which warmed me nicely; then I laid myself down to sleep. When I fell asleep, unfortunately a flame burnt the hair through, and, head over heels, I fell to the ground, and sank into the earth up to my girdle. I moved about to see how I could get out, and, when I found that I was tightly interred, I hurried home for a spade and came back and dug myself out. As soon as I was freed, I took the holy water and started for home. When I arrived reapers were working in the field. It was such a hot day, that I feared the poor men would burn to death, and called to them: 'Why do you not bring here our mare which is two days' journey long and half a day broad, and on whose back large willows are growing; she could make some shade where you are working?' My father hearing this, quickly brought the mare, and the reapers continued working in the shade. Then I took a jug in which to fetch some water. When I came to the well, I found the water was quite frozen, so I took my head off and broke the ice with it; then I filled the jug and carried the water to the reapers. When they saw me they asked me: 'Where is your head?' I lifted my hand, and, to my great surprise, my head was not upon my shoulders, and then I remembered having left it by the well. I went back at once, but found that a fox was there before me, and was busy devouring my head. I approached slowly and struck the beast fiercely with my foot, so that in great fear, it dropped a little book. This I picked up and on opening it, found written in it these words: 'The whole loaf is for thee, and Beardless is to get nothing!'"

Saying this, the boy took hold of the loaf and made off. As for Beardless, he was speechless, and remained gazing after the boy in astonishment.

"The whole loaf is for thee, and beardless is to get nothing!"

XII. The Maiden Wiser than the Tsar

Long ago there lived an old man, who dwelt in a poor cottage. He possessed one thing only in the world, and that was a daughter who was so wise that she could teach even her old father.

One day the man went to the tsar to beg, and the tsar, astonished at his cultivated speech, asked him whence he came and who had taught him to converse so well. He told the tsar where he lived, and that it was his daughter who had taught him to speak with eloquence.

"And where was your daughter taught?" asked the tsar.

"God and our poverty have made her wise," answered the poor man.

Thereupon the tsar gave him thirty eggs and said: "Take these to your daughter, and command her in my name to bring forth chickens from them. If she does this successfully I will give her rich presents, but if she fails you shall be tortured."

The poor man, weeping, returned to his cottage and told all this to his daughter. The maiden saw at once that the eggs which the tsar had sent were boiled, and bade her father rest while she considered what was to be done. Then while the old man was sleeping the girl filled a pot with water and boiled some beans.

Next morning she woke her father and begged him to take a plough and oxen and plough near the road where the tsar would pass. "When you see him coming," said she, "take a handful of beans, and while you are sowing them you must shout: 'Go on, my oxen, and may God grant that the boiled beans may bear fruit!' Then," she went on, "when the tsar asks you, 'How can you expect boiled beans to bear fruit?' answer him: 'just as from boiled eggs one can produce chicks!'"

The old man did as his daughter told him, and went forth to plough. When he saw the tsar he took out a handful of beans, and exclaimed: "Go on, my oxen! And may God grant that the boiled beans may bear fruit!" Upon hearing these words the tsar stopped his carriage, and said to the man: "My poor fellow, how can you expect boiled beans to bear fruit?"

"Just as from boiled eggs one can produce chicks!" answered the apparently simple old man.

The tsar laughed and passed on, but he had recognized the old man, and guessed that his daughter had instructed him to say this. He therefore sent officers to bring the peasant into his presence. When the old man came, the tsar gave him a bunch of flax, saying: "Take this, and make out of it all the sails necessary for a ship; if you do not, you shall lose your life."

The poor man took the flax with great fear, and went home in tears to tell his daughter of his new task. The wise maiden soothed him, and said that if he would rest she would contrive some plan. Next morning she gave her father a small piece of wood, and bade him take it to the tsar with the demand that from it should be made all the necessary tools for spinning and weaving, that he should thereby be enabled to execute his Majesty's order. The old man obeyed, and when the tsar heard the extraordinary request he was greatly astounded at the astuteness of the girl, and, not to be outdone, he took a small glass, saying: "Take this little glass to your daughter, and tell her she must empty the sea with it, so that dry land shall be where the ocean now is."

The old man went home heavily to tell this to his daughter. But the girl again reassured him, and next morning she gave him a pound of tow, saying: "Take this to the tsar and say, that when with this tow he dams the sources of all rivers and streams I will dry up the sea."

The Tsar Sends for the Girl

The father went back to the tsar and told him what his daughter had said, and the tsar, seeing that the girl was wiser than himself, ordered that she should be brought before him. When she appeared the tsar asked her: "Can you guess what it is that can be heard at the greatest distance?" and the girl answered: "Your Majesty, there are two things: the thunder and the lie can be heard at the greatest distance!"

The astonished tsar grasped his beard, and, turning to his attendants, exclaimed: "Guess what my beard is worth?" Some said so much, others again so much; but the maiden observed to the tsar that none of his courtiers had guessed right. "His Majesty's beard is worth as much as three summer rains," she said. The tsar, more astonished than ever, said: "The maiden has guessed rightly!" Then he asked her to become his wife, for "I love you," said he. The girl had become enamoured of the tsar, and she bowed low before him and said: "Your glorious Majesty! Let it be as you wish! But I pray that your Majesty may be graciously pleased to write with your own hand on a piece of parchment that should you or any of your courtiers ever be displeased with me, and in consequence banish me from the palace, I shall be allowed to take with me any one thing which I like best."

The tsar gladly consented, wrote out this declaration and affixed his signature.

Some years passed by happily but there came at last a day when the tsar was offended with the tsarina and he said angrily: "You shall be no longer my wife, I command you to leave my palace!"

The tsarina answered dutifully: "O most glorious tsar, I will obey; permit me to pass but one night in the palace, and to-morrow I will depart."

To this the tsar assented.

That evening, at supper, the tsarina mixed certain herbs in wine and gave the cup to the tsar, saying: "Drink, O most glorious tsar! And be of good cheer! I am to go away, but, believe me, I shall be happier than when I first met you!"

The tsar, having drunk the potion fell asleep. Then the tsarina who had a coach in readiness, placed the tsar in it and carried him off to her father's cottage.

When his Majesty awoke next morning and saw that he was in a cottage, he exclaimed: "Who brought me here?"

"I did," answered the tsarina.

The tsar protested, saying: "How have you dared do so? Did I not tell you that you are no longer my wife?"

Instead of answering the tsarina produced the parchment containing the tsar's promise and he could not find a word to say.

He could not find a word to say

Then the tsarina said: "As you see, you promised that should I be banished from your palace I should be at liberty to take with me that which I liked best!"

Hearing this, the tsar's love for his spouse returned, he took her in his arms, and they returned to the palace together.

XIII. Good Deeds Never Perish

Once upon a time there lived a man and woman who had one son. When the boy grew up his parents endeavoured to give him a suitable education which would be useful in his after life. He was a good, quiet boy, and above all he feared God. After he had completed his studies, his father intrusted him with a galley laden with various goods, so that he might trade with distant countries, and be the support of his parents' old age.

The First Voyage

On his first voyage he one day met with a Turkish ship, in which he heard weeping. So he called to the sailors on the Turkish vessel: "I pray you, tell me why there is such sorrow on board your ship!" And they answered: "We have many slaves whom we have captured in various parts of the world, and those who are chained are weeping and lamenting." Thereupon the young man said: "Pray, O brethren, ask your captain if he will allow me to ransom the slaves for a sum of money?" The sailors gladly called their captain, who was willing to bargain, and in the end the young man gave his ship with all its cargo to the Turk, in exchange for his vessel containing the slaves.

The young man asked each slave whence he came, and gave to all their freedom, and said that each might return to his own country.

Among the slaves was an old woman who held a most beautiful maiden by the arm. When he asked whence they came, the old woman answered through her tears: "We come from a far-away country. This young girl is the only daughter of the tsar, whom I have brought up from her infancy. One unlucky day she was walking in the palace gardens, and wandered to a lonely spot, where those accursed Turks saw her and seized her. She began to scream, and I, who happened to be near, ran to help her, but alas! I could not save her, and the Turks carried us both on board this galley." Then the good nurse and the beautiful girl, not knowing the way to their own country, and having no means of returning thither, implored the young man to take them with him. And this he was quite willing to do; indeed, he had immediately fallen in love with the princess, and he now married the poor homeless maiden, and, together with her and the old woman, returned home.

On their arrival, his father asked where his galley and its cargo were, and he told him how he had ransomed the slaves and set them at liberty. "This girl," said he, "is the daughter of a tsar, and this old woman is her nurse; as they could not return to their country I took them with me, and I have married the maiden." Thereupon his father grew very angry, and said: "O foolish son, what have you done? Why did you dispose so stupidly of my property without my permission?" and he drove him out of the house.

Fortunately for the young man, a good neighbour offered him hospitality, and, with his wife and her old nurse, he resided for a long time near by, endeavouring, through the influence of his mother and friends, to persuade his father to forgive him.

The Second Voyage

After some time the father relented, and received his son again in his house, together with his young wife and her nurse. Soon after, he purchased a second galley, larger and finer than the first, and loaded it with merchandise wherewith his son might trade to great profit, if so be that he were wise.

The young man sailed in this new vessel, leaving his wife and her nurse in the house of his parents, and soon came to a certain city, where he beheld a sorrowful sight. He saw soldiers busied in seizing poor peasants and throwing them into prison, and he asked: "Why, brethren, are you showing such cruelty to these unfortunate people?" And the soldiers replied: "Because they have not paid the tsar's taxes." The young man at once went to the officer and said: "I pray you, tell me how much these poor people must pay." The officer told him the amount due, and, without hesitation, the young man sold his galley and the cargo, and discharged the debts of all the prisoners. He now returned home, and, falling at the feet of his father, he told him the story and begged that he might be forgiven. But his father grew exceedingly angry this time, and drove him away from his house.

What could the unhappy son do in this fresh trouble? How could he beg, he whose parents were so well-to-do? Old friends of the family again used their influence with his father, urging that he should take pity on his son and receive him back, "for," said they, "it is certain that suffering has made him wiser, and that he will never again act so foolishly." At length his father yielded, took him again into his house, and prepared a third galley for him, much larger and finer than the two former ones.

The Third Voyage

The young man was overjoyed at his good fortune, and he had the portrait of his beloved wife painted on the helm, and that of the old nurse on the stern. When all the preparations for a new voyage were completed, he took leave of his parents, his wife, and other members of the family, and weighed anchor. After sailing for some time he arrived at a great city, in which there lived a tsar, and, dropping anchor, he fired his guns as a salute to the city. Toward evening the tsar sent one of his ministers to learn who the stranger was and whence he came, and to inform him that his master would come at nine o'clock next morning to visit the galley. The minister was astounded to see on the helm the portrait of the imperial princess—whom the tsar had promised to him in marriage when she was still a child—and on the stern that of the old nurse; but he did not make any remark, nor did he tell anyone at the palace what he had seen. At nine o'clock next morning the tsar came on board the galley with his ministers, and, as he paced the deck, conversing with the captain, he also saw the portrait of the maiden painted on the helm and that of the old woman on the stern, and he recognized at once the features of his only daughter and her nurse, whom the Turks had captured. At once he conceived the hope that his beloved child was alive and well, but he could not trust himself to speak, so great was his emotion. Composing himself as best he could, he invited the captain to come at two o'clock that afternoon to his palace, intending to question him, hoping thus to confirm the hopes of his heart.

Punctually at two o'clock the captain appeared at the palace, and the tsar at once began to question him in a roundabout manner as to the maiden whose portrait he had seen on the helm of his galley. Was she one of his relations, and, if so, in what degree? He was also curious concerning the old woman whose likeness was painted on the stern.

The young captain guessed at once that the tsar must be his wife's father, and he related to him word by word all his adventures, not omitting to say that, having found that the young maiden and her nurse had forgotten the way back to their country, he had taken pity on them and later had espoused the maiden. Hearing this the tsar exclaimed: "That girl is my only child and the old woman is her nurse; hasten and bring my daughter here that I may see her once more before I die. Bring here also your parents and all your family; your father will be my brother and your mother my sister, for you are my son and the heir to my crown. Go and sell all your property and come that we may live together in my palace!" Then he called the tsarina, his wife, and all his ministers, that they might hear the joyful news, and there was great joy in the court.

After this the tsar gave the captain a magnificent ship requesting him to leave his own galley behind. The young man was, of course, very grateful, but he said: "O glorious tsar! My parents will not believe me, if you do not send one of your ministers to accompany me." Thereupon the tsar appointed as his companion for the voyage, the very minister to whom he had formerly promised his daughter in marriage.

The captain's father was greatly surprised to see his son return so soon and in such a magnificent ship. Then the young man related to his father and others all that had happened, and the imperial minister confirmed all his statements. When the princess saw the minister she exclaimed joyfully: "Yes, indeed, all that he has said is true; this is my father's minister, who was to be my betrothed." Then the man and his family sold all their property and went on board the ship.

The Treacherous Minister

Now the minister was a wicked man, and he had formed a design to kill the young husband of the princess that he might espouse her and one day become tsar. Accordingly during the voyage he called the young man on deck one night to confer with him. The captain had a quiet conscience and did not suspect evil, wherefore he was entirely unprepared when the minister seized him and threw him swiftly overboard. The ship was sailing fast; it was impossible that he could reach it, so he fell gradually behind. By great good luck he was very near to land and soon he was cast ashore by the waves. But, alas! this land was but a bare uninhabited rock.

Meantime the minister had stolen back to his cabin and next morning when it was found that the captain had disappeared, all began to weep and wail, thinking that he had fallen overboard in the night and been drowned. His family would not be consoled, more especially his wife, who loved him so much. When they arrived at the tsar's palace and reported that the young man had been accidentally drowned, the entire court mourned with them.

For fifteen days the tsar's unhappy son-in-law was condemned to a bare subsistence upon the scanty grass which grew upon the rocky islet. His skin was tanned by the hot sun and his garments became soiled and torn, so that no one could have recognized him. On the morrow of the fifteenth day, he had the good fortune to perceive an old man on the shore, leaning on a stick, engaged in fishing. He began at once to hail the old man and to beseech him to help him off the rock. The old fisherman said: "I will save you, if you will pay me!" "How can I pay you," answered the castaway, "when, as you see, I have only these rags, and nothing more?" "Oh, as for that," replied the old man, "you can write and sign a promise to give me a half of everything that you may ever possess." The young man gladly made this promise. Then the old man produced writing materials and the young man signed the agreement, after which they both sailed in the old man's fishing boat to the mainland. After that the young man wandered from house to house and from village to village, a barefoot beggar, in rags, sunburnt, and hungry.

The Young Man's Return

After thirty days' journeying, good luck led him to the city of the tsar and he sat him down, staff in hand, at the gates of the palace, still wearing on his finger his wedding-ring, on which was engraved his name and that of his wife. The servants of the tsar, pitying his sad plight, offered him shelter for the night in the palace and gave him to eat fragments from their own dinner. Next morning he went to the garden of the palace, but the gardener came and drove him away, saying that the tsar and his family were soon coming by. He moved from that spot and sat down in a corner on the grass, when suddenly he saw the tsar walking with his own mother and father, who had remained at the court as the tsar's guests, and his beloved wife walking arm in arm with his enemy, the minister. He did not yet wish to reveal himself, but as the tsar and his train passed by and gave him alms, he stretched out his hand to receive it and the wedding-ring upon his finger caught the princess's eye. She recognized it at once, but it was incredible that the beggar could be her husband, and she said to him: "Pray, give me your hand that I may see your ring!" The minister protested, but the princess did not pay any attention to him, and proceeded to examine the ring, to find there her own name and that of her husband. Her heart was greatly agitated at the sight, but she made an effort to control her feelings and said nothing. Upon her return to the palace she appeared before her father and told him what she had seen. "Please send for him," said she, "and we may find out how the ring came into his possession!" The tsar immediately sent an attendant to fetch the beggar. The order was executed at once, and, when the stranger appeared the tsar asked him his name, whence he came, and in what manner he obtained the ring. The unfortunate young man could no longer maintain his disguise, so telling the tsar who he was, he went on to relate all his adventures since the minister treacherously threw him into the sea. "Behold!" said he at last, "Our gracious Lord and my right-dealing has brought me back to my parents and my wife." Almost beside themselves for joy, the tsar called for the young man's parents and imparted to them the good news. Who could express the joy of the aged couple when they identified their son? Words fail, also, to describe adequately the rejoicing which filled the hearts of the entire court. The servants prepared perfumed baths for the young man and brought him sumptuous new garments. The tsar gave orders that he should be crowned as tsar, and for several days there were wonderful festivities, in which the whole city joined; everywhere was singing, dancing and feasting. The old tsar summoned the wicked minister to appear before his son-in-law, to be dealt with according to his will. But the young tsar had a kind heart, so he forgave him upon the condition that he should leave the tsardom without delay, and never come back during his reign.

"Pray, give me your hand that I may see your ring!"

The new tsar had hardly began to rule, when the old fisherman who had saved him from the rocky isle came and craved audience. The tsar at once received his deliverer who produced the written promise. "Very well, old man," said the tsar; "to-day I am ruler, but I will as readily fulfil my word as if I were a beggar with little to share; so let us divide my possessions in two equal parts." Then the tsar took the books and began to divide the cities, saying: "This is for you—this is for me." So he marked all on a map, till the whole tsardom was divided between them, from the greatest city to the poorest hut.

When the tsar had finished the old man said: "Take all back! I am not a man of this world; I am an angel from God, who sent me to save you on account of your good deeds. Now reign and be happy, and may you live long in complete prosperity!" So saying, he vanished suddenly, and the young tsar ruled in great happiness ever after.

XIV. He Whom God Helps No One Can Harm

Once upon a time there lived a man and his wife, and they were blessed with three sons. The youngest son was the most handsome, and he possessed a better heart than his brothers, who thought him a fool. When the three brothers had arrived at the man's estate, they came together to their father, each of them asking permission to marry. The father was embarrassed with this sudden wish of his sons, and said he would first take counsel with his wife as to his answer.

The First Quest

A few days later the man called his sons together and told them to go to the neighbouring town and seek for employment. "He who brings me the finest rug will obtain my permission to marry first," he said.

The brothers started off to the neighbouring town together. On the way the two elder brothers began to make fun of the youngest, mocking his simplicity, and finally they forced him to take a different road.

Abandoned by his malicious brothers, the young man prayed God to grant him good fortune. At length he came to a lake, on the further shore of which was a magnificent castle. The castle belonged to the daughter of a tyrannous and cruel prince who had died long ago. The young princess was uncommonly beautiful, and many a suitor had come there to ask for her hand. The suitors were always made very welcome, but when they went to their rooms at night the late master of the castle would invariably come as a vampire and suffocate them.

As the youngest brother stood upon the shore wondering how to cross the lake, the princess noticed him from her window and at once gave an order to the servants to take a boat and bring the young man before her. When he appeared he was a little confused, but the noble maiden reassured him with some kind words—for he had, indeed, made a good impression upon her and she liked him at first sight. She asked him whence he came and where he intended to go, and the young man told her all about his father's command.

When the princess heard that, she said to the young man: "You will remain here for the night, and to-morrow morning we will see what we can do about your rug."

After they had supped, the princess conducted her guest to a green room, and bidding him "good-night," said: "This is your room. Do not be alarmed if during the night anything unusual should appear to disturb you."

Being a simple youth, he could not even close his eyes, so deep was the impression made by the beautiful things which surrounded him, when suddenly, toward midnight, there was a great noise. In the midst of the commotion he heard distinctly a mysterious voice whisper: "This youth will inherit the princely crown, no one can do him harm!" The young man took refuge in earnest prayer, and, when day dawned, he arose safe and sound.

When the princess awoke, she sent a servant to summon the young man to her presence, and he was greatly astonished to find the young man alive; so also was the princess and every one in the castle.

After breakfast the princess gave her guest a rich rug, saying: "Take this rug to your father, and if he desires aught else you have only to come back." The young man thanked his fair hostess and with a deep bow took his leave of her.

When he arrived home he found his two brothers already there; they were showing their father the rugs they had brought. When the youngest exhibited his they were astounded, and exclaimed: "How did you get hold of such a costly rug? You must have stolen it!"

The Second Quest

At length the father, in order to quieten them, said: "Go once more into the world, and he who brings back a chain long enough to encircle our house nine times shall have my permission to marry first!" Thus the father succeeded in pacifying his sons. The two elder brothers went their way, and the youngest hurried back to the princess. When he appeared she asked him: "What has your father ordered you to do now?" And he answered: "That each of us should bring a chain long enough to encircle our house nine times." The princess again made him welcome and, after supper, she showed him into a yellow room, saying: "Somebody will come again to frighten you during the night, but you must not pay any attention to him, and to-morrow we will see what we can do about your chain."

And sure enough, about midnight there came many ghosts dancing round his bed and making fearful noises, but he followed the advice of the princess and remained calm and quiet. Next morning a servant came once more to conduct him to the princess, and, after breakfast, she gave him a fine box, saying: "Take this to your father, and if he should desire anything more, you have but to come to me." The young man thanked her, and took his leave.

Again he found that his brothers had reached home first with their chains, but these were not long enough to encircle the house even once, and they were greatly astonished when their youngest brother produced from the box the princess had given an enormous gold chain of the required length. Filled with envy, they exclaimed: "You will ruin the reputation of our house, for you must have stolen this chain!"

The Third Quest

At length the father, tired of their jangling, sent them away, saying: "Go; bring each of you his sweetheart, and I will give you permission to marry." Thereupon the two elder brothers went joyfully to fetch the girls they loved, and the youngest hurried away to the princess to tell her what was now his father's desire. When she heard, the princess said: "You must pass a third night here, and then we shall see what we can do."

So, after supping together, she took him into a red room. During the night he heard again a blood-curdling noise, and from the darkness a mysterious voice said: "This young man is about to take possession of my estates and crown!" He was assaulted by ghosts and vampires, and was dragged from his bed; but through all the young man strove earnestly in prayer, and God saved him.

The young man strove earnestly in prayer

Next morning when he appeared before the princess, she congratulated him on his bravery, and declared that he had won her love. The young man was overwhelmed with happiness, for although he would never have dared to reveal the secret of his heart, he also loved the princess. A barber was now summoned to attend upon the young man, and a tailor to dress him like a prince. This done, the couple went together to the castle chapel and were wedded.

A few days later they drove to the young man's village, and as they stopped outside his home they heard great rejoicing and music, whereat they understood that his two elder brothers were celebrating their marriage feasts. The youngest brother knocked on the gate, and when his father came he did not recognize his son in the richly attired prince who stood before him. He was surprised that such distinguished guests should pay him a visit, and still more so when the prince said: "Good man, will you give us your hospitality for to-night?" The father answered: "Most gladly, but we are having festivities in our house, and I fear that these common people will disturb you with their singing and music." To this the young prince said: "Oh, no; it would please me to see the peasants feasting, and my wife would like it even more than I."

They now entered the house, and as the hostess curtsied deeply before them the prince congratulated her, saying: "How happy you must be to see your two sons wedded on the same day!" The woman sighed. "Ah," said she, "on one hand I have joy and on the other mourning: I had a third son, who went out in the world, and who knows what ill fate may have befallen him?"

After a time the young prince found an opportunity to step into his old room, and put on one of his old suits over his costly attire. He then returned to the room where the feast was spread and stood behind the door. Soon his two brothers saw him, and they called out: "Come here, father, and see your much-praised son, who went and stole like a thief!" The father turned, and seeing the young man, he exclaimed: "Where have you been for so long, and where is your sweetheart?"

Then the youngest son said: "Do not reproach me; all is well with me and with you!" As he spake he took off his old garments and stood revealed in his princely dress. Then he told his story and introduced his wife to his parents.

The brothers now expressed contrition for their conduct, and received the prince's pardon, after which they all embraced; the feasting was renewed, and the festivities went on for several days. Finally the young prince distributed amongst his father and brothers large portions of his new lands, and they all lived long and happily together.

XV. Animals as Friends and as Enemies[7]

Once upon a time, a long while ago, there lived in a very far-off country, a young nobleman who was so exceedingly poor that all his property was an old castle, a handsome horse, a trusty hound, and a good rifle.

This nobleman spent all his time in hunting and shooting, and lived entirely on the produce of the chase.

One day he mounted his well-kept horse and rode off to the neighbouring forest, accompanied, as usual, by his faithful hound. When he came to the forest he dismounted, fastened his horse securely to a young tree, and then went deep into the thicket in search of game. The hound ran on at a distance before his master, and the horse remained all alone, grazing quietly. Now it happened that a hungry fox came by that way and, seeing how well-fed and well-trimmed the horse was, stopped a while to admire him. By and by she was so charmed with the handsome horse, that she lay down in the grass near him to bear him company.

Some time afterward the young nobleman came back out of the forest, carrying a stag that he had killed, and was extremely surprised to see the fox lying so near his horse. So he raised his rifle with the intention of shooting her; but the fox ran up to him quickly and said, "Do not kill me! Take me with you, and I will serve you faithfully. I will take care of your fine horse whilst you are in the forest."

The fox spoke so pitifully that the nobleman was sorry for her, and agreed to her proposal. Thereupon he mounted his horse, placed the stag he had shot before him, and rode back to his old castle, followed closely by his hound and his new servant, the fox.

When the young nobleman prepared his supper, he did not forget to give the fox a due share, and she congratulated herself that she was never likely to be hungry again, at least so long as she served so skilful a hunter.

The next morning the nobleman went out again to the chase; the fox also accompanied him. When the young man dismounted and bound his horse, as usual, to a tree, the fox lay down near it to keep it company.

Now, whilst the hunter was far off in the depth of the forest looking for game, a hungry bear came by the place where the horse was tied, and, seeing how invitingly fat it looked, ran up to kill it. The fox hereupon sprang up and begged the bear not to hurt the horse, telling him if he was hungry he had only to wait patiently until her master came back from the forest, and then she was quite sure that the good nobleman would take him also to his castle and feed him, and care for him, as he did for his horse, his hound, and herself.

The bear pondered over the matter very wisely and deeply for some time, and at length resolved to follow the fox's advice. Accordingly he lay down quietly near the horse, and waited for the return of the huntsman. When the young noble came out of the forest he was greatly surprised to see so large a bear near his horse, and, dropping the stag he had shot from his shoulders, he raised his trusty rifle and was about to shoot the beast. The fox, however, ran up to the huntsman and entreated him to spare the bear's life, and to take him, also, into his service. This the nobleman agreed to do; and, mounting his horse, rode back to his castle, followed by the hound, the fox, and the bear.

The next morning, when the young man had gone again with his dog into the forest, and the fox and the bear lay quietly near the horse, a hungry wolf, seeing the horse, sprang out of a thicket to kill it. The fox and the bear, however, jumped up quickly and begged him not to hurt the animal, telling him to what a good master it belonged, and that they were sure, if he would only wait, he also would be taken into the same service, and would be well cared for. Thereupon the wolf, hungry though he was, thought it best to accept their counsel, and he also lay down with them in the grass until their master come out of the forest.

You can imagine how surprised the young nobleman was when he saw a great gaunt wolf lying so near his horse! However, when the fox had explained the matter to him, he consented to take the wolf also into his service. Thus it happened that this day he rode home followed by the dog, the fox, the bear, and the wolf. As they were all hungry, the stag he had killed was not too large to furnish their suppers that night, and their breakfasts next morning. Not many days afterward a mouse was added to the company, and after that a mole begged so hard for admission that the good nobleman could not find in his heart to refuse her. Last of all came the great bird, the kumrekusha—so strong a bird that she can carry in her claws a horse with his rider! Soon after a hare was added to the company, and the nobleman took great care of all his animals and fed them regularly and well, so that they were all exceedingly fond of him.

The Animals' Council

One day the fox said to the bear, "My good Bruin, pray run into the forest and bring me a nice large log, on which I can sit whilst I preside at a very important council we are going to hold."

Bruin, who had a great respect for the quick wit and good management of the fox, went out at once to seek the log, and soon came back bringing a heavy one, with which the fox expressed herself quite satisfied. Then she called all the animals about her, and, having mounted the log, addressed them in these words:

"You know all of you, my friends, how very kind and good a master we have. But, though he is very kind, he is also very lonely. I propose, therefore, that we find a fitting wife for him."

The assembly was evidently well pleased with this idea, and responded unanimously, "Very good, indeed, if we only knew any girl worthy to be the wife of our master; which, however, we do not."

Then the fox said, "*I* know that the king has a most beautiful daughter, and I think it will be a good thing to take her for our lord; and therefore I propose, further, that our friend the kumrekusha should fly at once to the king's palace, and hover about there until the princess comes out to take her walk. Then she must catch her up at once, and bring her here."

As the kumrekusha was glad to do anything for her kind master, she flew away at once, without even waiting to hear the decision of the assembly on this proposal.

Just before evening set in, the princess came out to walk before her father's palace: whereupon the great bird seized her and placed her gently on her outspread wings, and thus carried her off swiftly to the young nobleman's castle.

The king was exceedingly grieved when he heard that his daughter had been carried off, and sent out everywhere proclamations promising rich rewards to any one who should bring her back, or even tell him where he might look for her. For a long time, however, all his promises were of no avail, for no one in the kingdom knew anything at all about the princess.

At last, however, when the king was well-nigh in despair, an old gipsy woman came to the palace and asked the king, "What will you give me if I bring back to you your daughter, the princess?"

The king answered quickly, "I will gladly give you whatever you like to ask, if only you bring me back my daughter!"

Then the old gipsy went back to her hut in the forest, and tried all her magical spells to find out where the princess was. At last she found out that she was living in an old castle, in a very distant country, with a young nobleman who had married her.

The Magic Carpet

The gipsy was greatly pleased when she knew this, and taking a whip in her hand seated herself at once in the middle of a small carpet, and lashed it with her whip. Then the carpet rose up from the ground and bore her swiftly through the air, toward the far country where the young nobleman lived, in his lonely old castle, with his beautiful wife, and all his faithful company of beasts.

When the gipsy came near the castle she made the carpet descend on the grass among some tress, and leaving it there went to look about until she could meet the princess walking about the grounds. By and by the beautiful young lady came out of the castle, and immediately the ugly old woman went up to her, and began to fawn on her and to tell her all kinds of strange stories. Indeed, she was such a good story-teller that the princess grew quite tired of walking before she was tired of listening; so, seeing the soft carpet lying nicely on the green grass, she sat down on it to rest awhile. The moment she was seated the cunning old gipsy sat down by her, and, seizing her whip, lashed the carpet furiously. In the next minute the princess found herself borne upon the carpet far away from her husband's castle, and before long the gipsy made it descend into the garden of the king's palace.

You can easily guess how glad he was to see his lost daughter, and how he generously gave the gipsy even more than she asked as a reward. Then the king made the princess live from that time in a very secluded tower with only two waiting-women, so afraid was he lest she would again be stolen from him.

Meanwhile the fox, seeing how miserable and melancholy her young master appeared after his wife had so strangely been taken from him, and having heard of the great precautions which the king was using in order to prevent the princess being carried off again, summoned once more all the animals to a general council.

When all of them were gathered about her, the fox thus began: "You know all of you, my dear friends, how happily our kind master was married; but you know, also, that his wife has been unhappily stolen from him, and that he is now far worse off than he was before we found the princess for him. *Then* he was lonely; *now* he is more than lonely—he is desolate! This being the case, it is clearly our duty, as his faithful servants, to try in some way to bring her back to him. This, however, is not a very easy matter, seeing that the king has placed his daughter for safety in a strong tower. Nevertheless, I do not despair, and my plan is this: I will turn myself into a beautiful cat, and play about in the palace gardens under the windows of the tower in which the princess lives. I dare say she will long for me greatly the moment she sees me, and will send her waiting-women down to catch me and take me up to her. But I will take good care that the maids do not catch me, so that, at last, the princess will forget her father's orders not to leave the tower, and will come down herself into the gardens to see if she may not be more successful. I will then make believe to let her catch me, and at this moment our friend, the kumrekusha, who must be hovering over about the palace, must fly down quickly, seize the princess, and carry her off as before. In this way, my dear friends, I hope we shall be able to bring back to our kind master his beautiful wife. Do you approve of my plan?"

Of course, the assembly were only too glad to have such a wise counsellor, and to be able to prove their gratitude to their considerate master. So the fox ran up to the kumrekusha, who flew away with her under her wing, both being equally eager to carry out the project, and thus to bring back the old cheerful look to the face of their lord.

When the kumrekusha came to the tower wherein the princess dwelt she set the fox down quietly among the trees, where it at once changed into a most beautiful cat, and commenced to play all sorts of graceful antics under the window at which the princess sat. The cat was striped all over the body with many different colours, and before long the king's daughter noticed her, and sent down her two women to catch her and bring her up in the tower.

The two waiting-women came down into the garden, and called, "Pussy! pussy!" in their sweetest voices; they offered her bread and milk, but they offered it all in vain. The cat sprang merrily about the garden, and ran round and round them, but would on no account consent to be caught.

At length the princess, who stood watching them at one of the windows of her tower, became impatient, and descended herself into the garden, saying petulantly, "You only frighten the cat; let me try to catch her!" As she approached the cat, who seemed now willing to be caught, the kumrekusha darted down quickly, seized the princess by the waist, and carried her high up into the air.

The frightened waiting-women ran to report to the king what had happened to the princess; whereupon the king immediately let loose all his greyhounds to seize the cat which had been the cause of his daughter's being carried off a second time. The dogs followed the cat closely, and were on the point of catching her, when she, just in the nick of time, saw a cave with a very narrow entrance and ran into it for shelter. There the dogs tried to follow her, or to widen the mouth of the cave with their claws, but all in vain; so, after barking a long time very furiously, they at length grew weary, and stole back ashamed and afraid to the king's stables.

When all the greyhounds were out of sight the cat changed herself back into a fox, and ran off in a straight line toward the castle, where she found her young master very joyful, for the kumrekusha had already brought back to him his beautiful wife.

The King makes War on the Animals

Now the king was exceedingly angry to think that he had again lost his daughter, and he was all the more angry to think that such poor creatures as a bird and a cat had succeeded in carrying her off after all his precautions. So, in his great wrath, he resolved to make a general war on the animals, and entirely exterminate them.

To this end he gathered together a very large army, and determined to be himself their leader. The news of the king's intention spread swiftly over the whole kingdom, whereupon for the third time the fox called together all her friends—the bear, the wolf, the kumrekusha, the mouse, the mole, and the hare—to a general council.

When all were assembled the fox addressed them thus: "My friends, the king has declared war against us, and intends to destroy us all. Now it is our duty to defend ourselves in the best way we can. Let us each see what number of animals we are able to muster. How many of your brother bears do you think *you* can bring to our help, my good Bruin?"

The bear got up as quickly as he could on his hind legs and called out, "I am sure I can bring a hundred."

"And how many of your friends can *you* bring, my good wolf?" asked the fox anxiously.

"I can bring at least five hundred wolves with me," said the wolf with an air of importance.

The fox nodded her satisfaction and continued, "And what can *you* do for us, dear master hare?"

"Well, I think, I can bring about eight hundred," said the hare cautiously.

"And what can *you* do, you dear little mouse?"

"Oh, *I* can certainly bring three thousand mice."

"Very well, indeed!—and you Mr. Mole?"

"I am sure I can gather eight thousand."

"And now what number do you think you can bring us, my great friend, kumrekusha?"

"I fear not more than two or three hundred, at the very best," said the kumrekusha sadly.

"Very good; now all of you go at once and collect your friends; when you have brought all you can, we will decide what is to be done," said the fox; whereupon the council broke up, and the animals dispersed in different directions throughout the forest.

Not very long after, very unusual noises were heard in the neighbourhood of the castle. There was a great shaking of trees; and the growling of bears and the short sharp barking of wolves broke the usual quiet of the forest. The army of animals was gathering from all sides at the appointed place. When all were gathered together the fox explained to them her plans in these words: "When the king's army stops on its march to rest the first night, then you, bears and wolves, must be prepared to attack and kill all the horses. If, notwithstanding this, the army proceeds farther, you mice must be ready to bite and destroy all the saddle-straps and belts while the soldiers are resting the second night, and you hares must gnaw through the ropes with which the men draw the cannon. If the king still persists in his march, you moles must go the third night and dig out the earth under the road they will take the next day, and must make a ditch full fifteen yards in breadth and twenty yards in depth all round their camp. Next morning, when the army begins to march over this ground which has been hollowed out, you kumrekushas must throw down on them from above heavy stones while the earth will give way under them."

The plan was approved, and all the animals went off briskly to attend to their allotted duties.

When the king's army awoke, after their first night's rest on their march, they beheld, to their great consternation, that all the horses were killed. This sad news was reported at once to the king; but he only sent back for more horses, and, when they came late in the day, pursued his march.

The second night the mice crept quietly into the camp, and nibbled diligently at the horses' saddles and at the soldiers' belts, while the hares as busily gnawed at the ropes with which the men drew the cannon.

Next morning the soldiers were terrified, seeing the mischief the animals had done. The king, however, reassured them, and sent back to the city for new saddles and belts. When they were at length brought he resolutely pursued his march, only the more determined to revenge himself on these presumptuous and despised enemies.

On the third night, while the soldiers were sleeping, the moles worked incessantly in digging round the camp a wide and deep trench underground. About midnight the fox sent the bears to help the moles, and to carry away the loads of earth.

Next morning the king's soldiers were delighted to find that no harm seemed to have been done on the previous night to their horses or straps, and started with new courage on their march. But their march was quickly arrested, for soon the heavy horsemen and artillery began to fall through the hollow ground, and the king, when he observed that, called out, "Let us turn back. I see God himself is against us, since we have declared war against the animals. I will give up my daughter."

Then the army turned back, amidst the rejoicings of the soldiers. The men found, however, to their great surprise and fear, that whichever way they turned, they fell through the earth. To make their consternation yet more complete, the kumrekushas now began to throw down heavy stones on them, which crushed them completely. In this way the king, as well as his whole army, perished.

Very soon afterward the young nobleman, who had married the king's daughter, went to the enemy's capital and took possession of the king's palace, taking with him all his animals; and there they all lived long and happily together.

XVI. The Three Suitors

In a very remote country there formerly lived a king who had only one child—an exceedingly beautiful daughter. The princess had a great number of suitors, and amongst them were three young noblemen, whom the king loved much. As, however, the king liked the three nobles equally well, he could not decide to which of the three he should give his daughter as wife. One day, therefore, he called the three young noblemen to him, and said, "Go, all of you, and travel about the world. The one of you who brings home the most remarkable thing shall be my son-in-law!"

The three suitors started at once on their travels, each of them taking opposite ways, and going in search of remarkable things into far different countries.

A long time had not passed before one of the young nobles found a wonderful carpet which would carry rapidly through the air whoever sat upon it.

Another of them found a marvellous telescope, through which he could see everybody and everything in the world, and even the many-coloured sands at the bottom of the great deep sea.

The third found a wonder-working ointment, which could cure every disease in the world, and even bring dead people back to life again.

Now the three noble travellers were far distant from each other when they found these wonderful things. But when the young man who had found the telescope looked through it, he saw one of his former friends and present rivals walking with a carpet on his shoulder, and so he set out to join him. As he could always see, by means of his marvellous telescope, where the other nobleman was, he had no great difficulty in finding him, and when the two had met, they sat side by side on the wonderful carpet, and it carried them through the air until they had joined the third traveller. One day, when each of them had been telling of the remarkable things he had seen in his travels, one of them exclaimed suddenly, "Now let us see what the beautiful princess is doing, and where she is." Then the noble who had found the telescope, looked through it and saw, to his great surprise and dismay, that the king's daughter was lying very sick and at the point of death. He told this to his two friends and rivals, and they, too, were thunderstruck at the bad news—until the one who had found the wonder-working ointment, remembering it suddenly, exclaimed, "I am sure I could cure her, if I could only reach the palace soon enough!" On hearing this the noble who had found the wonderful carpet cried out, "Let us sit down on my carpet, and it will quickly carry us to the king's palace!"

Thereupon the three nobles gently placed themselves in the carpet, which rose instantly in the air, and carried them direct to the king's palace.

The king received them immediately; but said very sadly, "I am sorry for you: for all your travels have been in vain. My daughter is just dying, so she can marry none of you!"

But the nobleman who possessed the wonder-working ointment said respectfully, "Do not fear, sire, the princess will not die!" And on being permitted to enter the apartment where she lay sick, he placed the ointment so that she could smell it. In a few moments the princess revived, and when her waiting-women had rubbed a little of the ointment in her skin she recovered so quickly that in a few days she was better than she had been before she was taken ill.

The king was so glad to have his daughter given back to him, as he thought, from the grave, that he declared that she should marry no one but the young nobleman whose wonderful ointment had cured her.

The Dispute

But now a great dispute arose between the three young nobles: the one who possessed the ointment affirmed that had he not found it the princess would have died, and could not, therefore, have married any one; the noble who owned the telescope declared that had he not found the wonderful telescope they would never have known that the princess was dying, and so his friend would not have brought the ointment to cure her; whilst the third noble proved to them that had he not found the wonderful carpet neither the finding of the ointment nor the telescope would have helped the princess, since they could not have travelled such a great distance in time to save her.

The king, overhearing this dispute, called the young noblemen to him, and said to them, "My lords, from what you have said, I see that I cannot, with justice, give my daughter to any of you; therefore, I pray you to give up altogether the idea of marrying her, and that you continue friends as you always were before you became rivals."

The three young nobles saw that the king had decided justly; so they all left their native country, and went into a far-off desert to live like hermits. And the king gave the princess to another of his great nobles.

Many, many years had passed away since the marriage of the princess, when her husband was sent by her father to a distant country with which the king was waging war. The nobleman took his wife, the princess, with him, as he was uncertain how long he might be forced to remain abroad. Now it happened that a violent storm arose just as the vessel which carried the princess and her husband was approaching a strange coast; and in the height of the great tempest the ship dashed on some rocks, and went to pieces instantly. All the people on board perished in the waves, excepting only the princess, who clung very fast to a boat and was carried by the wind and the tide to the shore. There she found what seemed to be an uninhabited country, and, discovering a small cave in a rock, she lived alone in it for three years, feeding on wild herbs and fruits. She searched every day to find some way out of the forest which surrounded her cave, but could find none. One day, however, when she had wandered farther than usual from the cave where she lived, she came suddenly on another cave which, to her great astonishment, had a small door. She tried over and over again to open the door, thinking she would pass the night in the cave; but all her efforts were unavailing, it was shut so fast. At length, however, a deep voice from within the cave called out, "Who is at the door?"

At this the princess was so surprised that she could not answer for some moments; when, however, she had recovered a little, she said, "Open me the door!" Immediately the door was opened from within, and she saw, with sudden terror, an old man with a thick grey beard reaching below his waist and long white hair flowing over his shoulders.

What frightened the princess the more was her finding a man living here in the same desert where she had lived herself three years without seeing a single soul.

The hermit and the princess looked at each long and earnestly without saying a word. At length, however, the old man said, "Tell me, are you an angel or a daughter of this world?"

Then the princess answered, "Old man, let me rest a moment, and then I will tell you all about myself, and what brought me here." So the hermit brought out some wild pears, and when the princess had taken some of them, she began to tell him who she was, and how she came in that desert. She said, "I am a king's daughter, and once, many years ago, three young nobles of my father's court asked the king for my hand in marriage. Now the king had such an equal affection for all these three young men that he was unwilling to give pain to any of them, so he sent them to travel into distant countries, and promised to decide between them when they returned.

"The three noblemen remained a long time away; and whilst they were still abroad somewhere, I fell dangerously ill. I was just at the point of death, when they all three returned suddenly; one of them bringing a wonderful ointment, which cured me at once; the two others brought each equally remarkable things—a carpet that would carry whoever sat on it through the air, and a telescope with which one could see everybody and everything in the world, even to the sands at the bottom of the sea."

The Recognition

The princess had gone on thus far with her story, when the hermit suddenly interrupted her, saying: "All that happened afterward I know as well as you can tell me. Look at me, my daughter! I am one of those noblemen who sought to win your hand, and here is the wonderful telescope." And the hermit brought out the instrument from a recess in the side of his cave before he continued; "My two friends and rivals came with me to this desert. We parted, however, immediately, and have never met since. I know not whether they are living or dead, but I will look for them."

Then the hermit looked through his telescope, and saw that the other two noblemen were living in caves like his, in different parts of the same desert. Having found this out, he took the princess by the hand, and led her on until they found the other hermits. When all were reunited, the princess related her adventures since the foundering of the ship, in which her husband had gone down, and from which she alone had been saved.

The three noble hermits were pleased to see her alive once again, but at once decided that they ought to send her back to the king, her father.

Then they made the princess a present of the wonderful telescope, and the wonder-working ointment, and placed her on the wonderful carpet, which carried her and her treasures quickly and safely to her father's palace. As for the three noblemen, they remained, still living like hermits, in the desert, only they visited each other now and then, so that the years seemed no longer so tedious to them. For they had many adventures to relate to each other.

The king was exceedingly glad to receive his only child back safely, and the princess lived with her father many years; but neither the king nor his daughter could entirely forget the three noble friends who, for her sake, lived like hermits in a wild desert in a far-off land.

XVII. The Dream of the King's Son

There was once a king who had three sons. One evening, when the young princes were going to sleep, the king ordered them to take good note of their dreams and come and tell them to him next morning. So, the next day the princes went to their father as soon as they awoke, and the moment the king saw them he asked of the eldest, "Well, what have you dreamt?"

The prince answered, "I dreamt that I should be the heir to your throne."

And the second said, "And I dreamt that I should be the first subject in the kingdom."

Then the youngest said, "*I* dreamt that I was going to wash my hands, and that the princes, my brothers, held the basin, whilst the queen, my mother, held fine towels for me to dry my hands with, and your majesty's self poured water over them from a golden ewer."

The king, hearing this last dream, became very angry, and exclaimed, "What! I—the king—pour water over the hands of my own son! Go away this instant out of my palace, and out of my kingdom! You are no longer my son."

The poor young prince tried hard to make his peace with his father, saying that he was really not to be blamed for what he had only dreamed; but the king grew more and more furious, and at last actually thrust the prince out of the palace.

So the young prince was obliged to wander up and down in different countries, until one day, being in a large forest, he saw a cave, and entered it to rest. There, to his great surprise and joy, he found a large kettle full of Indian corn, boiling over a fire: and, being exceedingly hungry, began to help himself to the corn. In this way he went until he was shocked to see he had nearly eaten up all the maize, and then, being afraid some mischief would come of it, he looked about for a place in which to hide himself. At this moment, however, a great noise was heard at the cave-mouth, and he had only time to hide himself in a dark corner before a blind old man entered, riding on a great goat and driving a number of goats before him.

The old man rode straight up to the kettle, but as soon as he found that the corn was nearly all gone, he began to suspect some one was there, and groped about the cave until he caught hold of the prince.

"Who are you?" asked he sharply; and the prince answered, "I am a poor, homeless wanderer about the world, and have come now to beg you to be good enough to receive me."

"Well," said the old man, "why not? I shall at least have some one to mind my corn whilst I am out with my goats in the forest."

So they lived together for some time; the prince remaining in the cave to boil the maize, whilst the old man drove out his goats every morning into the forest.

One day, however, the old man said to the prince, "I think you shall take out the goats to-day, and I will stay at home to mind the corn."

This the prince consented to very gladly, as he was tired of living so long quietly in the cave. But the old man added, "Mind only one thing! There are nine different mountains, and you can let the goats go freely over eight of them, but you must on no account go on the ninth. The veele live there, and they will certainly put out your eyes as they have put out mine, if you venture on their mountain." The prince thanked the old man for his warning, and then, mounting the great goat, drove the rest of the goats before him out of the cave.

Following the goats, he had passed over all the mountains to the eighth, and from this he could see the ninth mountain, and could not resist the temptation he felt to go upon it. So he said to himself, "I will venture up, whatever happens!"

The Prince and the Veele

Hardly had he stepped on the ninth mountain before the fairies surrounded him, and prepared to put out his eyes. But, happily, a thought came into his head, and he exclaimed, quickly, "Dear veele, why take this sin on your heads? Better let us make a bargain, that if you spring over a tree that I will place ready to jump over, you shall put out my eyes, and I will not blame you!"

So the veele consented to this, and the prince went and brought a large tree, which he cleft down the middle almost to the root; this done, he placed a wedge to keep the two halves of the trunk open a little.

When it was fixed upright, he himself first jumped over it, and then he said to the veele, "Now it is your turn. Let us see if you can spring over the tree!"

One veele attempted to spring over, but the same moment the prince knocked the wedge out, and the trunk closing at once held the veele fast. Then all the other fairies were alarmed, and begged him to open the trunk and let their sister free, promising, in return, to give him anything he might ask. The prince said, "I want nothing except to keep my own eyes, and to restore eyesight to that poor old man." So the fairies gave him a certain herb, and told him to lay it over the old man's eyes, and then he would recover his sight. The prince took the herb, opened the tree a little so as to let the fairy free, and then rode back on the goat to the cave, driving the other goats before him. When he arrived there he placed at once the herb on the old man's eyes, and in a moment his eyesight came back, to his exceeding surprise and joy.

Next morning the old man, before he drove out his goats, gave the prince the keys of eight closets in the cave, but warned him on no account to open the ninth closet, although the key hung directly over the door. Then he went out, telling the prince to take good care that the corn was ready for their suppers.

Left alone in the cave, the young man began to wonder what might be in the ninth closet, and at last he could not resist the temptation to take down the key and open the door to look in.

The Golden Horse

What was his surprise to see there a golden horse, with a golden greyhound beside him, and near them a golden hen and golden chickens were busy picking up golden millet-seeds.

The young prince gazed at them for some time, admiring their beauty, and then he spoke to the golden horse, "Friend, I think we had better leave this place before the old man comes back again."

"Very well," answered the golden horse, "I am quite willing to go away, only you must take heed to what I am going to tell. Go and find linen cloth enough to spread over the stones at the mouth of the cave, for if the old man hears the ring of my hoofs he will be certain to kill you. Then you must take with you a little stone, a drop of water, and a pair of scissors, and the moment I tell you to throw them down you must obey me quickly, or you are lost."

The prince did everything that the golden horse had ordered him, and then, taking up the golden hen with her chickens in a bag, he placed it under his arm, and mounted the horse and rode quickly out of the cave, leading with him, in a leash, the golden greyhound. But the moment they were in the open air the old man, although he was very far off, tending his goats on a distant mountain, heard the clang of the golden hoofs, and cried to his great goat, "They have run away. Let us follow them at once."

In a wonderfully short time the old man on his great goat came so near the prince on his golden horse, that the latter shouted, "Throw now the little stone!"

The moment the prince had thrown it down, a high rocky mountain rose up between him and the old man, and before the goat had climbed over it, the golden horse had gained much ground. Very soon, however, the old man was so nearly catching them that the horse shouted, "Throw, now, the drop of water!" The prince obeyed instantly, and immediately saw a broad river flowing between him and his pursuer.

It took the old man on his goat so long to cross the river that the prince on his golden horse was far away before them; but for all that it was not very long before the horse heard the goat so near behind him that he shouted, "Throw the scissors." The prince threw them, and the goat, running over them, injured one of his fore legs very badly. When the old man saw this, he exclaimed, "Now I see I cannot catch you, so you may keep what you have taken. But you will do wisely to listen to my counsel. People will be sure to kill you for the sake of your golden horse, so you had better buy at once a donkey, and take the hide to cover your horse. And do the same with your golden greyhound."

Having said this, the old man turned and rode back to his cave; and the prince lost no time in attending to his advice, and covered with donkey-hide his golden horse and his golden hound.

After travelling a long time the prince came unawares to the kingdom of his father. There he heard that the king had had a ditch dug, three hundred yards wide and four hundred yards deep, and had proclaimed that whosoever should leap his horse over it, should have the princess, his daughter, for wife.

Almost a whole year had elapsed since the proclamation was issued, but as yet no one had dared to risk the leap. When the prince heard this, he said, "*I* will leap over it with my donkey and my dog!" and he leapt over it.

But the king was very angry when he heard that a poorly dressed man, on a donkey, had dared to leap over the great ditch which had frightened back his bravest knights; so he had the disguised prince thrown into one of his deepest dungeons, together with his donkey and his dog.

Next morning the king sent some of his servants to see if the man was still living, and these soon ran back to him, full of wonder, and told him that they had found in the dungeon, instead of a poor man and his donkey, a young man, beautifully dressed, a golden horse, a golden greyhound, and a golden hen, surrounded by golden chickens, which were picking up golden millet-seeds from the ground. Then the king said, "That must be some powerful prince." So he ordered the queen, and the princes, his sons, to prepare all things for the stranger to wash his hands. Then he went down himself into the dungeon, and led the prince up with much courtesy, desiring to make thus amends for the past ill-treatment.

The king himself took a golden ewer full of water, and poured some over the prince's hands, whilst the two princes held the basin under them, and the queen held out fine towels to dry them on.

This done, the young prince exclaimed, "Now, my dream is fulfilled"; and they all at once recognized him, and were very glad to see him once again amongst them.

XVIII. The Biter Bit

Once upon a time there was an old man who, whenever he heard anyone complain how many sons he had to care for, always laughed and said, "I wish that it would please God to give me a hundred sons!"

This he said in jest; as time went on, however, he had, in reality, neither more nor less than a hundred sons.

He had trouble enough to find different trades for his sons, but when they were once all started in life they worked diligently and gained plenty of money. Now, however, came a fresh difficulty. One day the eldest son came in to his father and said, "My dear father, I think it is quite time that I should marry."

Hardly had he said these words before the second son came in, saying, "Dear father, I think it is already time that you were looking out for a wife for me."

A moment later came in the third son, asking, "Dear father, don't you think it is high time that you should find me a wife?" In like manner came the fourth and fifth, until the whole hundred had made a similar request. All of them wished to marry, and desired their father to find wives for them as soon as he could.

The old man was not a little troubled at these requests; he said, however, to his sons, "Very well, my sons, I have nothing to say against your marrying; there is, however, I foresee, one great difficulty in the way. There are one hundred of you asking for wives, and I hardly think we can find one hundred marriageable girls in all the fifteen villages which are in our neighbourhood."

To this the sons, however, answered, "Don't be anxious about that, but mount your horse and take in your sack sufficient engagement-cakes. You must take, also, a stick in your hand so that you can cut a notch in it for every girl you see. It does not signify whether she be handsome or ugly, or lame or blind, just cut a notch in your stick for every one you meet with."

The old man said, "Very wisely spoken, my sons! I will do exactly as you tell me."

Accordingly he mounted his horse, took a sack full of cakes on his shoulder and a long stick in his hand, and started off at once to beat up the neighbourhood for girls to marry his sons.

The old man had travelled from village to village during a whole month, and whenever he had seen a girl he cut a notch in his stick. But he was getting pretty well tired, and he began to count how many notches he had already made. When he had counted them carefully over and over again, to be certain that he had counted all, he could only make out seventy-four, so that still twenty-six were wanting to complete the number required. He was, however, so weary with his month's ride that he determined to return home. As he rode along, he saw a priest driving oxen yoked to a plough, and seemingly very deep in anxious thought about something. Now the old man wondered a little to see the priest ploughing his own corn-fields without even a boy to help him; he therefore shouted to ask him why he drove his oxen himself. The priest, however, did not even turn his head to see who called to him, so intent was he in urging on his oxen and in guiding his plough.

The old man thought he had not spoken loud enough, so he shouted out again as loud as he could, "Stop your oxen a little, and tell me why you are ploughing yourself without even a lad to help you, and this, too, on a holy-day!"

Now the priest—who was in a perspiration with his hard work—answered testily, "I conjure you by your old age leave me in peace! I cannot tell you my ill-luck."

The Hundred Daughters

At this answer, however, the old man was only the more curious, and persisted all the more earnestly in asking questions to find out why the priest ploughed on a saint's day. At last the priest, tired with his importunity, sighed deeply and said, "Well, if you *will* know: I am the only man in my household, and God has blessed me with a hundred daughters!"

The old man was overjoyed at hearing this, and exclaimed cheerfully, "That's very good! It is just what I want, for *I* have a hundred sons, and so, as you have a hundred daughters, we can be friends!"

The moment the priest heard this he became pleasant and talkative, and invited the old man to pass the night in his house. Then, leaving his plough in the field, he drove the oxen back to the village. Just before reaching his house, however, he said to the old man, "Go yourself into the house whilst I tie up my oxen."

No sooner, however, had the old man entered the yard than the wife of the priest rushed at him with a big stick, crying out, "We have not bread enough for our hundred daughters, and we want neither beggars nor visitors," and with these words she drove him away.

Shortly afterwards the priest came out of the barn, and, finding the old man sitting on the road before the gate, asked him why he had not gone into the house as he had told him to do. Whereupon the old man replied, "I went in, but your wife drove me away!"

Then the priest said, "Only wait here a moment till I come back to fetch you." He then went quickly into his house and scolded his wife right well, saying, "What have you done? What a fine chance you have spoiled! The man who came in was going to be our friend, for he has a hundred sons who would gladly have married our hundred daughters!"

When the wife heard this she changed her dress hastily, and arranged her hair and head-dress in a different fashion. Then she smiled very sweetly, and welcomed with the greatest possible politeness the old man, when her husband led him into the house. In fact, she pretended that she knew nothing at all of anyone having been driven away from their door. And as the old man wanted much to find wives for his sons, he also pretended that he did not know that the smiling house-mistress and the woman who drove him away with a stick were one and the selfsame person.

So the old man passed the night in the house, and next morning asked the priest formally to give him his hundred daughters for wives for his hundred sons. Thereupon the priest answered that he was quite willing, and had already spoken to his daughters about the matter, and that they, too, were all quite willing. Then the old man took out his "engagement-cakes," and put them on the table beside him, and gave each of the girls a piece of money to *mark*. Then each of the engaged girls sent a small present by him to that one of his sons to whom she was thus betrothed. These gifts the old man put in the bag wherein he had carried the "engagement-cakes." He then mounted his horse, and rode off merrily homewards. There were great rejoicings in his household when he told how successful he had been in his search, and that he really had found a hundred girls ready and willing to be married; and these hundred, too, a priest's daughters.

The sons insisted that they should begin to make the wedding preparations without delay, and commenced at once to invite the guests who were to form part of the wedding procession to go to the priest's house and bring home the brides.

Here, however, another difficulty occurred. The old father must find two hundred bride-leaders (two for each bride); one hundred kooms; one hundred starisvats; one hundred chaious (running footmen who go before the processions); and three hundred vojvodes (standard-bearers); and, besides these, a respectable number of other non-official guests. To find all these persons the father had to hunt throughout the neighbourhood for three years; at last, however, they were all found, and a day was appointed when they were to meet at his house, and go thence in procession to the house of the priest.

The Wedding Procession

On the appointed day all the invited guests gathered at the old man's house. With great noise and confusion, after a fair amount of feasting, the wedding procession was formed properly, and set out for the house of the priest, where the hundred brides were already prepared for their departure for their new home.

So great was the confusion, indeed, that the old man quite forgot to take with him one of the hundred sons, and never missed him in the greeting and talking and drinking he was obliged, as father of the bridegrooms, to go through. Now the young man had worked so long and so hard in preparing for the wedding-day that he never woke up till long after the procession had started; and every one had had, like his father, too much to do and too many things to think of to miss him.

The wedding procession arrived in good order at the priest's house, where a feast was already spread out for them. Having done honour to the various good things, and having gone through all the ceremonies usual on such occasions, the hundred brides were given over to their "leaders," and the procession started on its return to the old man's house. But, as they did not set off until pretty late in the afternoon, it was decided that the night should be spent somewhere on the road. When they came, therefore, to a certain river named "Luckless," as it was already dark, some of the men proposed that the party should pass the night by the side of the water without crossing over. However, some others of the chief of the party so warmly advised the crossing the river and encamping on the other bank, that this course was at length, after a very lively discussion, determined on; accordingly the procession began to move over the bridge.

Just, however, as the wedding party were half-way across the bridge its two sides began to draw nearer each other, and pressed the people so close together that they had hardly room to breathe—much less could they move forwards or backwards.

The Black Giant

They were kept for some time in this position, some shouting and scolding, others quiet because frightened, until at length a black giant appeared, and shouted to them in a terribly loud voice, "Who are you all? Where do you come from? Where are you going?"

Some of the bolder among them answered, "We are going to our old friend's house, taking home the hundred brides for his hundred sons; but unluckily we ventured on this bridge after nightfall, and it has pressed us so tightly together that we cannot move one way or the other."

"And where is your old friend?" inquired the black giant.

Now all the wedding guests turned their eyes towards the old man. Thereupon he turned towards the giant, who instantly said to him, "Listen, old man! Will you give me what you have forgotten at home, if I let your friends pass over the bridge?"

The old man considered some time what it might be that he had forgotten at home, but, at last, not being able to recollect anything in particular that he had left, and hearing on all sides the groans and moans of his guests, he replied, "Well, I will give it you, if you will only let the procession pass over."

Then the black giant said to the party, "You all hear what he has promised, and are all my witnesses to the bargain. In three days I shall come to fetch what I have bargained for."

Having said this, the black giant widened the bridge and the whole procession passed on to the other bank in safety. The people, however, no longer wished to spend the night on the way, so they moved on as fast as they could, and early in the morning reached the old man's house.

As everybody talked of the strange adventure they had met with, the eldest son, who had been left at home, soon began to understand how the matter stood, and went to his father saying, "O my father! you have sold *me* to the black giant!"

Then the old man was very sorry, and troubled; but his friends comforted him, saying, "Don't be frightened! nothing will come of it."

The marriage ceremonies were celebrated with great rejoicings. Just, however, as the festivities were at their height, on the third day, the black giant appeared at the gate and shouted, "Now, give me at once what you have promised."

The old man, trembling all over, went forward and asked him, "What do you want?"

"Nothing but what you have promised me!" returned the black giant.

As he could not break his promise, the old man, very distressed, was then obliged to deliver up his eldest son to the giant, who thereupon said, "Now I shall take your son with me, but after three years have passed you can come to the Luckless River and take him away."

Having said this the black giant disappeared, taking with him the young man, whom he carried off to his workshop as an apprentice to the trade of witchcraft.

From that time the poor old man had not a single moment of happiness. He was always sad and anxious, and counted every year, and month, and week, and even every day, until the dawn of the last day of the three years. Then he took a staff in his hand and hurried off to the bank of the river Luckless. As soon as he reached the river, he was met by the black giant, who asked him, "Why are you come?" The old man answered that he come to take home his son, according to his agreement.

Thereupon the giant brought out a tray on which stood a sparrow, a turtle-dove, and a quail, and said to the old man, "Now, if you can tell which of these is your son, you may take him away."

The poor old father looked intently at the three birds, one after the other, and over and over again, but at last he was forced to own that he could not tell which of them was his son. So he was obliged to go away by himself, and was far more miserable than before. He had hardly, however, got half-way home when he thought he would go back to the river and take one of the birds which remembered and looked at him intently.

When he reached the river Luckless he was again met by the black giant, who brought out the tray again, and placed on it this time a partridge, a tit-mouse, and a thrush, saying, 'Now, my old man, find out which is your son!'

The anxious father again looked at one bird after the other, but he felt more uncertain than before, and so, crying bitterly, again went away.

The Old Woman

Just as the old man was going through a forest, which was between the river Luckless and his house, an old woman met him, and said, "Stop a moment! Where are you hurrying to? And why are you in such trouble?" Now, the old man was so deeply musing over his great unhappiness that he did not at first attend to the old woman; but she followed him, calling after him, and repeating her questions with more earnestness. So he stopped at last, and told her what a terrible misfortune had fallen upon him. When the old woman had listened to the whole story, she said cheerfully, "Don't be cast down! Don't be afraid! Go back again to the river, and, when the giant brings out the three birds, look into their eyes sharply. When you see that one of the birds has a tear in one of its eyes, seize that bird and hold it fast, for it has a human soul."

The old man thanked her heartily for her advice, and turned back, for the third time, towards the Luckless River. Again the black giant appeared, and looked very merry whilst he brought out his tray and put upon it a sparrow, a dove, and a woodpecker, saying, "My old man! find out which is your son!" Then the father looked sharply into the eyes of the birds, and saw that from the right eye of the dove a tear dropped slowly down. In a moment he grasped the bird tightly, saying, "This is my son!" The next moment he found himself holding fast his eldest son by the shoulder, and so, singing and shouting in his great joy, took him quickly home, and gave him over to his eldest daughter-in-law, the wife of his son.

Now, for some time they all lived together very happily. One day, however, the young man said to his father, "Whilst I was apprentice in the workshop of the black giant, I learned a great many tricks of witchcraft. Now I intend to change myself into a fine horse, and you shall take me to market and sell me for a good sum of money. But be sure not to give up the halter."

The father did as the son had said. Next market day he went to the city with a fine horse which he offered for sale. Many buyers came round him, admiring the horse, and bidding some sums for it, so that at last the old man was able to sell it for two thousand ducats. When he received the money, he took good care not to let go the halter, and he returned home far richer than he ever dreamt of being.

A few days later, the man who had bought the horse sent his servant with it to the river to bathe, and, whilst in the water, the horse got loose from the servant and galloped off into the neighbouring forest. There he changed himself back into his real shape, and returned to his father's house.

After some time had passed, the young man said one day to his father, "Now I will change myself into an ox, and you can take me to market to sell me; but take care not to give up the rope with which you lead me."

So next market-day the old man went to the city leading a very fine ox, and soon found a buyer, who offered ten times the usual price paid for an ox. The buyer asked also for the rope to lead the animal home, but the old man said, "What do you want with such an old thing? You had better buy a new one!" and he went off taking with him the rope.

That evening, whilst the servants of the buyer were driving the ox to the field, he ran away into a wood near, and, having taken there his human shape, returned home to his father's house.

On the eve of the next market-day, the young man said to his father: "Now I will change myself into a cow with golden horns, and you can sell me as before, only take care not to give up the string."

Accordingly he changed himself next morning into a cow, and the old man took it to the market-place, and asked for it three hundred crowns.

But the black giant had learnt that his former apprentice was making a great deal of money by practising the trade he had taught him, and, being jealous at this, he determined to put an end to the young man's gains.

The Giant buys the Cow

Therefore, on the third day he came to the market himself as a buyer, and the moment he saw the beautiful cow with golden horns he knew that it could be no other than his former apprentice. So he came up to the old man, and, having outbid all the other would-be purchasers, paid at once the price he had agreed on. Having done this, he caught the string in his hand, and tried to wrench it from the terrified old man, who called out, "I have not sold you the string, but the cow!" and held the string as fast as he could with both hands.

"Oh, no!" said the buyer, "I have the law and custom on my side! Whoever buys a cow, buys also the string with which it is led!" Some of the amused and astonished lookers-on said that this was quite true, therefore the old man was obliged to give up the string.

The black giant, well satisfied with his purchase, took the cow with him to his castle, and, after having put iron chains on her legs, fastened her in a cellar. Every morning the giant gave the cow some water and hay, but he never unchained her.

One evening, however, the cow, with incessant struggles, managed to get free from the chains, and immediately opened the cellar-door with her horns and ran away.

Next morning the black giant went as usual into the cellar, carrying the hay and water for the cow; but seeing she had got free and run away, he threw the hay down, and started off at once to pursue her.

When he came within sight of her, he turned himself into a wolf and ran at her with great fury; but his clever apprentice changed himself instantly from a cow into a bear, whereupon the giant turned himself from a wolf into a lion; the bear then turned into a tiger, and the lion changed into a crocodile, whereupon the tiger turned into a sparrow. Upon this the giant changed from the form of a crocodile into a hawk, and the apprentice immediately changed into a hare; on seeing which the hawk became a greyhound. Then the apprentice changed from a hare into a falcon, and the greyhound into an eagle; whereupon the apprentice changed into a fish. The giant then turned from an eagle into a mouse, and immediately the apprentice, as a cat, ran after him; then the giant turned himself into a heap of millet, and the apprentice transformed himself into a hen and chickens, which very greedily picked up all the millet except one single seed, in which the master was, who changed himself into a squirrel; instantly, however, the apprentice became a hawk, and, pouncing on the squirrel, killed it.

In this way the apprentice beat his master, the black giant, and revenged himself for all the sufferings he had endured whilst learning the trade of witchcraft. Having killed the squirrel, the hawk took his proper shape again, and the young man returned joyfully to his father, whom he made immensely rich.

XIX. The Trade that No One Knows

A long while ago there lived a poor old couple, who had an only son. The old man and his wife worked very hard to nourish their child well and bring him up properly, hoping that he, in return, would take care of them in their old age.

When, however, the boy had grown up, he said to his parents, "I am a man now, and I intend to marry, so I wish you to go at once to the king and ask him to give me his daughter for wife." The astonished parents rebuked him, saying: "What can you be thinking of? We have only this poor hut to shelter us, and hardly bread enough to eat, and we dare not presume to go into the king's presence, much less can we venture to ask for his daughter to be your wife."

The son, however, insisted that they should do as he said, threatening that if they did not comply with his wishes he would leave them, and go away into the world. Seeing that he was really in earnest in what he said, the unhappy parents promised him they would go and ask for the king's daughter. Then the old mother made a wedding cake in her son's presence, and, when it was ready, she put it in a bag, took her staff in her hand, and went straight to the palace where the king lived. There the king's servants bade her come in, and led her into the hall where his Majesty was accustomed to receive the poor people who came to ask alms or to present petitions.

The poor old woman stood in the hall, confused and ashamed at her worn-out, shabby clothes, and looking as if she were made of stone, until the king said to her kindly: "What do *you* want from me, old mother?"

She dared not, however, tell his Majesty why she had come, so she stammered out in her confusion: "Nothing, your Majesty."

Then the king smiled a little and said, "Perhaps you come to ask alms?"

Then the old woman, much abashed, replied: "Yes, your Majesty, if you please!"

Thereupon the king called his servants and ordered them to give the old woman ten crowns, which they did.

Having received this money, she thanked his Majesty, and returned home, saying to herself: "I dare say when my son sees all this money he will not think any more of going away from us."

In this thought, however, she was quite mistaken, for no sooner had she entered the hut than the son came to her and asked impatiently: "Well, mother, have you done as I asked you?"

At this she exclaimed: "Do give up, once for all, this silly fancy, my son. How could you expect me to ask the king for his daughter to be your wife? That would be a bold thing for a rich nobleman to do, how then can *we* think of such a thing? Anyhow, *I* dared not say one word to the king about it. But only look what a lot of money I have brought back. Now you can look for a wife suitable for you, and then you will forget the king's daughter."

When the young man heard his mother speak thus, he grew very angry, and said to her: "What do I want with the king's money? I don't want his money, but I *do* want his daughter! I see you are only playing with me, so I shall leave you. I will go away somewhere—anywhere—wherever my eyes lead me."

Then the poor old parents prayed and begged him not to go away from them, and leave them alone in their old age; but they could only quiet him by promising faithfully that the mother should go again next day to the king, and this time really ask him to give his daughter to her son for a wife.

In the morning, therefore, the old woman went again to the palace, and the servants showed her into the same hall she had been in before. The king, seeing her stand there, inquired: "What want you, my old woman, now?" She was, however, so ashamed that she could hardly stammer, "Nothing, please your Majesty."

The king, supposing that she came again to beg, ordered his servants to give this time also ten crowns.

With this money the poor woman returned to her hut, where her son met her, asking: "Well, mother, *this* time I hope you have done what I asked you?" But she replied: "Now, my dear son, do leave the king's daughter in peace. How can you really think of such a thing? Even if she would marry you, where is the house to bring her to? So be quiet, and take this money which I have brought you."

At these words the son was more angry than before, and said sharply: "As I see you will not let me marry the king's daughter, I will leave you this moment and never come back again;" and, rushing out of the hut, he ran away. His parents hurried after him, and at length prevailed on him to return, by swearing to him that his mother should go again to the king next morning, and really and in truth ask his Majesty this time for his daughter.

So the young man agreed to go back home and wait until the next day.

On the morrow the old woman, with a heavy heart, went to the palace, and was shown as before into the king's presence. Seeing her there for the third time, his Majesty asked her impatiently: "What do you want this time, old woman?" And she, trembling all over, said: "Please your Majesty—nothing." Then the king exclaimed: "But it cannot be nothing. Something you must want, so tell me truth at once, if you value your life!" Thereupon the old woman was forced to tell all the story to the king; how her son had a great desire to marry the princess, and so had forced her to come and ask the king to give her him to wife.

When the king had heard everything, he said: "Well, after all, *I* shall say nothing against it if my daughter will consent to it." He then told his servants to lead the princess into his presence. When she came he told her all about the affair, and asked her, "Are you willing to marry the son of this old woman?"

The Condition

The princess answered: "Why not? If only he learns first the trade that no one knows!" Thereupon the king bade his attendants give money to the poor woman, who now went back to her hut with a light heart.

The moment she entered her son asked her: "Have you engaged her?" And she returned: "Do let me get my breath a little! Well, *now* I have really asked the king: but it is of no use, for the princess declares she will not marry you until you have learnt the trade that no one knows!"

"Oh, that matters nothing!" exclaimed the son. "Now I only know the condition, it's all right!" The next morning the young man set out on his travels through the world in search of a man who could teach him the trade that no one knows. He wandered about a long time without being able to find out where he could learn such a trade. At length one day, being quite tired out with walking and very sad, he sat down on a fallen log by the wayside.

After he had sat thus a little while, an old woman came up to him, and asked: "Why art thou so sad, my son?" And he answered: "What is the use of your asking, when you cannot help me?" But she continued: "Only tell me what is the matter, and perhaps I can help you." Then he said: "Well, if you must know, the matter is this: I have been travelling about the world a long time to find a master who can teach me the trade that no one knows." "Oh, if it is only that," cried the old woman, "just listen to me! Don't be afraid, but go straight into the forest which lies before you, and there you will find what you want."

The young man was very glad to hear this, and got up at once and went to the forest. When he had gone pretty far in the wood he saw a large castle, and whilst he stood looking at it and wondering what it was, four giants came out of it and ran up to him, shouting: "Do you wish to learn the trade that no one knows?" He said: "Yes; that is just the reason why I come here." Whereupon they took him into the castle.

Next morning the giants prepared to go out hunting, and, before leaving, they said to him: "You must on no account go into the first room by the dining-hall." Hardly, however, were the giants well out of sight before the young man began to reason thus with himself: "I see very well that I have come into a place from which I shall never go out alive with my head, so I may as well see what is in the room, come what may afterwards." So he went and opened the door a little and peeped in. There stood a golden ass, bound to a golden manger. He looked at it a little, and was just going to shut the door when the ass said: "Come and take the halter from my head, and keep it hidden about you. It will serve you well if you only understand how to use it." So he took the halter, and, after fastening the room-door, quickly concealed it under his clothes. He had not sat very long before the giants came home. They asked him at once if he had been in the first room, and he, much frightened, replied: "No, I have not been in." "But we know that you have been!" said the giants in great anger, and seizing some large sticks they beat him so severely that he could hardly stand on his feet. It was very lucky for him that he had the halter wound round his body under his clothes, or else he would certainly have been killed.

The next day the giants again prepared to go out hunting, but before leaving him they ordered him on no account to enter the second room.

Almost as soon as the giants had gone away he became so very curious to see what might be in the second room, that he could not resist going to the door. He stood there a little, thinking within himself, "Well, I am already more dead than alive, much worse cannot happen to me!" and so he opened the door and looked in. There he was surprised to see a very beautiful girl, dressed all in gold and silver, who sat combing her hair, and setting in every tress a large diamond. He stood admiring her a little while, and was just going to shut the door again, when she spoke, "Wait a minute, young man. Come and take this key, and mind you keep it safely. It will serve you some time, if you only know how to use it." So he went in and took the key from the girl, and then, going out, fastened the door and went and sat down in the same place he had sat before.

He had not remained there very long before the giants came home from hunting. The moment they entered the house they took up their large sticks to beat him, asking, at the same time, whether he had been in the second room. Shaking all over with fear, he answered them, "No, I have not!"

"But we know you have been," shouted the giants in great anger, and they then beat him worse than on the first day.

The Third Room

The next morning, as the giants went out as usual to hunt, they said to him: "Do not go into the third room, for anything in the world; for if you do go in we shall not forgive you as we did yesterday, and the day before! We shall kill you outright!" No sooner, however, had the giants gone out of sight, than the young man began to say to himself, "Most likely they will kill me, whether I go into the room or not. Besides, if they do not kill me, they have beaten me so badly already that I am sure I cannot live long, so, anyhow, I will go and see what is in the third room." Then he got up and went and opened the door.

He was quite shocked, however, when he saw that the room was full of human heads! These heads belonged to young men who had come, like himself, to learn the trade that no one knows, and who, having obeyed faithfully and strictly the orders of the giants, had been killed by them.

The young man was turning quickly to go away when one of the heads called out: "Don't be afraid, but come in!" Thereupon he went into the room. Then the head gave him an iron chain, and said: "Take care of this chain, for it will serve you some time if you know how to use it!" So he took the chain, and going out fastened the door.

He went and sat down in the usual place to wait for the coming home of the giants, and, as he waited, he grew quite frightened, for he fully expected that they would really kill him this time.

The instant the giants came home they took up their thick sticks and began to beat him without stopping to ask anything. They beat him so terribly that he was all but dead; then they threw him out of the house, saying to him: "Go away now, since you have learnt the trade that no one knows!" When he had lain a long time on the ground where they had thrown him, feeling very sore and miserable, at length he tried to move away, saying to himself: "Well, if they really have taught me the trade that no one knows for the sake of the king's daughter I can suffer gladly all this pain, if I can only win her."

After travelling for a long time, the young man came at last to the palace of the king whose daughter he wished to marry. When he saw the palace, he was exceedingly sad, and remembered the words of the princess; for, after all his wanderings and sufferings, he had learnt no trade, and had never been able to find what trade it was "that no one knows." Whilst considering what he had better do, he suddenly recollected the halter, the key and the iron chain, which he had carried concealed about him ever since he left the castle of the four giants. He then said to himself, "Let me see what these things can do!" So he took the halter and struck the earth with it, and immediately a handsome horse, beautifully caparisoned, stood before him. Then he struck the ground with the iron chain, and instantly a hare and a greyhound appeared, and the hare began to run quickly and the greyhound to follow her. In a moment the young man hardly knew himself, for he found himself in a fine hunting-dress, riding on the horse after the hare, which took a path that passed immediately under the windows of the king's palace.

Now, it happened that the king stood at a window looking out, and noticed at once the beautiful greyhound which was chasing the hare, and the very handsome horse which a huntsman in a splendid dress was mounted on. The king was so pleased with the appearance of the horse and the greyhound that he called instantly some of his servants, and, sending them after the strange rider, bade them invite him to come to the palace. The young man, however, hearing some people coming behind him calling and shouting, rode quickly behind a thick bush, and shook a little the halter and the iron chain. In a moment the horse, the greyhound, and the hare had vanished, and he found himself sitting on the ground under the trees dressed in his old shabby clothes. By this time the king's servants had come up, and, seeing him sit there, they asked him whether he had seen a fine huntsman on a beautiful horse pass that way. But he answered them rudely: "No! I have not seen any one pass, neither do I care to look to see who passes!"

Then the king's servants went on and searched the forest, calling and shouting as loudly as they could, but it was all in vain; they could neither see nor hear anything of the hunter. At length they went back to the king, and told him that the horse the huntsman rode was so exceedingly quick that they could not hear anything of him in the forest.

The Son Returns

The young man now resolved to go to the hut where his old parents lived; and they were glad to see that he had come back to them once more.

Next morning, the son said to his father: "Now, father, I will show you what I have learned. I will change myself into a beautiful horse, and you must lead me into the city and sell me, but be very careful not to give away the halter, or else I shall remain always a horse!" Accordingly, in a moment he changed himself into a horse of extraordinary beauty, and the father took him to the market-place to sell him. Very soon a great number of people gathered round the horse, wondering at his unusual beauty, and very high prices were offered for him; the old man, however, raised the price higher and higher at every offer. The news spread quickly about the city that a wonderfully handsome horse was for sale in the market-place, and at length the king himself heard of it, and sent some servants to bring the horse, that he might see it. The old man led the horse at once before the palace, and the king, after looking at it for some time with great admiration, could not help exclaiming, "By my word, though I am a king, I never yet saw, much less rode, so handsome a horse!" Then he asked the old man if he would sell it him. "I will sell it to your Majesty, very willingly," said the old man; "but I will sell only the horse, and not the halter." Thereupon the king laughed, saying: "What should I want with your dirty halter? For such a horse I will have a halter of gold made!" So the horse was sold to the king for a very high price, and the old man returned home with the money.

Next morning, however, there was a great stir and much consternation in the royal stables, for the beautiful horse had vanished somehow during the night. And at the time when the horse disappeared, the young man returned to his parents' hut.

A day or two afterwards the young man said to his father: "Now I will turn myself into a fine church not far from the king's palace, and if the king wishes to buy it you may sell it him, only be sure not to part with the key or else I must remain always a church!"

When the king got up that morning, and went to his window to look out, he saw a beautiful church which he had never noticed before. Then he sent his servants out to see what it was, and soon after they came back saying, that "the church belonged to an old pilgrim, who told them that he was willing to sell it if the king wished to buy it." Then the king sent to ask what price he would sell it for, and the pilgrim replied: "It is worth a great deal of money."

The King Outbid

Whilst the servants were bargaining with the father an old woman came up. Now this was the same old woman who had sent the young man to the castle of the four giants, and she herself had been there and had learnt the trade that no one knew. As she understood at once all about the church, and had no mind to have a rival in the trade, she resolved to put an end to the young man. For this purpose she began to outbid the king, and offered, at last, so very large a sum of ready money, that the old man was quite astonished and confused at seeing the money which she showed him. He accordingly accepted her offer, but whilst he was counting the money, quite forgot about the key. Before long, however, he recollected what his son had said, and then, fearing some mischief, he ran after old woman and demanded the key back. But the woman could not be persuaded to give back the key, and said it belonged to the church which she had bought and paid for. Seeing she would not give up the key, the old man grew more and more alarmed, lest some ill should befall his son, so he took hold of the old woman by the neck and forced her to drop the key. She struggled very hard to get it back again, and, whilst the old man and she wrestled together, the key changed itself suddenly into a dove and flew away high in the air over the palace gardens.

When the old woman saw this, she changed herself into a hawk, and chased the dove. Just, however, as the hawk was about to pounce upon it, the dove turned itself into a beautiful bouquet, and dropped down into the hand of the king's daughter, who happened to be walking in the garden. Then the hawk changed again into the old woman, who went to the gate of the palace and begged very hard that the princess would give that bouquet, or, at least, one single flower from it.

But the princess said, "No! not for anything in the world! These flowers fell to me from heaven!" The old woman, however, was determined to get one flower from the bouquet, so, seeing the princess would not hear her, she went straight to the king, and begged piteously that he would order his daughter to give her one of the flowers from her bouquet. The king, thinking the old woman wanted one of the flowers to cure some disease, called his daughter to him, and told her to give one to the beggar.

But just as the king said this, the bouquet changed itself into a heap of millet-seed and scattered itself all over the ground. Then the old woman quickly changed herself into a hen and chickens, and began greedily to pick up the seeds. Suddenly, however, the millet vanished, and in its place appeared a fox, which sprang on the hen and killed her.

Then the fox changed into the young man, who explained to the astonished king and princess that he it was who had demanded the hand of the princess, and that, in order to obtain it he had wandered all over the world in search of some one who could teach him "the trade that no one knows."

When the king and his daughter heard this, they gladly fulfilled their part of the bargain, seeing how well the young man had fulfilled his.

Then, shortly afterwards, the king's daughter married the son of the poor old couple; and the king built for the princess and her husband a palace close to his own. There they lived long and had plenty of children, and people say that some of their descendants are living at present, and that these go constantly to pray in the church, which is always open because the key of it turned itself into a young man who married the king's daughter, after he had shown to her that he had done as she wished, and learnt, for her sake, "the trade that no one knows."

XX. The Golden-haired Twins

Once upon a time, a long, long while ago, there lived a young king who wished very much to marry, but could not decide where he had better look for a wife.

One evening as he was walking disguised through the streets of his capital, as it was his frequent custom to do, he stopped to listen near an open window where he heard three young girls chatting gaily together.

The girls were talking about a report which had been lately spread through the city, that the king intended soon to marry.

One of the girls exclaimed: "If the king would marry me I would give him a son who should be the greatest hero in the world."

The second girl said: "And if I were to be his wife I would present him with two sons at once—the twins with golden hair."

And the third girl declared that were the king to marry *her*, she would give him a daughter so beautiful that there should not be her equal in the whole wide world!

The young king listened to all this, and for some time thought over their words, and tried to make up his mind which of the three girls he should choose for a wife. At last he decided that he would marry the one who had said she would bring him twins with golden hair.

Having once settled this in his own mind, he ordered that all preparations for his marriage should be made forthwith, and shortly after, when all was ready, he married the second girl of the three.

Several months after his marriage the young king, who was at war with one of the neighbouring princes, received tidings of the defeat of his army, and heard that his presence was immediately required in the camp. He accordingly left his capital and went to his army, leaving the young queen in his palace to the care of his stepmother.

Now the king's stepmother hated her daughter-in-law very much indeed, so when the young queen was near her confinement, the old queen told her that it was always customary in the royal family for the heirs to the throne to be born in a garret.

The young queen (who knew nothing about the customs in royal families except what she had learnt from hearing or seeing since her marriage to the king) believed implicitly what her mother-in-law told her, although she thought it a great pity to leave her splendid apartments and go up into a miserable attic.

Now when the golden-haired twins were born, the old queen contrived to steal them out of their cradle, and put in their place two ugly little dogs. She then caused the two beautiful golden-haired boys to be buried alive in an out-of-the-way spot in the palace gardens, and then sent word to the king that the young queen had given him two little dogs instead of the heirs he was hoping for. The wicked stepmother said in her letter to the king that she herself was not surprised at this, though she was very sorry for his disappointment. As to herself, she had a long time suspected the young queen of having too great a friendship for goblins and elves, and all kinds of evil spirits.

When the king received this letter, he fell into a frightful rage, because he had only married the young girl in order to have the golden-haired twins she had promised him as heirs to his throne.

So he sent word back to the old queen that his wife should be put at once into the dampest dungeon in the castle, an order which the wicked woman took good care to see carried out without delay. Accordingly the poor young queen was thrown into a miserably dark dungeon under the palace, and kept on bread and water.

The Plight of the Young Queen

Now there was only a very small hole in this prison—hardly enough to let in light and air—yet the old queen managed to cause a great many people to pass by this hole, and whoever passed was ordered to spit at and abuse the unhappy young queen, calling out to her, "Are you really the queen? Are you the girl who cheated the king in order to be a queen? Where are your golden-haired twins? You cheated the king and your friends, and now the witches have cheated you!"

But the young king, though terribly angry and mortified at his great disappointment, was, at the same time, too sad and troubled to be willing to return to his palace. So he remained away for fully nine years. When he at last consented to return, the first thing he noticed in the palace gardens were two fine young trees, exactly the same size and the same shape.

These trees had both golden leaves and golden blossoms, and had grown up of themselves from the very spot where the stepmother of the king had buried the two golden-haired boys she had stolen from their cradle.

The king admired these two trees exceedingly, and was never weary of looking at them. This, however, did not at all please the old queen, for she knew that the two young princes were buried just where the trees grew, and she always feared that by some means what she had done would come to the king's ears. She therefore pretended that she was very sick, and declared that she was sure she should die unless her stepson, the king, ordered the two golden-leaved trees to be cut down, and a bed made for her out of their wood.

As the king was not willing to be the cause of her death, he ordered that her wishes should be attended to, notwithstanding he was exceedingly sorry to lose his favourite trees.

A bed was soon made from the two trees, and the seemingly sick old queen was laid on it as she desired. She was quite delighted that the golden-leaved trees had disappeared from the garden; but when midnight came, she could not sleep a bit, for it seemed to her that she heard the boards of which her bed was made in conversation with each other!

At last it seemed to her, that one board said, quite plainly, "How are you, my brother?" And the other board answered: "Thank you, I am very well; how are you?"

"Oh, I am all right," returned the first board; "but I wonder how our poor mother is in her dark dungeon! Perhaps she is hungry and thirsty!"

The wicked old queen could not sleep a minute all night, after hearing this conversation between the boards of her new bed; so next morning she got up very early and went to see the king. She thanked him for attending to her wish, and said she already was much better, but she felt quite sure she would never recover thoroughly unless the boards of her new bed were cut up and thrown into a fire. The king was sorry to lose entirely even the boards made out of his two favourite trees, nevertheless he could not refuse to use the means pointed out for his step-mother's perfect recovery.

So the new bed was cut to pieces and thrown into the fire. But whilst the boards were blazing and crackling, two sparks from the fire flew into the courtyard, and in the next moment two beautiful lambs with golden fleeces and golden horns were seen gambolling about the yard.

The king admired them greatly, and made many inquiries who had sent them there, and to whom they belonged. He even sent the public crier many times through the city, calling on the owners of the golden-fleeced lambs to appear and claim them; but no one came, so at length he thought he might fairly take them as his own property.

The king took very great care of these two beautiful lambs, and every day directed that they should be well fed and attended to; this, however, did not at all please his stepmother. She could not endure even to look on the lambs with their golden fleeces and golden horns, for they always reminded her of the golden-haired twins. So, in a little while she pretended again to be dangerously sick, and declared she felt sure that she should soon die unless the two lambs were killed and cooked for her.

The king was even fonder of his golden-fleeced lambs than he had been of the golden-leaved trees, but he could not long resist the tears and prayers of the old queen, especially as she seemed to be very ill. Accordingly, the lambs were killed, and a servant was ordered to carry their golden fleeces down to the river and to wash the blood well out of them. But whilst the servant held them under the water, they slipped, in some way or other, out of his fingers, and floated down the stream, which just at that place flowed very rapidly. Now it happened that a hunter was passing near the river a little lower down, and, as he chanced to look in the water, he saw something strange in it. So he stepped into the stream, and soon fished out a small box which he carried to his house, and there opened it. To his unspeakably great surprise, he found in the box two golden-haired boys. Now the hunter had no children of his own; he therefore adopted the twins he had fished out of the river, and brought them up just as if they had been his own sons. When the twins were grown up into handsome young men, one of them said to his foster-father, "Make us two suits of beggar's clothes, and let us go and wander a little about the world!" The hunter, however, replied and said: "No, I will have a fine suit made for each of you, such as is fitting for two such noble-looking young men." But as the twins begged hard that he should not spend his money uselessly in buying fine clothes, telling him that they wished to travel about as beggars, the hunter—who always liked to do as his two handsome foster-sons wished—did as they desired, and ordered two suit of clothes, like those worn by beggars, to be prepared for them. The two sons then dressed themselves up as beggars, and as well as they could hid their beautiful golden locks, and then set out to see the world. They took with them a goussle and cymbal, and maintained themselves with their singing and playing.

The King's Sons

They had wandered about in this way some time when one day they came to the king's palace. As the afternoon was already pretty far advanced, the young musicians begged to allowed to pass the night in one of the outbuildings belonging to the court, as they were poor men, and quite strangers in the city. The old queen, however, who happened to be just then in the courtyard, saw them, and hearing their request said sharply that beggars could not be permitted to enter any part of the king's palace. The two travellers said they had hoped to pay for their night's lodging by their songs and music, as one of them played and sung to the goussle, and the other to the cymbal.

The old queen, however, was not moved by this, but insisted on their going away at once. Happily for the two brothers, the king himself came out into the courtyard just as his stepmother angrily ordered them to go away, and at once directed his servants to find a place for the musicians to sleep in, and ordered them to provide the brothers with a good supper. After they had supped, the king commanded them to be brought before him that he might judge of their skill as musicians, and that their singing might help him to pass the time more pleasantly.

Accordingly, after the two young men had taken the refreshment provided for them, the servants took them into the king's presence, and they began to sing this ballad:—

"The pretty bird, the swallow, built her nest with care in the palace of the king. In the nest she reared up happily two of her little ones. A black, ugly-looking bird, however came to the swallow's nest to mar her happiness and to kill her two little ones. And the ugly black bird succeeded in destroying the happiness of the poor little swallow; the little ones, however, although yet weak and unfledged were saved, and, when they were grown up and able to fly, they came to look at the palace where their mother, the pretty swallow, had built her nest."

This strange song the two minstrels sung so very sweetly that the king was quite charmed, and asked them the meaning of the words.

Whereupon the two meanly dressed young men took off their hats, so that the rich tresses of their golden hair fell down over their shoulders, and the light glanced so brightly upon it that the whole hall was illuminated by the shining. They then stepped forward together, and told the king all that had happened to them and to their mother, and convinced him that they were really his own sons.

The king was exceedingly angry when he heard all the cruel things his stepmother had done, and he gave orders that she should be burnt to death. He then went with the two golden-haired princes to the miserable dungeon wherein his unfortunate wife had been confined so many years, and brought her once more into her beautiful palace. There, looking on her golden-haired sons, and seeing how much the king, their father, loved them, she soon forgot all her long years of misery. As to the king, he felt that he could never do enough to make amends for all the misfortunes his queen had lived through, and all the dangers to which his twin sons had been exposed. He felt that he had too easily believed the stories of the old queen, because he would not trouble himself to inquire more particularly into the truth or falsehood of the strange things she had told him.

After all this mortification, and trouble, and misery, everything came right at last. So the king and his wife, with their golden-haired twins, lived together long and happily.

---

[1] This legend was written and contributed to Vouk St. Karadgitch by Prince Michel Obrenovitch III, who had heard it in his childhood from the lips of his nurse.

[2] The Christians of the Balkans usually make the sign of the cross before and after every meal.

[3] A golden coin worth about 10s.

[4] The apple is a symbolic gift, which a wooer offers to the maiden of his choice.

[5] It is the custom with Serbians, for one of her brothers to present the bride to her wooer.

[6] Beardless is used as the personification of craftiness and sharpness.

[7] This and the remaining stories in this chapter are reprinted from *Serbian Folk-Lore*, by Madame C. Mijatovitch, by kind permission of M. Chedo Miyatovich.

Chapter XV: Some Serbian Popular Anecdotes

St. Peter and the Sand

A townsman went one day to the country to hunt and came at noon to the house of a peasant whom he knew. The man asked him to share his dinner, and while they were eating, the townsman looked around him and noticed that there was but little arable land to be seen. There were rocks and stones in abundance, however. Surprised at this, the townsman exclaimed: "In the name of all that is good, my friend, how on earth can you good people of this village exist without arable land! and whence these heaps of rocks and stones?" "It is, indeed, a great misfortune!" answered the peasant. "People say that our ancestors heard from their fore-fathers that when our Lord walked on this earth, St. Peter accompanied Him carrying on his back a sack full of sand. Occasionally our Lord would take a grain of sand and throw it down to make a mountain, saying: 'May this grain multiply!' When they arrived here St. Peter's sack burst and half of its contents poured out in our village."

Why the Serbian People are Poor

The nations of the world met together one day on the middle of the earth to divide between themselves the good things in life. First they deliberated upon the methods of procedure. Some recommended a lottery, but the Christians, well knowing that they, as the cleverest, would be able to obtain the most desirable gifts, and not wishing to be at the mercy of fortune, suggested (and the idea was instantly adopted by all) that each should express a wish for some good thing and it would be granted to him. The men of Italy were allowed to express their wish first, and they desired Wisdom. The Britons said: "We will take the sea." The Turks: "And we will take fields." The Russians: "We will take the forests and mines." The French: "And we will have money and war." "And what about you Serbians?" asked the nations, "What do you wish for?" "Wait till we make up our mind!" answered the Serbians; and they have not yet agreed upon their reply.

The Gipsies and the Nobleman

A very rich and powerful nobleman was one day driving through his vast estates. From afar four *Tzigans*[1] noted that he was alone, and greedily coveting his fine carriage horses, determined to deprive him of them. As the carriage approached, they rushed on to the road, respectfully took off their hats, knelt before him, and one of them began to speak, saying: "O how happy we are to have an opportunity of manifesting to you, O most gracious lord, our deep gratitude for the noble deeds and many acts of kindness with which your late and generous father used to overwhelm us! As we have no valuable presents to offer you, allow us to harness ourselves to your carriage and draw you home." The haughty nobleman, proud of his father's good deeds, was pleased to assent to this unusual form of courtesy. Two gipsies thereupon detached the horses, harnessed themselves to the carriage and drew it for some distance. Suddenly, however, they cut themselves loose and ran back to the two other rascals who by this time had got clear away with the horses.

Why the Priest was drowned

A few peasants and a priest were once crossing a river. Suddenly a tempest arose and overturned the boat. All were good swimmers except the poor priest, and when the peasants regained their boat and righted it, which they did very soon, they approached the struggling preacher and called to him to give them his hand that they might save him; but he hesitated and was drowned. The peasants went to impart the sad news to the priest's widow who, hearing it, exclaimed: "What a pity! But had you offered him *your* hands, he would surely have accepted them, and thus his precious life would have been saved—for it was ever his custom to *receive*."

The Era from the other World[2]

A Turk and his wife halted in the shadow of a tree. The Turk went to the river to water his horse, and his wife remained to await his return. Just then an Era passed by and saluted the Turkish woman: "Allah help you, noble lady." "May God aid you," she returned; "whence do you come?" "I come from the Other World, noble lady." "As you have been in the Other World, have you not, perchance, seen there my son Mouyo, who died a few months ago?" "Oh, how could I help seeing him? He is my immediate neighbour." "Happy me! How is he, then?" "He is well, may God be praised! But he could stand just a little more tobacco and some more pocket-money to pay for black coffee." "Are you going back again? And if so, would you be so kind as to deliver to him this purse with his parent's greetings?" The Era took the money protesting that he would be only too glad to convey so pleasant a surprise to the youth, and hurried away. Soon the Turk came back, and his wife told him what had transpired. He perceived at once that she had been victimized and without stopping to reproach her, he mounted his horse and galloped after the Era, who, observing the pursuit, and guessing at once that the horseman was the husband of the credulous woman, made all the speed that he could. There was a mill near by and making for it, the Era rushed in and addressed the miller with: "For Goodness' sake, brother, fly! There is a Turkish horseman coming with drawn sword; he will kill you. I heard him say so and have hurried to warn you in time." The miller had no time to ask for particulars; he knew how cruel the Turks were, and without a word he dashed out of the mill and fled up the adjacent rocks.

Meantime the Era placed the miller's hat upon his own head and sprinkled flour copiously over his clothes, that he might look like a miller. No sooner was this done than the Turk came up. Alighting from his horse, he rushed into the mill and hurriedly asked the Era where he had hidden the thief. The Era pointed indifferently to the flying miller on the rock, whereupon the Turk requested him to take care of his horse while he ran and caught the swindler. When the Turk was gone some distance up the hill our Era brushed his clothes, swiftly mounted the horse and galloped away. The Turk caught the real miller, and demanded: "Where is the money you took from my wife, swindler?" The poor miller made the sign of the cross3 and said: "God forbid! I never saw your noble lady, still less did I take her money."

He asked the Era where he had hidden the thief

After about half an hour of futile discussion, the Turk was convinced of the miller's innocence, and returned to where he had left his horse. But lo! There was no sign of a horse! He walked sadly back to his wife, and she, seeing that her husband had no horse, asked in surprise: "Where did you go, and what became of your horse?" The Turk replied: "You sent money to our darling son; so I thought I had better send him the horse that he need not go on foot in the Other World!"

A Trade before Everything

Once upon a time a king set out in his luxurious pleasure-galley accompanied by his queen and a daughter. They had proceeded a very little way from the shore when a powerful wind drove the galley far out to sea, where at last it was dashed upon a barren rock. Fortunately there was a small boat upon the galley, and the king, being a good sailor, was able to launch this frail bark, and he rescued his wife and daughter from the waves. After long tossing and drifting, good fortune smiled upon the wanderers; they began to see birds and floating leaves, which indicated that they were approaching dry land. And, indeed, they soon came in sight of shore, and, as the sea was now calm, were able to land without further adventure. But, alas, the king knew no trade, and had no money upon his person. Consequently he was forced to offer his services as a shepherd to a rich landowner, who gave him a hut and a flock of sheep to tend. In these idyllic and simple conditions they lived contentedly for several years, undisturbed by regrets for the magnificence of their past circumstances.

One day the only son of the ruler of that strange country lost his way while riding in the neighbourhood after a fox, and presently he beheld the beautiful daughter of our shepherd. No sooner did his eyes fall upon the maiden than he fell violently in love with her, and she was not unwilling to receive the protestations of undying affection which he poured into her ears. They met again and again, and the maiden consented to marry the prince, provided her parents would approve the match.

The prince first declared his wish to his own parents, who, of course, were greatly astonished at their son's apparently foolish selection, and would not give their consent. But the prince protested solemnly that his resolution was unshakable; he would either marry the girl he loved or remain single all his days. Finally his royal father took pity on him, and sent his first adjutant to the shepherd secretly to ask the hand of his daughter for the prince.

The Condition

When the adjutant came and communicated the royal message, the shepherd asked him: "Is there any trade with which the royal prince is familiar?" The adjutant was amazed at such a question. "Lord forbid, foolish man!" he exclaimed, "how could you expect the heir-apparent to know a trade? People learn trades in order to earn their daily bread; princes possess lands and cities, and so do not need to work."

But the shepherd persisted, saying: "If the prince knows no trade, he cannot become my son-in-law."

The royal courier returned to the palace and reported to the king his conversation with the shepherd, and great was the astonishment throughout the palace when the news became known, for all expected that the shepherd would be highly flattered that the king had chosen his daughter's hand for the prince in preference to the many royal and imperial princesses who would have been willing to marry him for the asking.

The king sent again to the shepherd, but the man remained firm in his resolution. "As long as the prince," said he, "does not know any trade, I shall not grant him the hand of my daughter."

When this second official brought back to the palace the same answer, the king informed his son of the shepherd's condition, and the royal prince resolved to put himself in the way of complying with it.

His first step was to go through the city from door to door in order to select some simple and easy trade. As he walked through the streets he beheld various craftsmen at their work, but he did not stay until he came to the workshop of a carpet-maker, and this trade appeared to him both easy and lucrative. He therefore offered his services to the master, who gladly undertook to teach him the trade. In due time the prince obtained a certificate of efficiency, and he went to the shepherd and showed it to him, together with samples of his hand work. The shepherd examined these and asked the prince: "How much could you get for this carpet?" The prince replied: "If it is made of grass, I could sell it for threepence." "Why, that is a splendid trade," answered the shepherd, "threepence to-day and another threepence to-morrow would make sixpence, and in two other days you would have earned a shilling! If I only had known this trade a few years ago I would not have been a shepherd." Thereupon he related to the prince and his suite the story of his past life, and what ill fate had befallen him, to the greatest surprise of all. You may be sure that the prince rejoiced to learn that his beloved was highly born, and the worthy mate of a king's son. As for his father, he was especially glad that his son had fallen in love, not with the daughter of a simple shepherd, but with a royal princess.

The marriage was now celebrated with great magnificence, and when the festivities came to an end, the king gave the shepherd a fine ship, together with a powerful escort, that he might go back to his country and reassume possession of his royal throne.

[1]*Tzigans* or Gipsies in Serbia, and indeed in the whole Balkan Peninsula, deal mostly with horses. Stealing and selling horses is their main occupation.

[2]*Era* is a name given to the peasants of the district of Ouzitze (Western Serbia). They are supposed to be very witty and shrewd, and might be called the Irishmen of Serbia.

[3]When Serbians are greatly surprised at anything they involuntarily make the sign of the cross.

Printed in Great Britain
by Amazon

41711433R00256